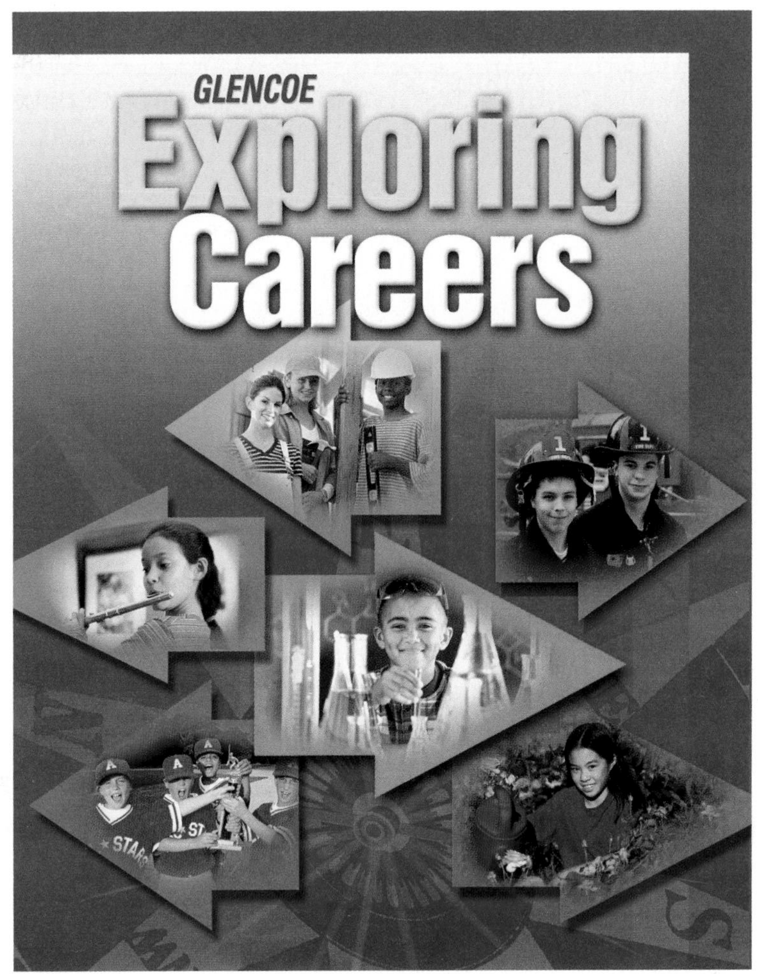

Fourth Edition

Joan Kelly-Plate
Career Educator
Lake Suzy, Florida

Ruth Volz-Patton
Career Consultant
Springfield, Illinois

New York, New York   Columbus, Ohio   Chicago, Illinois   Peoria, Illinois   Woodland Hills, California

The McGraw-Hill Companies

Printed in the United States of America.

Send all inquiries to:
Glencoe/McGraw-Hill
21600 Oxnard Street, Suite 500
Woodland Hills, CA 91367

ISBN 0-07-845644-4 (Student Text)
ISBN 0-07-846049-2 (Teacher Annotated Edition)

2 3 4 5 6 7 8 9 027 08 07 06 05 04 03

ADVISORY BOARD

To best research and address the needs of today's workplace, Glencoe/McGraw-Hill assembled an advisory board of industry leaders and educators. The board lent its expertise and experience to establish the foundation for this innovative, real-world, career education program. Glencoe/McGraw-Hill would like to acknowledge the following companies and individuals for their support and commitment to this project:

Mark Ballard
Director of Human Resources
Recruitment and Development
The Limited, Inc.
Columbus, OH

Michele Bina
Michele Bina and Associates
former Manager of Organizational Effectiveness
The Prudential Healthcare Group
Woodland Hills, CA

Joe Bryan
Industrial Cooperative Training Coordinator
Warsaw Community Schools
Warsaw, IN

Mary Sue Burkhardt
Career Specialist
Family and Consumer Sciences
Twin Lakes High School
Monticello, IN

Mable Burton
Career Development Specialist
Office of Education for Employment
Philadelphia, PA

Liz Lamatrice
Career Education Coordinator
Jefferson County, OH

Keith Mitchell
Manager, Testing and Assessment
Abbott Laboratories
Abbott Park, IL

James Murphy
Education Relations Manager
The Boeing Company
Seattle, WA

William M. Pepito
Manager, Lake County Skills Development Program
Abbott Laboratories
Abbott Park, IL

William J. Ratzburg
Director, Northern Kane County Regional Vocational System
Coordinator, Career & Technical Education School District U-46
Elgin, IL

Gary Schepf
Business Education Department Chair
Nimitz High School
Irving, TX

REVIEWERS

Becky Baker
School Counselor
Appling Middle School
Bartlett, TN

Jerry Balistreri
Retired, Vocational Education Director
Anchorage School District
Anchorage, AK

Toni Barrows
Teacher/Coordinator
Clay High School
Orange Park, FL

Claudene Bell
School-to-Career and Service Learning Coordinator
Burbank Unified School District
Burbank, CA

Karen Berbary
Family and Consumer Science Teacher
Broadway Middle School
Elmira, NY

Nathan Brubaker
Teacher
Putnam City High School
Oklahoma City, OK

Bea DeSapio
Teacher
Ditmas Intermediate School #62
Brooklyn, NY

Mary Hopple
School-to-Career Coordinator
Oxnard Union High School District
Oxnard, CA

Patricia Sue (Black) Locks
Vocational Counselor
Texas State Technical College
Brownwood, TX

Paula Smith Mendoza
Teacher
Bryan Adams High School
Dallas, TX

Judy C. Murphy, M.S.E.
Business Educator
Sylvan Hills Middle School
Sherwood, AR

Beverly Newton
Business Education Consultant
Nebraska Department of Education
Lincoln, NE

Margaret Peterson
Teacher
Marvin Sedway Middle School
Las Vegas, NV

Richard L. Rios
Coordinator, Career and Technology Education
Anchorage School District
Anchorage, AK

Irma Rosas
Teacher/Coordinator
El Paso High School
El Paso, TX

Allison Wyeth, M.Ed.
Teacher
Goleta Valley Junior High School
Goleta, CA

Susan Wilson
Curriculum Director
Monroe Local School District
Hamilton, OH

Table of Contents

UNIT 2 FINDING AND APPLYING FOR A JOB

UNIT 3 EMPLOYMENT SKILLS

Chapter 14 Managing Your Money 292

UNIT 5 LIFELONG LEARNING

Chapter 15 Living a Balanced Life 316

Features

The Global Workplace

Attitude Counts

Q&A

Career Opportunities

Welcome to *Exploring Careers!*

What do you enjoy? What are you good at? What do you want to do with your life? What do you dream of becoming? This book will help you begin to explore the answers to these questions.

Getting to Know You

If you really think about it, there is at least one thing, if not several things, that you really enjoy. Think of the things that make time fly for you, things that make you feel good about yourself. Maybe you love playing sports or acting in plays. Perhaps you like gardening or writing stories. The things you enjoy now and in the future will lead to various careers. Throughout this course, you will be exploring careers that match who you are. This book will help you get started.

First you'll take a look at yourself. You'll identify your interests and values. You'll think about your skills and aptitudes. You'll imagine your ideal lifestyle. Then you'll consider how each might affect your career choices one day.

Looking at Careers

You'll learn about the many career areas and begin to think about careers that best suit you. Let's say, for example, that you love animals and value education. A career working as an exhibit interpreter at a zoo or aquarium might interest you. A career as a dog obedience trainer might also appeal to you. There are all kinds of career possibilities to match who you are and what you believe is important. This book will introduce you to different ways to explore these possibilities now and in the future.

Planning for the Future

In this book, you will also learn how to make decisions, set goals, and plan for your future. You will consider the kind of education and training you will need for careers that interest you. You will learn how to find, apply, and interview for a job.

You'll get a glimpse of what it's like to be part of the work world. You'll learn what to expect and what will be expected of you. You'll find out why it's important to develop strong people skills and basic skills. You'll discover the part health and safety play in your life now and on the job.

You'll take a look at how business is organized and operates in our country. You'll find out how to manage your money and make wise purchases. You'll get valuable tips for balancing work and personal life. You'll learn how to give something back to your community.

Last but not least, you'll discover how to deal with the different kinds of changes life brings. You'll learn the importance of lifelong learning, a positive attitude, and planning. What you will learn will help you move toward your future with excitement and confidence.

Get ready for an exciting adventure with *Exploring Careers*. The adventure you are about to start is the beginning of a lifetime of career exploration!

Understanding the Text Structure

Exploring Careers is divided into five units: Career Exploration, Finding and Applying for a Job, Employment Skills, Business and Personal Finance, and Lifelong Learning. Within each unit there are two to five chapters. Each chapter is divided into lessons.

Discover lists what you will learn in the Lesson.

Why It's Important briefly states the Lesson's meaning and purpose.

Key Terms is a list of important vocabulary words. The Key Terms are also highlighted in yellow as they are introduced with the text and are accompanied by clear definitions.

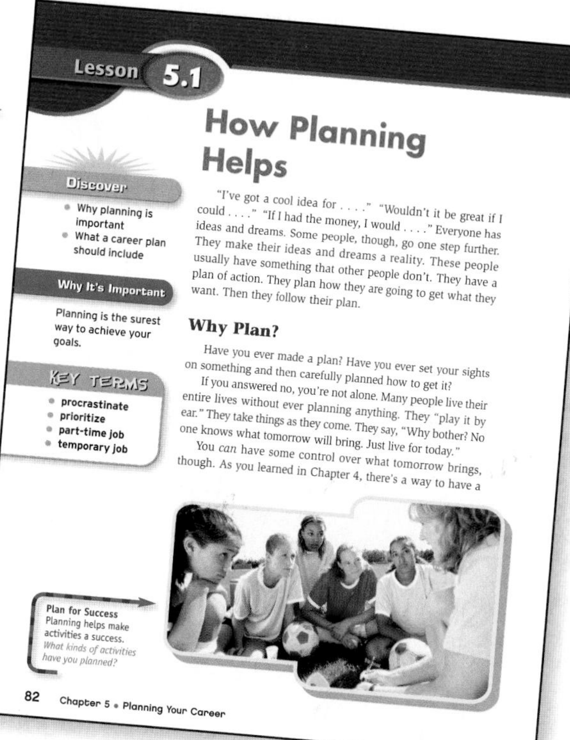

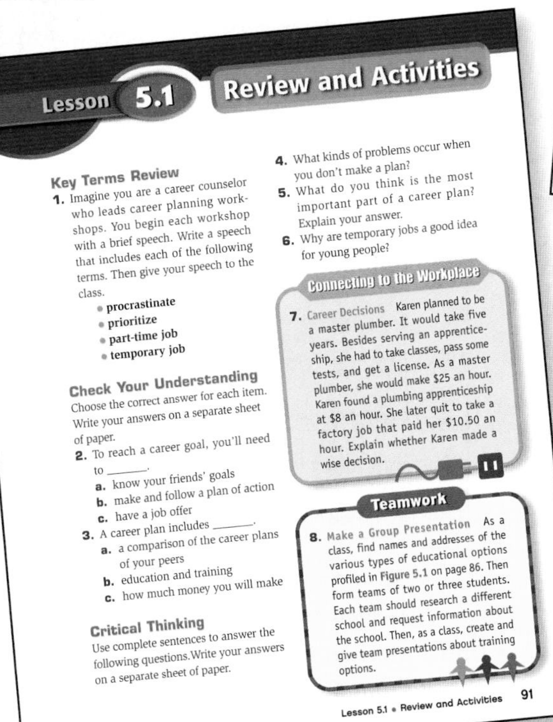

Lesson Review and Activities concludes each Lesson and helps to reinforce your understanding of the main points of the Lesson.

Focus on the Features

Text features in each chapter provide special insights into career topics and challenge your creativity and imagination.

The Global Workplace

Foreign Language Basics

Many people around the world speak some English. This makes traveling easier for native English speakers. However, before going to a foreign country, learn a few basic phrases of that country's language to help in routine situations. Pocket-size phrase books are easy to carry and usually list many useful words. Learning *thank you* is a good place to start.

- **Italy** .... *grazie*
- **Germany** .... *danke*
- **Latin America, Spain** ..... *gracias*
- **South Korea** .... *kamsa hamnida*
- **Somalia** .... *mahadsanid*

Internet Activity

Use Internet resources to learn a few basic phrases in a language that interests you. Learn *hello, good-bye, please, thank you*, and four other terms you think would be helpful. Go to the *Exploring Careers* Web site at exploring.glencoe.com for a list of Web sites to help you complete this activity.

The Global Workplace feature identifies work-related cultural differences to prepare you for the global workplace you will enter one day.

Make Your Goals Realistic

Q: If achieving my goals takes longer than I planned, does that mean my goals are unrealistic?

A: No, your goals can take longer than planned. It is important to be aware of what it will take to achieve your goals. If your goals are taking longer than you first estimated, then figure out why. Did you need more money? Did you forget to include the hours spent on chores? Periodically reevaluate your goals and adjust them to include the things you didn't consider.

Q & A feature anticipates questions about exploring careers that you might have as you read the text.

Attitude Counts

Teamwork

Working in teams can improve productivity and creativity. The right attitude will make your team a success. A good tip for effective teamwork: Respect your teammates and you'll find they will do the same for you.

Cooperative Learning Activity

- Work with a small group of classmates to brainstorm three important rules for successful teamwork.
- Share your results with the class.

Attitude Counts feature provides tips for building a positive attitude.

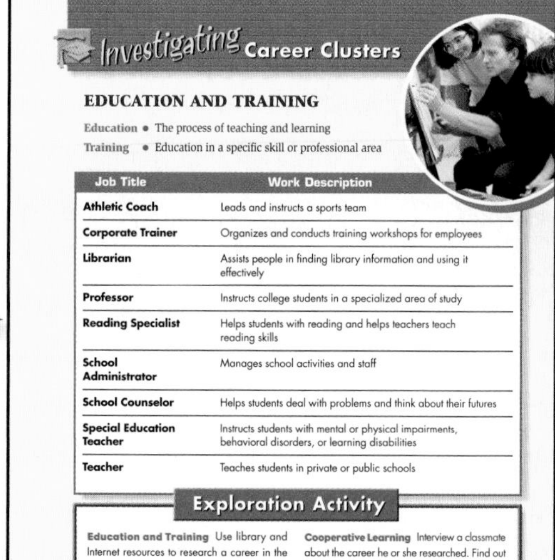

Investigating Career Clusters

EDUCATION AND TRAINING

Education • The process of teaching and learning

Training • Education in a specific skill or professional area

Job Title	Work Description
Athletic Coach	Leads and instructs a sports team
Corporate Trainer	Organizes and conducts training workshops for employees
Librarian	Assists people in finding library information and using it effectively
Professor	Instructs college students in a specialized area of study
Reading Specialist	Helps students with reading and helps teachers teach reading skills
School Administrator	Manages school activities and staff
School Counselor	Helps students deal with problems and think about their futures
Special Education Teacher	Instructs students with mental or physical impairments, behavioral disorders, or learning disabilities
Teacher	Teaches students in private or public schools

Exploration Activity

Education and Training Use library and Internet resources to research a career in the Education and Training career cluster. Write a report on your findings. Include information about the kinds of work, skills required, working conditions, training and education required, and career outlook.

Cooperative Learning Interview a classmate about the career he or she researched. Find out as much information about that career as you can during the interview. Then have your classmate interview you about the career you researched. Afterward, share what you learned with the class.

Investigating Career Clusters • Education and Training 99

Investigating Career Clusters feature offers more detailed information about a career cluster and an exploration activity to learn more.

Career Opportunities

Education and Training

If you enjoy working with people and are enthusiastic, creative, patient, and flexible, then a career in education and training may be right for you. You can find jobs of different skill levels in the Education and Training career cluster.

Critical Thinking

Why are good communication skills and time management skills important for educators?

ELEMENTARY SCHOOL TEACHER

A local elementary school seeks an experienced teacher. Applicants must have experience teaching science, language arts, math, and social studies. They may also teach other subjects such as music and art.

Career Opportunities feature offers a brief description of a career cluster and a job within the cluster.

Reviewing What You've Learned

Each chapter in *Exploring Careers* concludes with a Chapter Review and Activities.

Chapter Review and Activities is designed to help you recall, use, and expand on the concepts presented in the chapter.

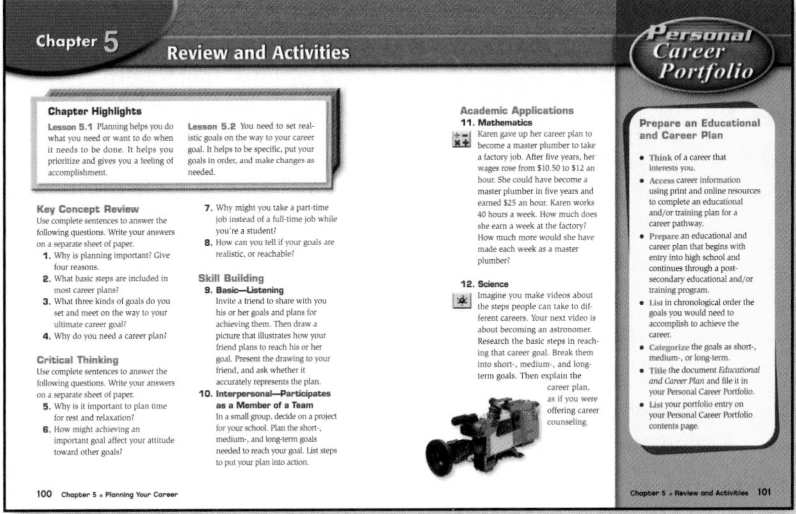
Chapter 5 Review and Activities

Chapter Highlights

Lesson 5.1 Planning helps you do what you need or want to do when it needs to be done. It helps you prioritize and gives you a feeling of accomplishment.

Lesson 5.2 You need to set realistic goals on the way to your career goal. It helps to be specific, put your goals in order, and make changes as needed.

Key Concept Review
Use complete sentences to answer the following questions. Write your answers on a separate sheet of paper.
1. Why is planning important? Give four reasons.
2. What basic steps are included in most career plans?
3. What three kinds of goals do you set and meet on the way to your ultimate career goal?
4. Why do you need a career plan?

Critical Thinking
Use complete sentences to answer the following questions. Write your answers on a separate sheet of paper.
5. Why is it important to plan time for rest and relaxation?
6. How might achieving an important goal affect your attitude toward other goals?
7. Why might you take a part-time job instead of a full-time job while you're a student?
8. How can you tell if your goals are realistic, or reachable?

Skill Building
9. **Basic—Listening**
Invite a friend to share with you his or her goals and plans for achieving them. Then draw a picture that illustrates how your friend plans to reach his or her goal. Present the drawing to your friend, and ask whether it accurately represents the plan.
10. **Interpersonal—Participates as a Member of a Team**
In a small group, decide on a project for your school. Plan the short-, medium-, and long-term goals needed to reach your goal. List steps to put your plan into action.

Academic Applications
11. **Mathematics**
Karen gave up her career plan to become a master plumber to take a factory job. After five years, her wages rose from $10.50 to $12 an hour. She could have become a master plumber in five years and earned $25 an hour. Karen works 40 hours a week. How much does she earn a week at the factory? How much more would she have made each week as a master plumber?
12. **Science**
Imagine you make videos about the steps people can take to different careers. Your next video is about becoming an astronomer. Research the basic steps in reaching that career goal. Break them into short-, medium-, and long-term goals. Then explain the career plan, as if you were offering career counseling.

Personal Career Portfolio

Prepare an Educational and Career Plan
- Think of a career that interests you.
- Access career information using print and online resources to complete an educational and/or training plan for a career pathway.
- Prepare an educational and career plan that begins with entry into high school and continues through a post-secondary educational and/or training program.
- List in chronological order the goals you would need to accomplish to achieve the career.
- Categorize the goals as short-, medium-, or long-term.
- Title the document *Educational and Career Plan* and file it in your Personal Career Portfolio.
- List your portfolio entry on your Personal Career Portfolio contents page.

100 Chapter 5 • Planning Your Career

Chapter 5 • Review and Activities 101

Resources to Help You Learn

The back of *Exploring Careers* contains resources that help you find and learn more information.

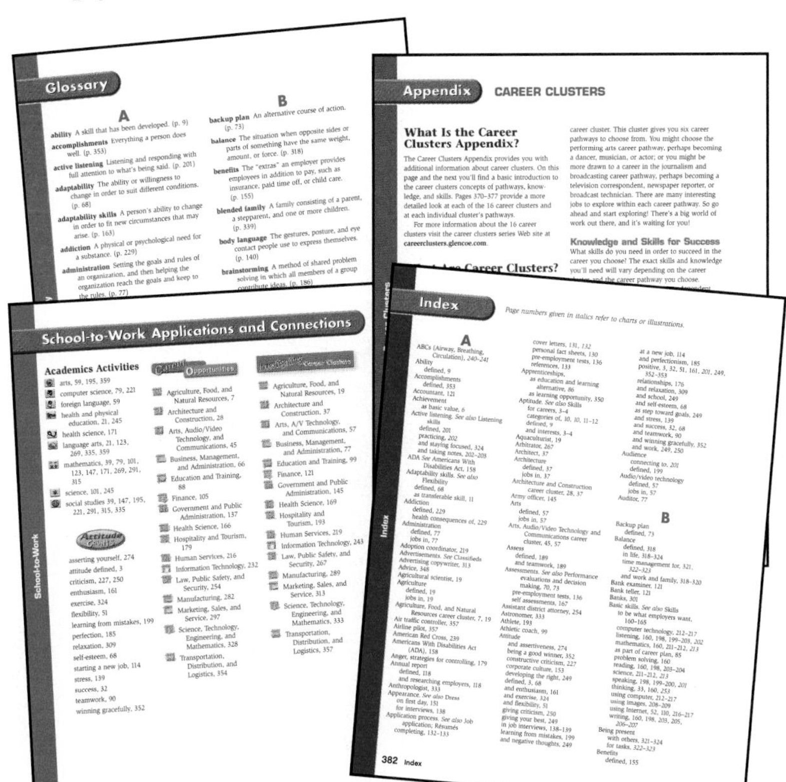

Glossary allows you to find definitions quickly and easily. Following each definition in parentheses is the page number on which the term is defined.

Career Clusters Appendix provides detailed information about each career cluster's pathways.

School-to-Work Applications and Connections helps you find activities that tie your classroom learning to the workplace.

Index lists key terms and ideas along with important graphs, charts, and other illustrations.

Chapter 1

Self Awareness

Lesson 1.1

Your Interests and Values

Lesson 1.2

Your Skills and Aptitudes

Lesson 1.3

Your Personality and Learning Styles

CAREER CLUSTER

You will explore the Agriculture, Food, and Natural Resources career cluster.

What You'll Learn

- You will explore who you are.
- You will discover your interests, values, skills, and aptitudes.
- You will learn how your personality and learning styles can affect your career choices.

Get Ready!

Describe Yourself

- Make a collage of five words that describe you.
- Share your collage with four or five people from different areas of your life. Ask each person to suggest words to add. Note these words.

Apply Compare the words on your collage to the words you noted. Add the noted words to your collage. Does your expanded collage create a more complete picture of you?

Lesson 1.1

Your Interests and Values

Discover

- What interests you
- The link between your interests and different careers
- What you value, or believe is important

Why It's Important

Your interests and values are at the heart of who you are and will help lead you to careers that are right for you.

KEY TERMS

- **interests**
- **technology**
- **interest inventory**
- **values**
- **work values**
- **economic values**

Who are you? Don't answer right away. Take some time to think about you. After all, most people spend their whole lives discovering who they are. Getting to know yourself is an important part of your journey. In fact, it can be the most exciting journey of your life.

On your journey, you'll try new ways of doing things. You'll look at things in different ways. You'll go down many paths. Some will lead to careers. How will you know the way? By exploring and finding who you are.

Discovering Your Interests

How do I like to spend my free time? What am I curious about? What do I find fascinating? These are questions you'll be asking yourself as you explore your **interests.** Your interests are your favorite activities. People have some interests in common. Look at **Figure 1.1**. Do you share any of these interests? Which ones?

Your Favorite Things

Make a list of your interests. How do you spend your time? What school subjects do you enjoy?

Discover Yourself Before thinking about your future, get to know yourself. Look in the mirror. *How would you describe the person you see?*

What are your favorite things to do? Perhaps you like to read, play sports, dance, cook, or surf the Web.

What do you talk about with your friends? What kinds of books and magazines do you read? What kinds of TV shows and movies do you watch? What do you daydream about? Your answers to all of these questions are your interests.

Where Do Your Interests Lead?

Now take a close look at your list of interests. You may begin to see patterns. Things you enjoy doing may fall into categories, or groups.

People, Information, or Technology

Do many or most of your interests fall into one of the groups shown in **Figure 1.2** on pages 4–5? Take a look.

The *people* category describes activities involving people. The *information* category has to do with using ideas, facts, words, and figures. The *technology* category involves working with things, such as tools, machines, and other equipment. **Technology** is the practical use of scientific knowledge (ideas, methods, tools, and materials) to get things done.

Matching Interests and Careers

So far you've made your own list of interests. You may also want to consider taking an interest inventory. An **interest inventory** is a checklist that points to your strongest interests.

Attitude Counts

What Is Attitude?

Attitude is a general outlook on life. A person with a positive attitude sees the good things and works to improve any negative things. A positive attitude makes life more enjoyable.

Cooperative Learning Activity

Raul spent two hours on the computer working on an assignment. Just as he finished, his computer crashed. Raul lost all his work. Discuss the following with a partner, then share your thoughts with the class:

- The good things in this situation.
- Ways to improve the negative parts of this situation.

Figure 1.1

SOME COMMON INTERESTS

MUSIC

OUTDOORS

SPORTS

ANIMALS

FASHION

Things You Enjoy Interests can lead to careers. *What careers might each of these interests lead to?*

You choose interests from groups of items. Then your interests are matched to possible careers. For example, if you're interested in engineering and astronomy, you might be matched to a career in aerospace engineering.

There are no right or wrong answers when you take an interest inventory. An interest inventory is just another way of exploring who you are. It is also a way of exploring possible careers. Ask your teacher or school counselor if you can fill out an interest inventory.

Figure 1.2 PEOPLE, INFORMATION, OR TECHNOLOGY

Many people strongly prefer people, information, or technology. *Which interests you?*

A

People

If you're interested in people, you may make friends easily. You probably get along well with others. You might enjoy helping your friends solve their problems. You're usually ready to drop everything to be with others. You might enjoy being a salesperson, a fitness trainer, or a police officer. **Many careers involve working with people.**

What Are Values?

Values also give you direction. Your **values** are what you believe is important. They are the beliefs and ideas you live by. Like your interests, your values are an important part of who you are. Your values help you to make all kinds of decisions, from choosing friends to choosing careers. Values can guide you as you make important decisions. They can help you make wise choices.

B

Information

Maybe you like information. If so, you probably enjoy reading. You may spend hours in the library or exploring sites on the Internet. You might be interested in history. You may know baseball scores and world records. Someday you might be a Web site designer, a detective, or a book editor. **Many careers are open to people who like information.**

C

Technology

If technology grabs your interest, you may enjoy making or fixing things. You may take things apart just to see how they work. Perhaps you can work on a computer for hours without even noticing the time. One day you might be a video producer, a recording engineer, or a lab technician. **There are many careers for people interested in technology.**

Your **work values** are the things about work that are important to you. Understanding your work values will help you select a career that suits you. For example, if you value independence, you might be happy working as an entrepreneur. If you value helping other people, you would probably enjoy a career as a social worker, a teacher, or a health care worker.

You also have economic values. Your **economic values** are how important money is to your happiness. Your economic values influence your economic goals.

Where do your values come from? You learn them from important people in your life—family members, teachers, religious leaders. The values of your culture or community may also influence your personal values.

Luis Ramos of Miami, Florida, gives his grandmother credit for many of his values.

> "My grandmother taught me to care about others, especially older people. When I was thinking about careers, I knew I wanted to help people."

Luis is a home health aide. He cares for an older man who lives on his own.

Figure 1.3

BASIC VALUES

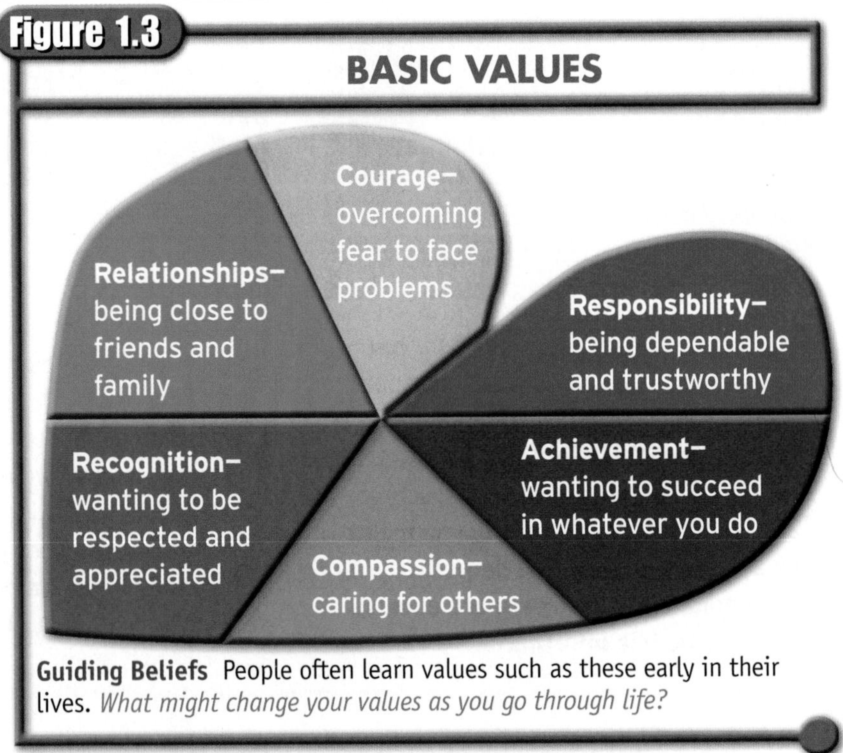

Guiding Beliefs People often learn values such as these early in their lives. *What might change your values as you go through life?*

Uncovering Your Values

People share many basic values. **Figure 1.3** shows some of them. Many values are taught by example. If your parents or family members always make an effort to be truthful with you, you'll probably be truthful, too. If you see them helping others, you'll learn by their example.

Try This Activity

Evaluate Your Values

Do you share any of the values listed in **Figure 1.3**? What other values do you have?

Make a Chart In the left-hand column of your chart, list your values. In the right-hand column, tell where these values came from. Are they personal values, family values, work values, economic values, or cultural values?

Compare Charts Compare your chart with a partner. Then keep it for later use. Add new values as you discover them.

Your values can guide you as you make important decisions. They can help you choose wisely.

Career Opportunities

Agriculture, Food, and Natural Resources

Do you enjoy farming? Mining? Ranching? Do you appreciate forests and natural parks? Then perhaps a career in the Agriculture, Food, and Natural Resources career cluster is for you. Many careers involve working outdoors.

ZOOKEEPER

Zoo seeks experienced keeper. Candidates must have at least 5 years of experience caring for animals in a zoo, ranch, or wildlife preserve. Keepers are responsible for feeding, watering, cleaning, and caring for animals. Experience with large mammals a plus.

Critical Thinking

Do you think zookeepers need to have good communication skills? Why?

Lesson 1.1 Review and Activities

Key Terms Review

1. On a separate sheet of paper, write six sentences that use the key terms. Draw a blank line in place of the key term in each sentence. Exchange sentences with a partner and complete each other's sentences.
   - **interests**
   - **technology**
   - **interest inventory**
   - **values**
   - **work values**
   - **economic values**

Check Your Understanding

Choose the correct answer for each item. Write your answers on a separate sheet of paper.

2. Two things you should consider about yourself when investigating careers are ______.
   a. teamwork and homework
   b. technology and people
   c. interests and values
3. Your values are ______.
   a. the beliefs and ideas you live by
   b. the items you buy at a store for a good price
   c. the things you like doing

Critical Thinking

Use complete sentences to answer the following questions. Write your answers on a separate sheet of paper.

4. How do you think you develop interests?
5. Why is it a good idea to think about your interests when making career choices?
6. Who might help you identify your values?

Connecting to the Workplace

7. **Interests and Values** Survey three teachers at your school to find out what interests and values can lead to a teaching career. Take notes during your interviews. Then, create a chart listing the interests and values mentioned by the teachers. When you are finished, write a job profile detailing some of the values and interests it takes to be a teacher.

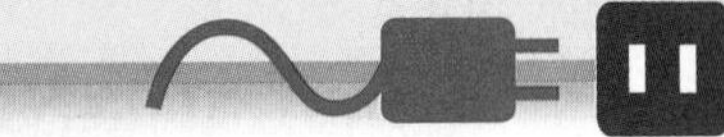

Teamwork

8. **Put Values Into Practice** Team up with a group of classmates. Choose one value you all share. Think of an idea for putting what you collectively value into practice. For example, your team's value might be protecting the environment. One way to put that value into practice would be to start a recycling program at your school. Create a poster that illustrates your value and idea for putting it into action. Share your team's poster with the class.

Lesson 1.2

Your Skills and Aptitudes

Now you've got some idea of your interests and values. Don't stop there. You're just getting to know yourself. What's next? You'll want to consider what you can learn to do.

Comparing Skills and Aptitudes

A **skill** is the ability to perform a task due to training and experience. Once you've learned something, it becomes a skill. You already have many skills. You can read and write. You may know how to play an instrument or a sport. These are skills. An **ability** is a skill you have already developed. An **aptitude** is your potential for learning a skill.

Use Your Skills
You may find a career some day that uses abilities you have now. *What is something you do well or know how to do? To what careers could it lead?*

Discover

- How skills and aptitudes differ
- What your skills and aptitudes are
- Where your skills and aptitudes might lead you

Why It's Important

Your skills and aptitudes are clues to what you can do. They can point you toward different careers.

KEY TERMS

- skill
- ability
- aptitude
- job-specific skills
- transferable skills

Having an aptitude is like having a knack for something, like drawing, or training pets. Aptitudes can be developed into skills. Micky Campbell showed an aptitude for building things when she was growing up.

"When I was a kid," Micky recalls, "all I wanted to do was put pieces of wood together. I made birdhouses, dollhouses, tree houses—anything I could think of." Today, Micky runs her own construction business near Charlotte, North Carolina. She builds houses—first homes, dream houses, and everything in between. Micky turned her aptitude into a skill by learning carpentry.

What Are Your Skills?

What skills do you have? How can you figure out what your aptitudes are? Start by making a list. Set up a chart like the one in **Figure 1.4**. Group your skills and aptitudes under the headings *Mental*, *Physical*, and *Social*. Write down all your skills and aptitudes that come to mind. Keep your list handy and add new skills and aptitudes as you think of them.

Figure 1.4

MY SKILLS AND APTITUDES

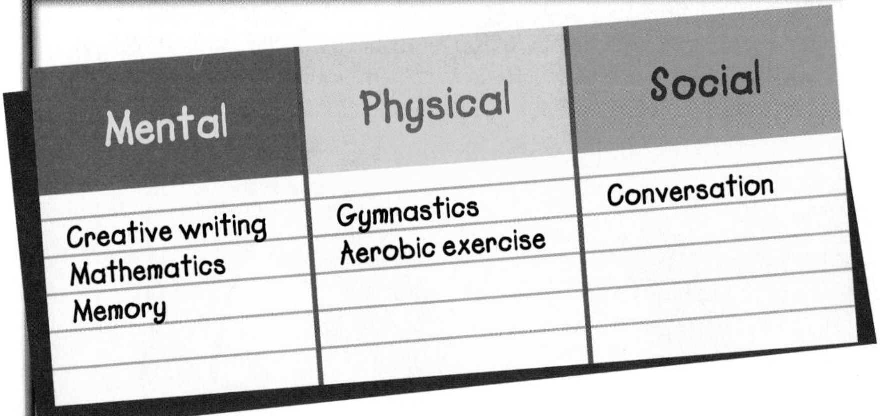

Mental	Physical	Social
Creative writing	Gymnastics	Conversation
Mathematics	Aerobic exercise	
Memory		

Skills and Aptitudes One way to analyze your skills and aptitudes is to think of them in groups. Make a chart with three headings: Mental, Physical, and Social. Then write your skills and aptitudes under the appropriate heading. *Are all three groups the same size, or do you have more skills and aptitudes in one area than in another?*

Understanding Different Kinds of Skills

Employers always want workers to have both job-specific skills and general transferable skills. **Job-specific skills** are the skills necessary to do a particular job, like balancing a budget or programming a computer. **Transferable skills** are general skills used in school and in various types of jobs. Transferable skills are always necessary, regardless of the career you choose. The following is a list of some of the most common transferable workplace skills:

- Communication skills
- Listening skills
- Problem-solving skills
- Technology skills
- Decision-making skills
- Organizing and planning skills
- Teamwork skills
- Social skills
- Adaptability skills

Q & A

Getting the Skills You'll Need

Q: I know exactly what job I want. Why should I waste time developing skills that don't seem related to this job?

A: It is important to get as many skills as you can. Although some skills might not seem necessary, most jobs require workers to have more than just one kind of skill. For example, chefs need cooking skills, but they also need math and planning skills. A variety of skills is necessary for succeeding and advancing in a job.

Apply Your Aptitudes Many people dream of being professional athletes. *In what other careers might you use your aptitude for a sport?*

Try This Activity

Assess Your Career Interests and Aptitudes

Understanding your personal interests and aptitudes will help you set and achieve realistic career and educational goals. Start by completing a formal career interest and aptitude assessment. Your teacher or school counselor should be able to give you such a test.

Match Interests and Aptitudes to Opportunities Once you've completed your self-assessment, match your interests and aptitudes to career opportunities. Make a list of your interests and aptitudes. Then write down several career opportunities that match your interests and aptitudes. Record why each career on your list might be a good fit for you.

Get Feedback Show your list of aptitudes, interests, and potential careers to a friend, a family member, a teacher, or someone else you trust. Ask whether he or she thinks the careers you have listed are right for you and why. Add this information to your list.

Develop Your Skills Select the career from your list that interests you most and consider what skills you would need to develop to achieve that career. Be sure to consider transferable workplace skills as well as job-specific skills. Write down the skills you need and how you can acquire them.

Thinking About the Future

Do you feel you know yourself any better now? Take a break and take stock. Review your list of skills and aptitudes. Allow yourself to dream a bit about where some of your strengths might lead you.

Here are a few thoughts to keep in mind as you think about the future.

- Everyone has different skills and aptitudes.
- Certain skills are more important in some careers than in others.
- Transferable skills are required in all careers.
- You need to develop skills in many areas. You will not have an aptitude for everything you want to learn. Don't let that stop you from developing the skills you want and need.

Lesson 1.2 Review and Activities

Key Terms Review

1. In your own words describe each of the key terms. Then explain how an aptitude differs from a skill and how a transferable skill differs from a job-specific skill.
   - **skill**
   - **ability**
   - **aptitude**
   - **job-specific skills**
   - **transferable skills**

Check Your Understanding

Determine whether each statement is true or false. Rewrite any false statement to make it true. Write your answers on a separate sheet of paper.

2. Once you've learned something, it becomes an aptitude.
3. An example of a skill is being able to play an instrument.
4. An aptitude is a well-developed skill.

Critical Thinking

Use complete sentences to answer the following questions. Write your answers on a separate sheet of paper.

5. Do you think it is important to try to develop skills related to your aptitudes? Why or why not?
6. What skills do you have now that are not connected to any of your aptitudes?

Connecting to the Workplace

7. **Understanding Skills** Use words and pictures to create a presentation about transferable skills. Explain the difference between job-specific skills and transferable skills. Then explain how transferable skills are used in school and in a variety of careers. In your presentation, define each type of transferable skill and describe how each can be used in several situations and among different careers. Tell why employers value workers with these transferable skills. Share your presentation with the class.

Character Building

8. **Career Advice** A school counselor told Raquel that her skills and aptitudes are perfect for a career in technology. He encouraged her to look for careers in this area. Raquel does like to instant message with friends over the Internet, but working on a computer is not her favorite activity. Her favorite activities are exercising and taking care of people. She dreams of a job in health care and thinks that a career as a physical therapist would be perfect for her. Write Raquel a letter offering her advice about choosing a career that's right for her.

Lesson 1.3

Your Personality and Learning Styles

Discover

- What kind of personality you have
- Your best ways of learning
- How your personality and learning styles can affect your career choices

Why It's Important

Your personality and learning style are both signs of how you think, act, and feel. They can help direct you to careers that match the kind of person you are.

KEY TERMS

- **personality**
- **learning styles**
- **self awareness**

"She's got a great personality." "He's got a great personality." How many times have you heard someone say that about someone else? Have you ever thought about what it really meant, though? Your personality is what makes you a special person. By that definition, we all have great personalities.

Exploring Personality

Your **personality** is what makes you different from everyone else. It's the sum total of your feelings, actions, habits, and thoughts. Your personality makes you a unique individual.

Who Do You Think You Are?

If someone asked you to describe your personality, what would you say? You might start naming some of your characteristics. What are some of the first words that come to mind?

Everyone Is Different Imagine a world in which everyone had the same personality. *What special quality of yours would people miss? What special quality of a friend would you miss?*

Describe Your Personality

Try This Activity

Here are a few ideas to get you started. Look at the words below. Which best fit your personality?

outgoing	loyal	confident
fun-loving	dependable	friendly
flexible	generous	creative
energetic	quiet	shy
caring	serious	self-directed

Express Yourself Write a paragraph about your personality. Include those words from the list above or any other words that describe your personality.

Look at Ways You Learn

How you think and learn is another part of your personality. The different ways people naturally think and learn are called **learning styles.** When you are aware of your own learning styles, you are able to determine the best approach for you to learn something new. You can also determine which career areas are right for you.

Take a look at the learning styles shown in **Figure 1.5** on page 16. Which type of learner are you? What do you like to do? What are the best ways for you to learn? Is there more than one learning style that applies to you?

Self Awareness and Career Strategy

Why think about your personality? Why figure out what kind of learner you are? Your personality will affect how you work and the people you work with. Knowing your learning styles will help you take the best approach to learning new things on the job.

Knowing your thoughts, feelings, and actions is **self awareness.** Self awareness is the key to career exploration and to a successful career strategy. To assess your strengths, weaknesses, and developmental needs, you must understand yourself. Self awareness is also an essential element of a successful career strategy. Self-aware people are able to effectively set and achieve goals.

Figure 1.5

EIGHT STYLES OF LEARNING

Type of Learner	Likes	Best Ways to Learn
Verbal/ Linguistic Learner	Likes to read, write, and tell stories; good at memorizing names and dates	Learns best by saying, hearing, and seeing words
Logical/ Mathematical Learner	Likes to ask questions, do experiments, work with numbers, explore patterns and relationships, and solve puzzles and problems	Learns best by making categories, classifying, and working with patterns
Visual/ Spatial Learner	Likes to draw, build, design, and create things; good at imagining, doing puzzles and mazes, and reading maps and charts	Learns best by using the mind's eye and working with colors and pictures
Musical/ Rhythmic Learner	Likes to sing, hum, play an instrument, and listen to music; good at remembering melodies, noticing pitches and rhythms, and keeping time	Learns best through rhythm and melody
Bodily/ Kinesthetic Learner	Likes to touch and move around; good at hands-on activities and crafts	Learns best by inter-acting with people and objects in a real space
Interpersonal Learner	Likes having lots of friends, talking to people, and joining groups; good at understanding people, leading, organizing, communicating, and mediating conflicts	Learns best by sharing, comparing, and cooperating
Intrapersonal Learner	Likes to work alone and pursue interests at own pace; good at self awareness, focusing on personal feelings, and following instincts to learn what needs to be known	Learns best through independent study
Naturalistic Learner	Likes spending time outdoors and working with plants, animals, and other parts of the natural environment; good at identifying plants and animals and at hearing and seeing connections to nature	Learns best by observing, collecting, identifying, sorting, and organizing patterns

Learning Styles Most people have more than one learning style. *Which learning styles would rank as your top two or three?*

The Global Workplace

How Do *You* Say It in English?

English is the official language spoken in England and Australia, but it might still sound like a foreign language to you on a visit there. Not all English-speaking countries use the same words you do. They may use local words in place of words that are familiar to you.

It's a good idea to know some local words when you do business in other English-speaking countries. If you're in need of a bathroom in England, ask for the "loo." If you are looking for the subway in London, ask for the "Tube." In Australia, ask where you can find some "tucker" if you are hungry and want food.

Internet Activity

Use Internet resources to find out what other countries use English as the official language. Learn some common unique local words used in these countries. Go to the *Exploring Careers* Web site at exploring.glencoe.com for a list of Web sites to help you complete this activity.

Considering Career Options

Now that you've started getting to know yourself, you should also get to know your career options. A great way to learn about career options is to study career clusters. A career cluster is a group of similar occupations and industries. Career clusters were developed by the U.S. Department of Education as a way to organize career planning. Each cluster covers a major segment of the economy, such as manufacturing, finance, or government and public administration.

In each chapter of this textbook you will learn about a different career cluster. The Investigating Career Clusters feature on page 19 will help you begin to explore career clusters. To learn more about career clusters in general, read Chapter 3. You can also find more detailed information about career clusters in the Career Clusters Appendix at the back of the book.

Lesson 1.3 Review and Activities

Key Terms Review

1. Imagine you are a crossword-puzzle writer. Write a clue for each of the following key terms.

- **personality**
- **learning styles**
- **self awareness**

Check Your Understanding

Choose the correct answer for each item. Write your answers on a separate sheet of paper.

2. Your personality is ______.

a. all your characteristics, or qualities
b. how you think about others
c. the type of people you know

3. If you learn best by working alone, your style of learning is ______.

a. musical
b. intrapersonal
c. interpersonal

Critical Thinking

Use complete sentences to answer the following questions. Write your answers on a separate sheet of paper.

4. How does self awareness benefit you?

5. Look at the learning styles chart on page 16. What careers would you match with the different learning styles?

6. Why might you do well in a career that uses your strongest learning style?

Connecting to the Workplace

7. **Personality and Careers** Work with a partner. Interview your partner to find out about his or her personality. Note several words that best describe your partner's personality, then think of a career that might fit this personality. Write a personalized career report for your partner explaining why the career would be right for him or her. Begin the report as follows: You would be a good __________ because you are . . . . Exchange reports and discuss them.

Teamwork

8. **Learning Styles** Choose one of the eight learning styles. Team up with other classmates who chose the same learning style. As a team write three sentences that are true about the learning style and two sentences that are false. Then play "Fact or Fiction" with the other teams. Read your sentences and have other teams guess which sentences about your team's learning style are "fiction."

Investigating Career Clusters

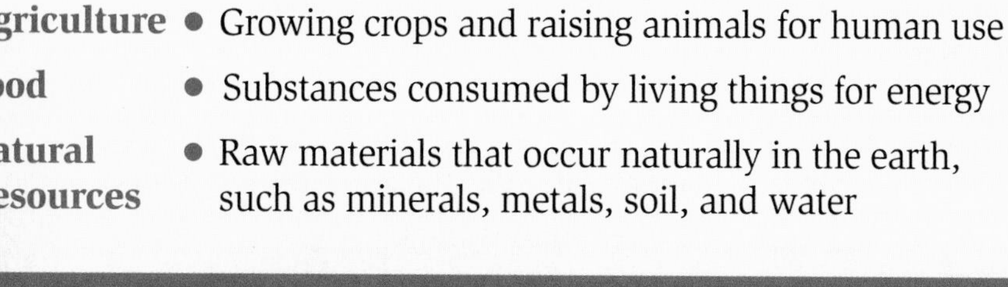

AGRICULTURE, FOOD, AND NATURAL RESOURCES

Agriculture • Growing crops and raising animals for human use

Food • Substances consumed by living things for energy

Natural Resources • Raw materials that occur naturally in the earth, such as minerals, metals, soil, and water

Job Title	Work Description
Agricultural Scientist	Studies farm crops and animals to develop ways of improving their quality and quantity
Aquaculturist	Raises fish such as trout, catfish, and salmon in stock ponds
Deckhand	Operates a fishing ship and its equipment
Ecologist	Studies the relationships between organisms and their environment and among groups of organisms
Farmer	Plants, cultivates, harvests, and stores crops; tends livestock and poultry
Forester	Manages, protects, and improves forested lands
Game Warden	Patrols and protects public areas and wildlife
Geologist	Studies the physical aspects of the earth

Exploration Activity

Agriculture, Food, and Natural Resources Use library and Internet resources to research a career in the Agriculture, Food, and Natural Resources career cluster. Write a report on your findings. Include information about the kinds of work, the skills required, the working conditions, the training and education required, and the career outlook.

Cooperative Learning Interview a classmate about the career he or she researched. Find out as much information about that career as you can during the interview. Then have your classmate interview you about the career you researched. Afterward, take turns sharing what you learned from each other with the class.

Chapter 1 Review and Activities

Chapter Highlights

Lesson 1.1 Your interests and values can lead you in many career directions.

Lesson 1.2 Your skills and aptitudes will be needed in a variety of careers.

Lesson 1.3 Your personality and learning style may fit some careers better than others.

Key Concept Review

Use complete sentences to answer the following questions. Write your answers on a separate sheet of paper.

1. How can you discover your interests?
2. Where do values come from?
3. How does an aptitude differ from a skill?
4. What makes up a personality?
5. What are the eight learning styles?

Critical Thinking

Use complete sentences to answer the following questions. Write your answers on a separate sheet of paper.

6. Which of your interests have to do with people? Information? Technology?
7. Why is it important to know what your values are before making career choices?
8. What is something you have an aptitude for? How would you go about developing an aptitude into a skill?
9. What do you think the world would be like if everyone had the same skills and aptitudes?
10. What careers do you think might fit your personality?

Skill Building

11. **Basic—Mathematics**
    Take a survey of the learning styles in your class. Ask each student to name his or her main learning style. Record your classmates' responses. Total the number of students for each learning style. Show the number of students for each style in a bar graph. Explain the results of your survey to the class.

12. Personal Qualities—Self-Esteem

Create an award for a part of your personality you wish to honor. Decorate the award with drawings that illustrate your personality.

Academic Applications

13. Language Arts

Write an essay about yourself. Describe your interests, values, skills, aptitudes, and personality. Tell about goals and dreams you have for your life. Discuss ways you plan to get to know yourself better.

14. Health and Physical Education

Ask a friend or family member to teach you a new physical activity this week. You might learn a new dance or a new sport. You might experiment with yoga or tai chi. Afterward, record your reaction. What did you like about the new activity? What did you dislike? What did it teach you about yourself?

Personal Career Portfolio

Begin Your Portfolio

- **Begin** to create a Personal Career Portfolio to showcase your skills and accomplishments.
- **Use** a folder with dividers to organize your portfolio materials.
- **Label** your folder *My Personal Career Portfolio*.
- **Create** a cover page with your name, class, teacher, and school.
- **Create** a contents page where you will list the contents of your portfolio as you build it.
- **Write** lists of your interests, aptitudes, skills, and values.
- **Categorize** your skills as Basic Skills, Thinking Skills, or Personal Qualities.
- **Title** the document *Inventory of Interests, Aptitudes, Skills, and Values* and file it in your Personal Career Portfolio.
- **Update** the inventory as you discover and gain new interests, aptitudes, skills, and values.
- **List** your portfolio entry on your Personal Career Portfolio contents page.

Chapter 2

Thinking About Work

Lesson 2.1

What Is Work All About?

Lesson 2.2

How Work Is Changing

CAREER CLUSTER

You will explore the Architecture and Construction career cluster.

What You'll Learn

- You will step inside the world of work.
- You will discover why people work and how work affects their lives.
- You will learn how the world of work is changing.
- You will begin to imagine yourself as part of that exciting world some time in the future.

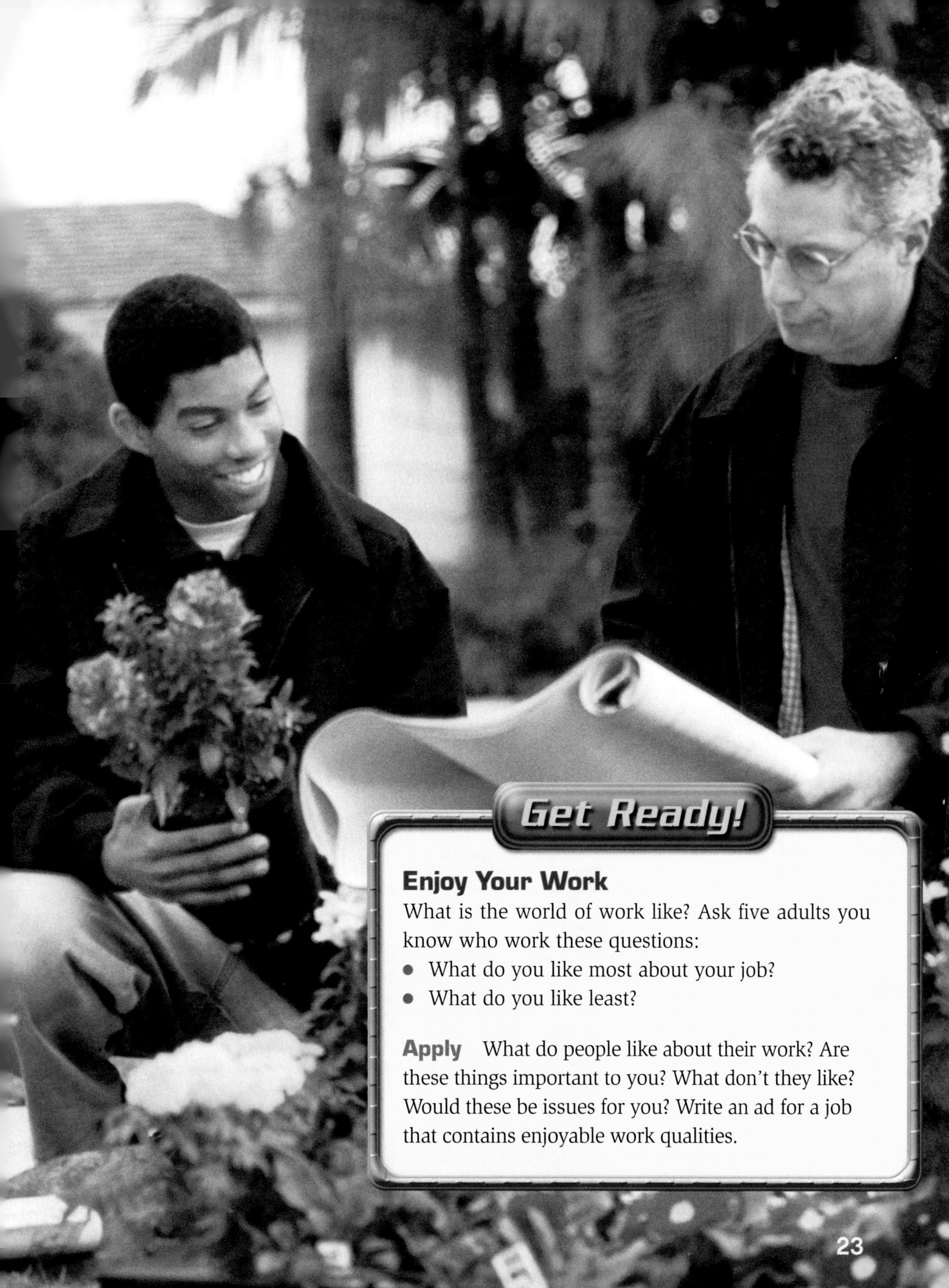

Get Ready!

Enjoy Your Work

What is the world of work like? Ask five adults you know who work these questions:

- What do you like most about your job?
- What do you like least?

Apply What do people like about their work? Are these things important to you? What don't they like? Would these be issues for you? Write an ad for a job that contains enjoyable work qualities.

Lesson 2.1

What Is Work All About?

Discover

- Why people work
- How work affects people's lives

Why It's Important

Choosing work that is right for you will be easier to do if you understand why people work and how work can affect your life.

KEY TERMS

- **job**
- **occupation**
- **career**
- **full-time**
- **lifestyle**

Think about your world—your everyday world. Where do you go? What do you do? Who are the people in your life?

You probably spend a lot of time at home and in school. The people around you are mostly family and friends. Your days are full. You have classes and homework. Maybe you take part in after-school activities.

This is the world you know—today. One day, though, your world will be different. Work will be part of your life.

What Is Work?

That's a good question. A quick, easy answer is that work is what people do to earn money. **Figure 2.1** shows that people need money to pay for their needs and wants. Money is not the whole story, though.

Make Friends
You're with all kinds of people at school each day. *Where do you think you'll meet people when you've finished school?*

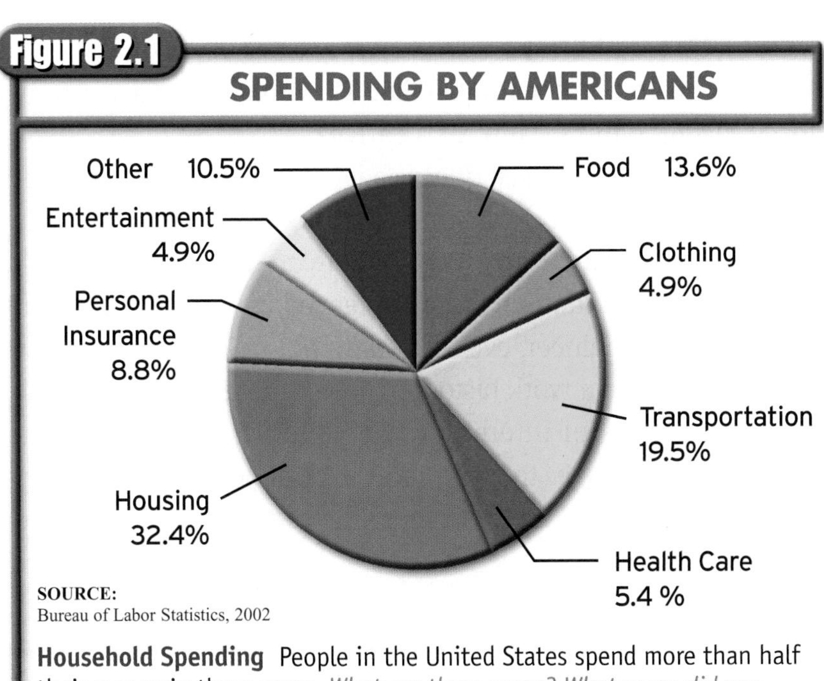

Household Spending People in the United States spend more than half their money in three areas. *What are those areas? What areas did you expect would be the top three? Why?*

Why Work?

People work for many reasons. Take Roberto Hernandez, a wildlife biologist. He has this to say about work.

> "Work isn't just about money. For me, it's about making a difference in the world. I use what I've learned about science to help animals. On the job I also get to meet people who are interested in the same things I am. It's great to work at something you like."

According to Roberto, there are many reasons for working. People work

- to make a contribution,
- to help others,
- to use skills and talents,
- to meet other people.

There are other reasons for working. Some people work so that they won't be bored. Others work to challenge their mind or feel good about themselves. What other reasons for working can you think of?

Jobs, Occupations, and Careers

How do you find work you like? Do you look for a job, train for an occupation, or aim for a career?

The answer to the last question is "all three." Work includes jobs, occupations, and careers. A **job** is work that people do for pay. An **occupation** is a set of related skills and experiences. If you are trained and experienced as an engineer, your occupation is engineer, even if you do not hold an engineering job. A **career** is a work history of one or more jobs in the same or related fields of interest. Each job in a career builds on interest, knowledge, training, and experience from the other jobs. Look at **Figure 2.2** to see how Roberto Hernandez arrived at his career.

Figure 2.2 JOBS LEAD TO CAREERS

Roberto Hernandez found jobs doing what he liked. A series of jobs led to his career as a wildlife biologist. *Which jobs interest you? What careers could they lead to?*

A

Roberto Hernandez began his career as a young child. He fed the wildlife in his neighborhood. Roberto volunteered to keep his neighbor's birdfeeder full.

B

While in high school, Roberto got a job cleaning out animal cages at the local animal shelter. In this job, he learned about animal behavior.

Your Work and Your Life

Like Roberto, you'll want to do work you enjoy. Did you know that you could spend 2,000 hours a year working? If you work **full-time,** you'll be on the job at least 40 hours a week. That's time you'll want to spend doing something you enjoy.

Choosing a Way of Life

There are other reasons to think carefully about career choices. For one, the work you do affects your lifestyle. Your **lifestyle** is the way you use your time, energy, and other resources. Many people use much of their time and energy at work.

C

In college he worked as a research assistant. This job taught him how to study animals in their natural habitats.

D

Now Roberto works as a wildlife biologist at the San Diego Zoo. His field studies with wildlife help maintain the delicate ecosystem balance.

Try This Activity

What Kind of Lifestyle Do You Want?

It is important to understand the impact of career choice on personal lifestyle. Think about the kind of lifestyle you want.

Lifestyle Budget Prepare a personal lifestyle budget reflecting your lifestyle desires. In what manner would you like to live? Write down your future lifestyle goals, and then create a detailed budget to show how much money you will need each month and each year to achieve those goals.

Think About Salaries Now that you have estimated how much it will cost to live the lifestyle you plan, use print and online resources to determine the monthly salaries of ten careers in which you are interested. Rank the careers according to salary needs and determine which of the careers will allow you to meet your lifestyle expectations. Select the career from your list that most closely matches your lifestyle budget.

Remain Flexible As you plan for your future, remember that adaptability and flexibility are vitally important. As you progress along your career path, you need to be able to recognize whether you need to make changes to your career plan to achieve the kind of lifestyle you want.

Career Opportunities

Architecture and Construction

If you enjoy making things, and are hardworking, detail-oriented, and good at visualization, then a career in architecture and construction may be right for you.

Critical Thinking

Do you think people working in construction need to be creative? Why?

LANDSCAPE ARCHITECT

Architectural firm seeks experienced landscape architect. Applicants must have experience with drafting blueprints, estimating costs, and analyzing environmental impact reports. Experience with drought-resistant gardens a plus.

Lesson 2.1 Review and Activities

Key Terms Review

1. Imagine you've written news articles on the following topics: jobs, careers, and lifestyles. Write five headlines for your articles. Each should include one of the key terms. The headlines should grab people's attention in as few words as possible.
   - **job**
   - **occupation**
   - **career**
   - **full-time**
   - **lifestyle**

Check Your Understanding

Determine whether each statement is true or false. Rewrite any false statement to make it true. Write your answers on a separate sheet of paper.

2. A career is many different jobs.
3. People work to make a contribution, to help others, to use skills and talents, and to meet other people.
4. People in the United States spend more than half their money on housing, food, and clothing.

Critical Thinking

Use complete sentences to answer the following questions. Write your answers on a separate sheet of paper.

5. What do you think is the most important reason for working? Explain your answer.
6. How might the kind of work you choose affect your lifestyle?

Connecting to the Workplace

7. **Why People Work** Make a list of the reasons people work. Then take a survey of five people who work. Give them each a copy of the list. At the top of the paper, have them write the kind of work they do. Then ask them to check their reasons for working. Tally your results. What do your results tell you? Share your findings with your classmates.

Community Involvement

8. **Make a Chart** Make a list of 10 jobs in your community. Then make a chart that has five columns. Use the following headings for the columns: *Make a Contribution, Help Others, Use Skills and Talents, Meet Other People,* and *Challenge the Mind*. Under each heading, list the jobs that fit the description. Some jobs may be listed under more than one heading. From the chart, choose a job you might like. Under which headings did you list this job? Explain to the class why you would like that job.

Lesson 2.2

How Work Is Changing

Discover

- How the global economy affects jobs
- How technology is changing the way people work
- How the working population is changing

Why It's Important

Being aware of changes in the work world will help you make sound decisions about career possibilities.

KEY TERMS

- **economy**
- **goods**
- **services**
- **global economy**
- **job market**
- **labor force**
- **e-commerce**
- **gender equity**
- **trend**
- **team**
- **workforce diversity**
- **job sharing**
- **outsourcing**
- **telecommute**
- **flextime**

You know what work is. You understand why people work. You see the link between work and lifestyle. What else would you like to know? How about what's going on in the world of work right now?

The world of work is constantly changing. Some businesses fail. New businesses start. Certain kinds of workers are no longer needed. Other kinds of workers are in demand. The way people work is also changing.

Shop the World
As part of the global economy, you can buy goods from around the world. *How do you decide what to buy?*

Economic Changes: The Global Economy

One big change for Americans is that today the world of work is no longer limited to businesses located in the United States. The world of work really does include the whole world. It's global.

It's a Small World

Have you ever noticed where things you own were made? Check the packaging or labels on things you use every day. That pair of jeans may have been made in Hong Kong. Your radio may be a product of Japan. The shampoo you use may have been made in Mexico or Canada. The label on your backpack may say "Made in the U.S.A."

The Global Workplace

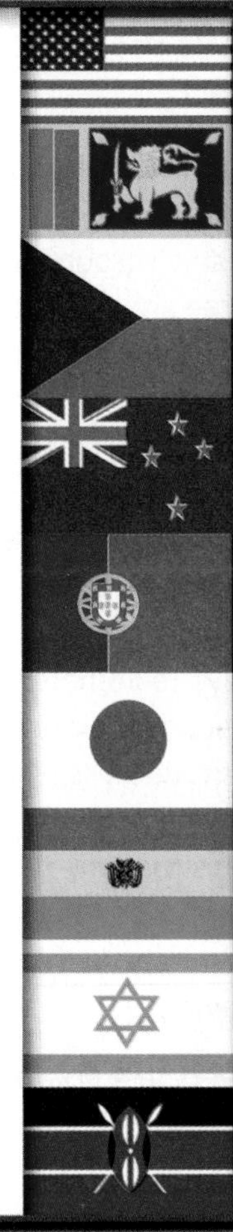

Trading Cards

Business cards are a quick way to give others your name, your company's name, and telephone number. Exchanging business cards in the United States is a casual affair. Today, you can e-mail electronic business cards to your associates or even "beam" the electronic cards to their personal digital assistants, or PDAs. In some countries though, trading business cards is a ritual. When doing business in Japan, always offer your business card with two hands. Make sure the words face the recipient. Accept a card with two hands and bow slightly to it. Then place the card in your jacket or shirt pocket. Never put it in your pants pocket or wallet.

Internet Activity

Use Internet resources to learn about some of the new technologies used today for business cards. Compare them with traditional business cards. Which kind of business card would you want? Why? Go to the *Exploring Careers* Web site at exploring.glencoe.com for a list of Web sites to help you complete this activity.

Attitude Counts

Recipe for Success

Success depends on more than hard work. Attitude is an essential ingredient in the recipe for success. You can start cultivating a positive attitude today. Positive attitude skills include enthusiasm, asserting yourself, managing stressful situations, flexibility, self-esteem, and treating people with respect.

Cooperative Learning Activity

- In small groups, list three situations to which you could respond with a positive or a negative attitude.
- Read one of the situations to the group.
- Have teammates practice their positive attitude skills by role-playing responses to the situation.
- Take turns reading situations and role-playing.

Work Abroad
Today, many jobs are available in other countries. *In what other country do you think you might like to work? Why?*

When you buy things that others make, you're taking part in the economy. The term **economy** refers to the ways people make, buy, and sell goods and services. **Goods** are items that people buy. **Services** are activities people do for others for a fee. When you buy goods made in other countries, you are part of the global economy. The **global economy** is all the world's economies and how they are linked. It's a small world—thanks to the global economy.

A World of Jobs

The global economy affects people around the world who buy goods. It also affects jobs around the world. In fact, the global economy affects the job market in each country. The **job market** is the need for workers and the kinds of work available to them. Each country has a labor force with unique skills and specialties. A **labor force** is all people over the age of 16 who work or are seeking work.

Some kinds of work may not be available in the United States. In recent years, some U.S. workers have lost their jobs to workers in other countries. Take the clothing industry, for instance. Many businesses in the United States have hired companies located in Asia to make clothing. U.S. businesses hire workers overseas because they will often work for less money than U.S. workers.

The global economy also creates jobs. People around the world want many goods and services U.S. businesses sell. Wheat, trucks, computer technology, and scientific instruments are just a few U.S. goods sold in other countries. That means jobs for workers in the United States.

Many businesses based in other countries have offices in the United States. They need people here to run them. Today, people in the United States find work in other countries more easily than in the past.

Technology Changes: Working in the Digital Age

Global is one buzzword. *Technology* is another. Technology has been part of your life since you were born. DVDs, satellite radio, the Internet, handheld computers, and cellular phones are nothing new to you. These and other forms of technology help people get information and do their work more quickly than before.

Technology has also fueled the development of e-commerce. **E-commerce** is the buying and selling of goods and services via the Internet. E-commerce has revolutionized the global marketplace. It has changed the way companies do business, and it has become a big part of the global economy.

Be Prepared for Lifelong Learning

If you're comfortable with both technology and change, you've got a head start on success. Today, workers need to be adaptable and willing to continually learn new technology and new ways of working.

One day, you will use the skills you're learning in school in the workplace. Every day you're improving basic skills, like reading, writing, mathematics, listening, and speaking. You are developing thinking skills, such as decision making and problem solving. You're also building personal skills, such as honesty and responsibility. You'll use these skills in all kinds of work later. They'll help you adjust to new technology and change, and they'll help you compete with others in the world of work.

Get a Head Start

Q: Why should I worry about changes happening now in the job I want? It'll be years before I'm working.

A: Keeping up with the changes happening today will give you a head start over others later. If you know what changes are taking place now, then you'll be able to plan to get the skills or knowledge you will need to do the job later. For instance, you can learn how to use a new software program, or you can take an extra course at school. So, be alert to what's happening now. Make it a habit to read stories about your job interest. Talk with those already in the field about the changes happening today.

Social Changes

You'll have a lot of company in the world of work. The number of people in the United States who work continues to increase. There are no signs that this growth is going to stop.

By 2010, there will be almost as many women as men working in the United States. The U.S. workplace has been moving toward having more gender equity. **Gender equity** is equal employment opportunity for all, regardless of gender.

There will also be more people of different backgrounds working. **Figure 2.3** shows the percentage of different groups in the work world. It also predicts how much each group will grow by the year 2010. The number of Hispanic and Asian workers will increase much faster than the number of workers from other groups.

People will also be staying in the labor force longer. You may hear less talk of retiring, or leaving work. People will think of work as something that lasts a lifetime.

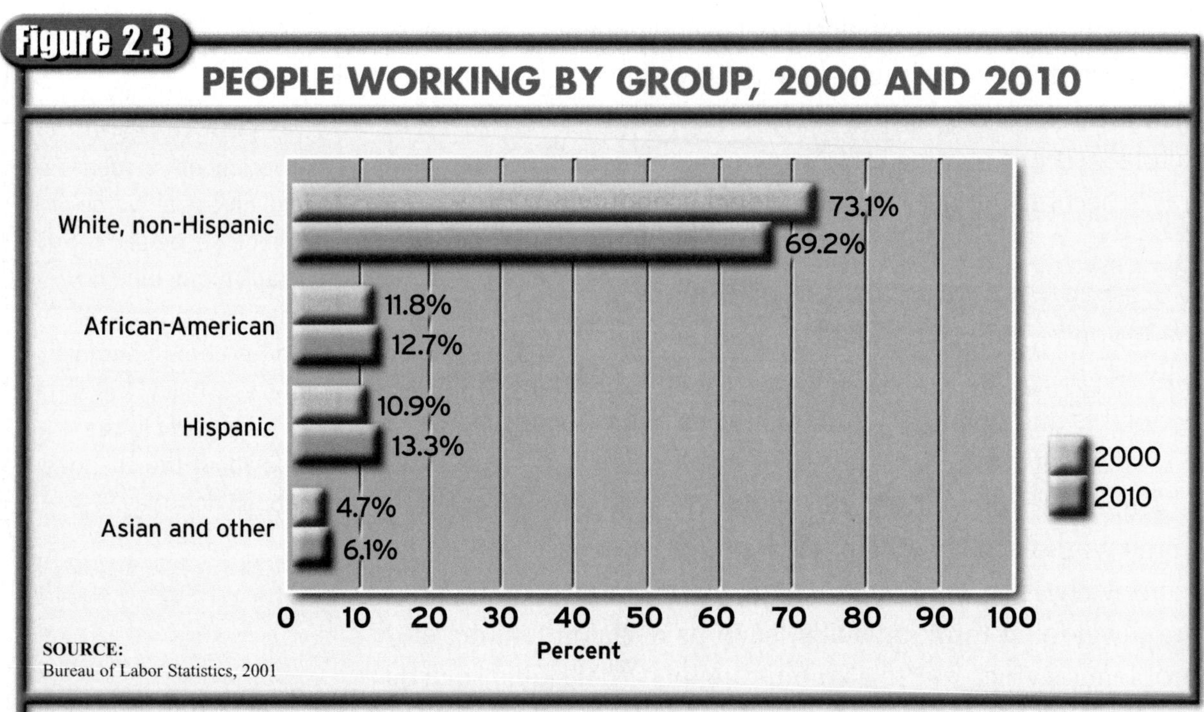

Americans Working The number of people working will continue to grow. *What group will represent most of the people at work in 2010? What group will represent a smaller group of working people than it did in 2000?*

Try This Activity

The Impact of Change

It is important to understand the effect change has on society and on career opportunities. Knowing about change helps you make sound decisions about your job, your career, and your future.

Compose a Report Write a report explaining positive and negative examples of societal change. Explain how each change affects society and career opportunities.

Workplace Trends

People today are working in new ways and places. Figure 2.4 shows just some of the trends that are important in the work world. A **trend** is a change over a period of time.

Figure 2.4

CHANGES IN HOW AND WHERE PEOPLE WORK

Teams	People today often work in teams. A **team** is a group of people who work together to set goals and make decisions to solve problems and put ideas into action. The growing importance of teamwork means that you will be evaluated on your team efforts as well as your individual accomplishments.
Workforce Diversity	Today's workplaces are more diverse. **Workforce diversity** is achieved by employing workers with different backgrounds, experiences, ideas, and skills.
Job Sharing	**Job sharing** is a flexible work arrangement that allows two part-time employees to divide one full-time job. The employees split duties, salaries, vacations, and other benefits. Job sharing allows people to combine careers with other commitments.
Outsourcing	Companies hire other companies for particular jobs. This is called outsourcing. **Outsourcing** is using outside resources to do tasks traditionally handled by internal staff. Outsourcing service providers are sometimes called independent contractors, contract workers, or vendors.
Telecommuting	More people are working at home than ever before. More than 30 million people **telecommute**, or work at home for a company. Computers, telephones, modems, and fax machines connect them to the company office. Others work for themselves. By 2010, more than 10 million Americans will be their own bosses.
Flextime	**Flextime** is a work schedule arrangement that allows workers to choose work hours that fit their particular needs. For example, a worker might want to start work early in the morning in order to leave in the mid-afternoon.

Modern Working There have been many changes in how and where people work. *Which new ways of working appeal to you? In what careers could you see yourself working in these ways?*

Lesson 2.2 Review and Activities

Key Terms Review

1. Write a speech about the changing world of work, using all the key terms for this lesson. Read your speech to the class.

- **economy**
- **goods**
- **services**
- **global economy**
- **job market**
- **labor force**
- **e-commerce**
- **gender equity**
- **trend**
- **team**
- **workforce diversity**
- **job sharing**
- **outsourcing**
- **telecommute**
- **flextime**

Check Your Understanding

Choose the correct answer for each item. Write your answers on a separate sheet of paper.

2. Three changes that will affect future careers include ______ changes.
   a. legal, technological, and ethical
   b. global, social, and typical
   c. global, technological, and social
3. The global economy is ______.
   a. the world environment
   b. the way the world's economies are linked and managed
   c. our world currency

Critical Thinking

Use complete sentences to answer the following questions. Write your answers on a separate sheet of paper.

4. How has technology changed work in a career that interests you?
5. How has diversity changed the workplace?
6. How have outsourcing and telecommuting changed work?

Character Building

7. **International Etiquette** You've found the perfect job in Singapore, but you don't know much about the culture. Use library and Internet resources to research business etiquette in Singapore. What are some of the differences you'll find when you get there? Write a paragraph explaining three ways you'll need to change your normal behavior and why these changes are necessary.

Teamwork

8. **Make a Presentation** Team up with other students to create a presentation about the Architecture and Construction career cluster. Use print or online resources to find out more about that career cluster. Make a presentation to your class about the career cluster and how change will affect it.

Investigating Career Clusters

ARCHITECTURE AND CONSTRUCTION

Architecture • Designing and constructing structures that enclose space to meet human needs

Construction • Building structures

Job Title	Work Description
Architect	Designs buildings and other structures
Building Inspector	Examines construction of buildings, highways, streets, or other structures
Carpenter	Cuts, fits, and assembles wood and other materials in the construction of buildings, highways, docks, boats, and other structures
Civil Engineer	Designs and supervises construction of roads, airports, tunnels, bridges, buildings, and other structures
Concrete Mason	Pours and finishes concrete to make patios, walkways, floors, roads, dams, and other areas
Drafter	Prepares technical plans that show how something should be built
Electrician	Installs, connects, tests, and maintains electrical systems
Landscape Architect	Designs landscaped areas that are functional and attractive and that fit in with the natural environment
Plumber	Installs, maintains, and repairs pipe systems
Roofer	Installs and repairs roofs

Exploration Activity

Architecture and Construction Use library and Internet resources to research a career in the Architecture and Construction career cluster. Write a report on the kinds of work, the skills required, the working conditions, the training and education required, and the career outlook.

Cooperative Learning Interview a classmate about the career he or she researched. Find out as much information about that career as you can during the interview. Then have your classmate interview you about the career you researched. Afterward, share what you learned with the class.

Chapter 2 Review and Activities

Chapter Highlights

Lesson 2.1 People work to earn money, to make a contribution, to help others, to use skills and talents, and to meet others.

Lesson 2.2 People today are working in new ways and places. The global economy affects jobs and job markets in every country.

Key Concept Review

Use complete sentences to answer the following questions. Write your answers on a separate sheet of paper.

1. List five reasons people work.
2. What is a lifestyle?
3. What is the global economy, and how does it affect jobs?
4. What are three social changes affecting the workplace today?
5. What are some recent changes in how and where people work?

Critical Thinking

Use complete sentences to answer the following questions. Write your answers on a separate sheet of paper.

6. Why would it help to have careers in mind when considering different jobs?
7. Why do you think many people spend much of their time and energy at work?
8. What does it mean to say that thanks to the global economy, it's a small world?
9. Why do you think some people are afraid of technology?
10. Why might an older person choose to continue to work?

Skill Building

11. **Basic—Reading**
    Read a daily newspaper for one week. Look for articles about the global economy. Make a news digest with summaries of each article. Circulate your news digest in class.
12. **Personal Qualities—Responsibility**
    Make a list of paid and volunteer jobs you've had. Then, describe your responsibilities in each job and the skills you used in each. Tell your classmates about your work experience.

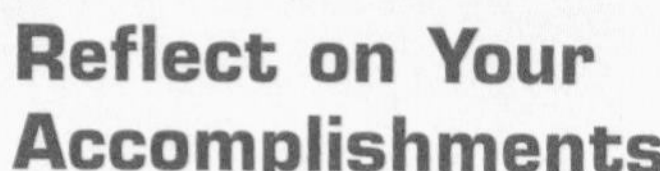

Personal Career Portfolio

Academic Applications

13. Social Studies

Imagine you're in charge of hiring at a car manufacturer. Sales of cars are down because many people are buying cars made overseas. Your company has to cut jobs. Research agencies that provide people with training or information about new jobs. Make a list of the agencies and what they do. Share your findings with the class.

14. Mathematics

Anita works as a project manager for an export company. Anita is responsible for hiring workers for the projects; each worker can produce $50,000 worth of goods for export. Her next project involves $900,000 worth of goods for export. How many people will she need to hire for the project?

Reflect on Your Accomplishments

- **List** the things you have accomplished in your life. This is a list of the things of which you are proud.
- **Write** a brief description of each of these accomplishments. Note why each was important to you. Did you have to work hard for it? Did it help others? Did it bring you a reward?
- **Title** your new document *Accomplishments* and file it in your Personal Career Portfolio.
- **List** the things you would like to accomplish in the future. Note why these are important to you.
- **Title** the document *Goals to Accomplish* and file it in your Personal Career Portfolio.
- **Update** your *Accomplishments* list each time you reach a goal you set in your *Goals to Accomplish* list.
- **List** your portfolio entries on your Personal Career Portfolio contents page.

Chapter 3

Researching Careers

Lesson 3.1

Career Choices

Lesson 3.2

Career Research

CAREER CLUSTER

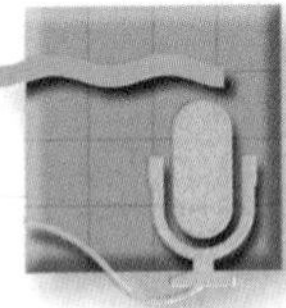

You will explore the Arts, Audio/Video Technology, and Communications career cluster.

What You'll Learn

- You will learn how to research careers.
- You will look at career clusters and kinds of activities people do in many careers.
- You will find out where to get information about careers that interest you.

Get Ready!

Choosing a Career

Survey three adults on how they chose their careers. Write down their answers to these questions:

- How did you learn about your career?
- What kinds of work do you do?
- What advice would you give someone thinking about entering your career?

Apply Review the responses and make a list of what you learned about choosing a career.

Lesson 3.1

Career Choices

Discover

- Which career clusters, or groups of related careers, interest you
- Career interest areas, or kinds of activities, that can direct you toward specific careers

Why It's Important

By looking at career clusters and career activities, you'll get an idea of the kinds of careers you might enjoy. Exploring all kinds of career possibilities now will help you make career choices later.

KEY TERMS

- career clusters
- career interest areas

When was the last time you went out for ice cream? Did it take you a long time to decide what you wanted? Chances are you had to choose from dozens of flavors. How did you ever make up your mind?

Now imagine yourself making a different kind of choice. This time you're considering different types of careers. There are more than 28,800 different careers to choose from. Do you know what you want to do for a living? How will you ever be able to decide?

Think About Your Choices
It's never too soon to start thinking about careers. You have many choices. *What careers do you have in mind?*

Why not take a taste? You'd ask for a taste if you weren't sure what flavor of ice cream to get. Of course, tasting all those flavors of ice cream might give you a stomachache. Just thinking about 28,800 careers might make your head ache. Luckily there is an easy way to think about careers. The U.S. Department of Education has organized careers into 16 career clusters.

Career Clusters

Career clusters are groups of similar occupations and industries. Career clusters will help you discover your interests and decide where you want your future to take you. **Figure 3.1** on page 44 lists the 16 career clusters. Which clusters appeal to you? Why?

The Global Workplace

The Perfect Gift

It's a nice gesture to give your host in a foreign country a gift for his or her hospitality. Choose your gift carefully though. Even the most well-intentioned gifts can be offensive in some countries. Never give a clock as a present in Hong Kong, as it connotes death. When you visit someone's home in Ecuador, never bring lilies or marigolds. These flowers are only for funerals. In Germany, avoid giving gifts such as perfume, soap, and clothing. These items are too personal.

So take the time to research and find that perfect gift. It will show that you understand and respect the customs of other countries.

Internet Activity

Use Internet resources to find out what business gifts are appropriate in one other country. Is there a special way in which you should present or receive a gift in this country? Go to the *Exploring Careers* Web site at exploring.glencoe.com for a list of Web sites to help you complete this activity.

Figure 3.1

U.S. DEPARTMENT OF EDUCATION CAREER CLUSTERS

Career Cluster	Job Examples
Agriculture, Food, and Natural Resources	Farmer, park ranger, animal trainer, food inspector, logger, ecologist, veterinarian, arborist, geologist, miner
Architecture and Construction	Building inspector, surveyor, architect, bricklayer, electrician, drywall installer, drafter, civil engineer, plumber
Arts, Audio/Video Technology, and Communications	Actor, computer animator, musician, camera operator, telephone technician, broadcast technician, choreographer
Business, Management, and Administration	Receptionist, business analyst, human resources manager, marketing manager, accounting clerk, controller, recruiter
Education and Training	Teacher, coach, corporate trainer, librarian, school principal
Finance	Stockbroker, banker, insurance agent, financial analyst, economist, auditor, accountant, tax preparer, loan officer
Government and Public Administration	City manager, customs inspector, legislator, urban planner, postal worker, army officer, meter reader, sanitation worker
Health Science	Paramedic, physician, nurse, pharmacist, physical therapist, dietician, dentist, home health aide, health educator
Hospitality and Tourism	Chef, caterer, lifeguard, professional athlete, hotel manager, housekeeper, travel agent, personal fitness trainer, concierge
Human Services	Child care worker, social worker, psychologist, counselor, consumer advocate, hairstylist, product safety tester
Information Technology	Computer programmer, e-commerce specialist, Web designer, systems analyst, network administrator
Law, Public Safety, and Security	Firefighter, security guard, bailiff, paralegal, attorney, judge, dispatcher, crime lab technician, detective, parole officer
Manufacturing	Machinist, welder, production manager, robotics engineer, model maker, baker, industrial designer, textile designer
Marketing, Sales, and Service	Cashier, inventory clerk, real estate broker, interior designer, model, retail salesperson, telemarketer, marketing researcher
Science, Technology, Engineering, and Mathematics	Engineer, astronomer, mathematician, physicist, microbiologist, chemist, aerospace engineer, oceanographer
Transportation, Distribution, and Logistics	Airline pilot, taxi driver, railroad conductor, cargo agent, shipping clerk, air traffic controller, vehicle mechanic

Career Clusters A career cluster is a group of jobs and industries that are similar. Grouping careers into clusters makes it easier to see the variety of careers that are available in the United States. *How are the jobs listed for each cluster alike?*

Career clusters are organized by industry and occupation. Industries, such as finance and manufacturing, produce products or services. An occupation, such as teacher, requires workers to have specific job skills and knowledge. For this reason, a career may fall into two different career clusters. Medical transcriptionists, for example, are part of both the Business, Management, and Administration career cluster and the Health Science career cluster. Workers in this career must use medical knowledge to provide transcription services.

Every career cluster is divided into career pathways. Each career pathway contains a group of careers requiring similar skills and education. You can learn more about career pathways in the Career Clusters Appendix at the back of the book.

Career Interest Areas

Here's another way to discover different kinds of careers. Try matching what you know about yourself to career interest areas. **Career interest areas** are general kinds of activities people do in many different careers.

Figure 3.2 on pages 46–47 shows six career interest areas. Take some time to think about each one.

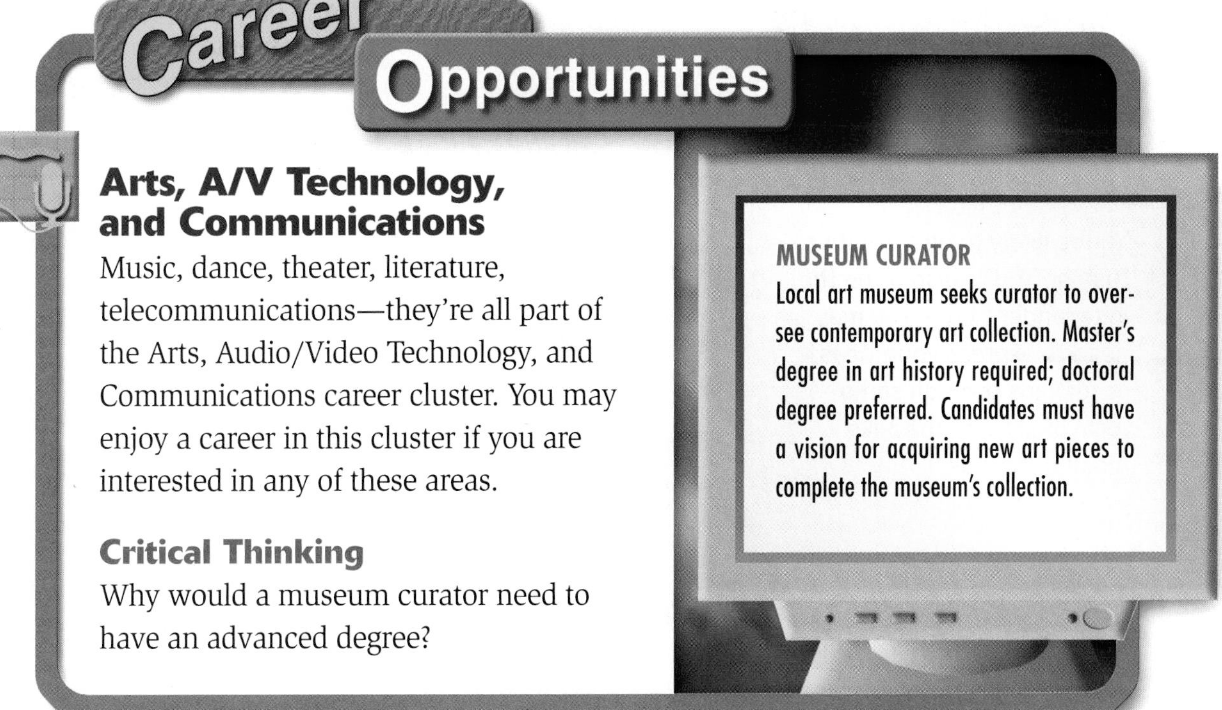

Arts, A/V Technology, and Communications

Music, dance, theater, literature, telecommunications—they're all part of the Arts, Audio/Video Technology, and Communications career cluster. You may enjoy a career in this cluster if you are interested in any of these areas.

Critical Thinking

Why would a museum curator need to have an advanced degree?

What's Your Match?

Did you see yourself in any of the career interest areas? You may actually have found more than one interest area that fits you. That's not surprising. There's a little bit of each type in all of us.

Focus on the one or two areas that describe you best. These areas help pinpoint your strongest interests, values, skills, and aptitudes. They will point you to careers you might like.

Figure 3.2 **CAREER INTEREST AREAS**

Think of career interest areas as kinds of activities you may or may not like to do. Look again at the lists you made of your interests, values, skills, and aptitudes. Now look at the six career interest areas. *Which sound like you?*

A

Creator

You're likely to be a creative thinker. You're also often the independent type. You may need to express your ideas or feelings through some form of art. You may like making things.

B

Investigator

You're probably a logical thinker. You may like testing theories and doing research. Discovering new ways of doing things may interest you. Your interests may include science, math, or history.

C

Organizer

You probably love working with information or numbers. You may be neat. Perhaps you find it easy to follow rules and directions. You may thrive on routine. You usually like working as part of a team.

Careers for All Types!

What careers do you suppose match the different career interest areas? You may be in for a surprise. Look at the *Creator*, for example. Creators work in many different careers. Sure, they might be actors, journalists, photographers, or songwriters. They can also be teachers, advertising executives, or plastic surgeons. City planners, robotics engineers, and even Webmasters would also consider themselves Creators.

D

Influencer

You're likely to be out in front and leading others. You're probably good at making a point. You usually have no problem persuading others to agree with you. You may be somewhat competitive.

E

Doer

You always seem busy. You appear to have endless energy. You may like working with your hands. You probably enjoy using tools and machinery. You may love the outdoors.

F

Helper

You tend to think of others before yourself. People may describe you as friendly, fun, or patient. You're always around to lend a hand. You probably work well in groups. You usually communicate well with people.

Do What You Love Many people find a match for themselves in more than one career interest area. *What career interest areas might describe the activities of this person?*

People in a variety of careers also represent the other career interest areas. *Investigators* include physicians, repair technicians, and librarians. They might design solar energy systems, write computer programs, or conduct experiments in laboratories. Lawyers, weather observers, and historians are also Investigators.

Organizers are everywhere, too. They are proofreaders, office managers, and reservation agents. They work as magazine editors, laboratory technicians, and food scientists. Organizers might keep a company's financial records or record research data. Financial consultants, word-processing specialists, and printing equipment operators are all Organizers.

Politicians, company presidents, marketing managers, and salespeople are obvious *Influencers*. Influencers also include restaurant managers, TV announcers, and small business owners. Even real estate agents, film producers, and building contractors would call themselves Influencers.

There are also *Doers* in many careers. Electricians, firefighters, and farmers are a few examples. Dental hygienists, forestry workers, and jewelers are others. Doers might spend their days outdoors repairing power lines or building roads and highways. They might also work indoors operating special machinery to build airplanes or automobiles. Automotive mechanics, hair stylists, and camera operators also are Doers.

Helpers are also all around. Nurses, teachers, ministers, and social workers help people every day. Other Helpers include wedding coordinators, travel agents, and environmental engineers. Career counselors, psychiatrists, and child care workers are also good examples of Helpers.

Take some time to review the job examples for the career clusters in **Figure 3.1** on page 44. What careers match the career interest areas that describe you? Do any of these careers appeal to you?

Remember, one of your best resources is exploring.glencoe.com

Lesson 3.1 Review and Activities

Key Terms Review

1. Make two flash cards, one for career clusters and one for career interest areas. On one side of each card, write the term. On the other side, write the definition. Use the cards to drill a classmate on the definitions.
   - **career clusters**
   - **career interest areas**

Check Your Understanding

Choose the correct answer for each item. Write your answers on a separate sheet of paper.

2. One of the 16 career clusters is _______.
   - **a.** Marine Science
   - **b.** Economic Policy
   - **c.** Manufacturing
3. One of the six career interest areas is _______.
   - **a.** Business
   - **b.** Creator
   - **c.** Ideals
4. If you tend to think of others before yourself, you are a _______.
   - **a.** Doer
   - **b.** Helper
   - **c.** Creator

Critical Thinking

Use complete sentences to answer the following questions. Write your answers on a separate sheet of paper.

5. Why are social workers and hairdressers part of the same career cluster, human services?
6. Which career interest area do you think would be most common for doctors?

Connecting to the Workplace

7. **Career Interest Inventory** Survey an adult about his or her career interest areas. Write the person's name and a brief description of the person's job. Also note the career cluster the job is in. Describe each interest area to the adult. Note the career interest areas the adult thinks describe him or her. Analyze the match between the adult's job and his or her career interest areas. Does the match seem like a good one? Why or why not?

Teamwork

8. **Create a Brochure** Work with a small group of classmates. As a group, choose one of the 16 career clusters. Have each member of the group research a career in the cluster. Work together to make a brochure, with visuals, that tells about careers in the cluster. Distribute copies of the finished brochure to your fellow classmates.

Lesson 3.2

Career Research

Discover

- Key questions to ask about careers that interest you
- Where to get information about careers

Why It's Important

By researching careers you'll get to know as much as you can about careers that interest you. The information you gather will help you decide which careers are right for you.

KEY TERMS

- research
- exploratory interview
- job shadowing
- internship
- volunteering
- service learning
- cooperative program

Once you identify interesting careers, it's time for some research. When you do **research,** you investigate a subject and gather information about it. The research you do now will pay off in many ways later.

What to Research

Before you begin, it helps to know what kind of information you're looking for. Be sure to keep your lists of interests, values, skills, and aptitudes handy also. The following 10 questions will help you gather basic information about careers.

1. What skills and aptitudes should I have?
2. What education and training would I need?
3. What would my work environment, or surroundings, be like?
4. What hours would I spend on the job?
5. What kinds of work would I do?
6. What responsibilities would I have?

Find Career Information
You won't have any trouble finding career information. You live in the information age, after all. *What resources do you use to find information on other topics? Which might also have information about careers?*

7. Would I be able to move ahead?
8. What will this career be like when I'm ready to work?
9. What does this career pay?
10. What other rewards would this career provide?

Where Do You Find It?

You know *what* you're looking for. Now you need to know *where* to look for it. Finding out about careers is easier than you might think. You can gather information in many places and many ways.

Check Out the Library

Your school or public library is a good place to start. First, see if your library has a job information or career center. If it does, you'll find reference books, magazines, videos, and other information on careers there.

Search the library catalog for the subject "careers." A librarian can also help you locate career reference materials. The following publications are especially useful:

- The ***Dictionary of Occupational Titles (DOT)***—a collection of 20,000 detailed job profiles. O*NET, the online version of the DOT, is a database of job profiles.
- The ***Occupational Outlook Handbook (OOH)***—a general source of information about hundreds of careers. It explains what workers in each career do and what education and training they need. The OOH also makes predictions about the future of each career. It is available in print and online.
- The ***Guide for Occupational Exploration***—a guide to exploring 12,000 careers grouped according to 12 major interest areas and subgroups within those areas. The guide cross-references jobs by interests, experience, skills, and training.
- The ***Occupational Outlook Quarterly***—a publication that provides current information on employment trends and outlooks. This update to the OOH comes out four times a year. It is available in print and online.
- The ***Reader's Guide to Periodical Literature***—a detailed index of magazine articles.

Flexibility

The one constant in life is change. Technology and jobs are always changing. What's the best method for dealing with change? Welcome it! Flexibility is crucial. Facing change with a positive attitude will help you learn new skills and adapt to new challenges.

Cooperative Learning Activity

- Team up with two or three classmates.
- Together, investigate one aspect of your school that has changed recently.
- Ask teachers and fellow students about the ways they have had to adapt to this change.
- As a group, write an article on the change you've investigated.

Global Connections
The Internet links you to people and sources of information around the world. *Why might career information from around the world be useful?*

Search the Internet

These days, the hottest place to research anything is the Internet. The World Wide Web offers a wide range of job recruitment and career research Web sites. These Web sites are run by various organizations and businesses. Many Web sites specialize in specific careers and industries.

You can also use the Internet to find career opportunities and information on a specific company's Web site. Most large companies now list their job openings either on their own Web page or with an online job listing service.

The federal government has many career research resources on the Internet. For links to online career research resources, go to the *Exploring Careers* Web site at exploring.glencoe.com.

Know Your Sources

No matter where you get your information, it's always important to check it. You want to be sure that the information you gathered is true and that it is still current. Make sure you can trust the source of your information. Compare your information with information from other sources. Check to see how up-to-date the information is.

Talk to People

You can ask family, friends, and neighbors to help you explore careers. With their help, build a list of people who work in interesting careers. Teachers and school counselors may also be able to add people to your list.

Then do what Michael Klein did. Arrange an exploratory interview. An **exploratory interview** is a short, informal talk with someone who works in a career that interests you. It's a good way to get an insider's view of a particular career.

Michael had always imagined himself in publishing. He grew up just outside New York City, a center of publishing.

When Michael discovered that his mother's friend was a magazine editor, he called the friend. She was more than happy to meet with him. The interview was a real eye-opener for Michael.

> "I sure learned a lot. My mom's friend was very open with me. She told me about the pluses and minuses of her job. I've got a much better idea of what I'd be getting into now."

Michael's interview paid off. His Mom's friend introduced him to the managing editor. The managing editor invited Michael to apply for a part-time job next summer.

Conduct Exploratory Interviews

Try This Activity

Now that you know how to locate, analyze, and apply career information, use that knowledge to create a Career Resource File.

Talk to People Ask your family, friends, neighbors, teachers, and counselors to help you build a list of people who work in careers and industries that you find interesting. Do some initial research online and at the library to learn more about the careers and industries in which you are interested. Then, call business and industry representatives to arrange exploratory interviews. Don't be afraid to ask people for interviews. They may have started out by receiving someone else's help and may be more than happy to pass the favor along.

Ask Questions During the interviews, ask questions such as these:

- How did you start in your career?
- What education and training did it require?
- What do you like about your job?
- What do you do on a typical day at your job?

Take Notes Take detailed notes during your interviews. Afterward, write your reflections on each interview experience. Place your reflections in your Career Resource File. As you gather more information about the careers and industries in which you are interested, add the information to your Career Resource File.

Check Your Information

Q: I found a chat room about a career I'm interested in. Several people said there was no future in this career. Should I forget about this career?

A: Absolutely not! You can't always trust what you find on the Internet. It's important to check any information you gather. Before you accept or act on any information you find, ask yourself these questions about the information:

- Is it a fact or one person's opinion?
- Is it current or is it out-of-date?
- Is it the same as what I find in sources that I trust?

Work!

Obviously, the best way to learn about a career from the inside is to work. A job in a particular career area can wait until you're in high school. Right now, though, you can take advantage of other kinds of work opportunities.

Try job shadowing, for instance. **Job shadowing** involves following someone for a few days on the job. You learn about a particular career by watching and listening.

Jana Davies got her first taste of the career she has today by doing just that. Jana is an accountant in Boston. Mathematics was Jana's favorite subject in school. When she was in middle school, she spent two days at her uncle's accounting firm. "It was tax season—the most hectic time of year," she recalls. "I remember loving the atmosphere. It was quiet but so busy. Even today I find tax season exciting."

Another way to learn about careers is to experience an internship. An **internship** is a temporary paid or unpaid position that involves direct work experience in a career field. The value of an internship is the experience and the contacts that you make. Internships can sometimes lead to job offers.

You might also consider **volunteering,** or working without pay. Volunteering is a great way to explore careers. Senior citizen centers, hospitals, museums, and libraries are always looking for volunteers. You'll get valuable experience, whether you choose that career later or not.

Ask and Explore
You'll ask most of the questions at an exploratory interview. *Why is it important to gather information before the interview?*

A service learning project can also be a useful experience for researching careers. **Service learning** is a learning method in which students learn and develop through thoughtfully organized service to the community. You will learn more about community service and service learning in Lesson 15.2.

Another option to gain first-hand experience on a job is to participate in a cooperative (co-op) program. A **cooperative program** combines school studies with paid work experience. Students in a co-op program use the skills they are learning in class in a job related to their career of interest. Participants of a co-op program receive school credit and pay. They also gain great insight into a possible future career.

Write Career Critiques

Select two careers that interest you. Research the careers. To make sure that your research is well-rounded, use a variety of research techniques, including job shadowing, volunteering, internships, real or simulated work experiences, interviewing people, attending career fairs, reading books, watching videos, or using technology such as the Internet, CD-ROMs, and DVDs.

Critique Careers Collect as much information as you can about the careers. Then write critiques of the careers. Write what you like and dislike about each career, and include information on the career outlook.

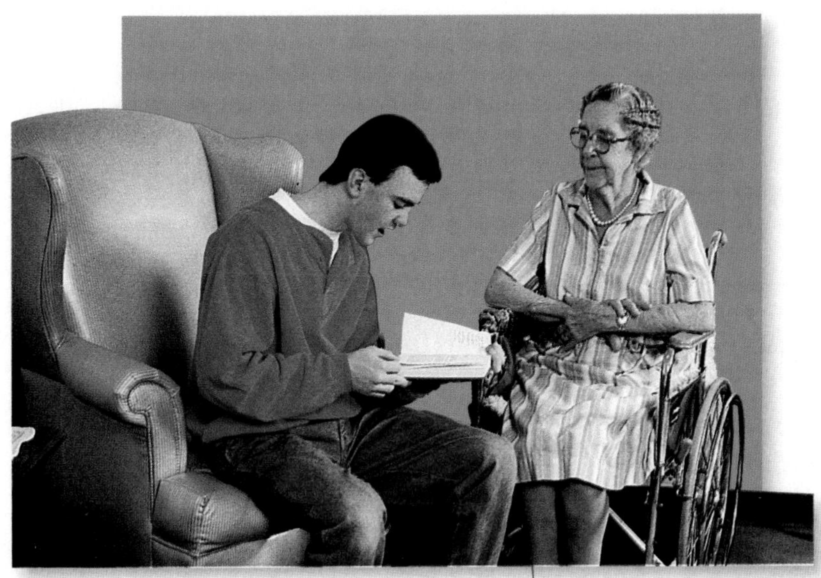

Help Others
When you volunteer, you give time and energy. In return, you get experience and much more. *Which career cluster might interest this volunteer?*

Lesson 3.2 Review and Activities

Key Terms Review

1. Write a letter to your grandparent or another adult describing the process of researching and exploring careers. In the letter, use and define each key term.
   - **research**
   - **exploratory interview**
   - **job shadowing**
   - **internship**
   - **volunteering**
   - **service learning**
   - **cooperative program**

Check Your Understanding

Tell whether each statement is true or false. Rewrite any false statement to make it true. Write your answers on a separate sheet of paper.

2. When doing career research, you should ask certain basic questions.
3. The library, the Internet, other people, and jobs are all sources of career information.
4. You can always trust information you find on the Internet.

Critical Thinking

Use complete sentences to answer the following questions. Write your answers on a separate sheet of paper.

5. What can you learn from an exploratory interview?
6. Why is it always important to gather up-to-date career information?

Character Building

7. **The Rewards of Volunteering** You and a classmate are volunteering at a local nursing home together. You've both agreed to work there for two months. However, your classmate always arrives late and leaves early, and she often works on her homework instead of spending time with the residents. She says that if she isn't getting paid, she doesn't need to work hard. Is this true? Explain your answer.

Community Involvement

8. **Research Volunteer Opportunities** Find out about local volunteer work that's available for someone your age. Look under the headings "Social Services" and "Human Services" in the Yellow Pages. Or, search the Internet for youth volunteer programs in your area. Contact an organization that sounds interesting. Ask questions about the work its volunteers do. Would this volunteer work help you in your career exploration? Share your research with the class.

Investigating Career Clusters

ARTS, AUDIO/VIDEO TECHNOLOGY, AND COMMUNICATIONS

- **Arts** • The performing and visual arts
- **A/V Technology** • The technology used to present sound or pictures
- **Communications** • The transmission of messages through technology

Job Title	Work Description
Choreographer	Creates original dances and instructs performers at rehearsals
Curator	Searches for, buys, and maintains art for museums
Dancer	Dances alone, with a partner, or in a group to entertain an audience
Director	Oversees the interpretation of plays and scripts for movies, TV, or theater
Illustrator	Paints or draws pictures for print or film media
Journalist	Gathers information and prepares stories about world events
Musician	Plays musical instruments, sings, composes, or conducts musical groups
Photographer	Photographs people, events, materials, and products with camera
Writer	Communicates through the written word

Exploration Activity

Arts, Audio/Video Technology, and Communications Use library and Internet resources to research a career in the Arts, A/V Technology, and Communications career cluster. Write a report on the kinds of work, skills required, working conditions, training and education required, and career outlook.

Cooperative Learning Interview a classmate about the career he or she researched. Find out as much information about that career as you can during the interview. Then have your classmate interview you about the career you researched. Afterward, share what you learned with the class.

Chapter 3 Review and Activities

Chapter Highlights

Lesson 3.1 There are thousands of different careers from which to choose. Exploring all kinds of career possibilities now will help you make career choices later.

Lesson 3.2 You can research careers at the library, on the Internet, by talking to people, and by working.

Key Concept Review

Use complete sentences to answer the following questions. Write your answers on a separate sheet of paper.

1. What is the difference between career clusters and career interest areas?
2. What kinds of career information should you research?
3. What are four places or ways to find career information?
4. How can you check the career information you gather?
5. What can you do now to explore working in a particular career?

Critical Thinking

Use complete sentences to answer the following questions. Write your answers on a separate sheet of paper.

6. Why are career clusters useful?
7. Why should you research a career before deciding on it?
8. What is the value of an internship?
9. What questions might you ask during an exploratory interview?
10. What can you learn about a career by job shadowing?

Skill Building

11. **Basic—Writing**
    Write a letter to someone who works in a career that interests you. Describe why you're interested in his or her career. Request an exploratory interview. Include a list of interview questions.
12. **Information—Acquires and Evaluates Information**
    Research a question you have about a career. Take notes on the information you find. Also record where you find it. Give a short oral report about your research. Compare doing research at the library with searching on the Internet.

Academic Applications

13. The Arts

You've been invited to have a booth at a career fair. You want to make buttons for visitors to your booth. The buttons will advertise your favorite career cluster. Design a button that tells about the cluster in words or pictures. Hand out paper copies of the button to your classmates.

14. Foreign Language

A career of interest to you requires knowledge of at least one language besides English. Find out about language classes at your school, your local high school, and in your community. Share your findings with the class.

Personal Career Portfolio

Conduct Career Research

- **Conduct** research on the career in which you are most interested.
- **Note** the specifics about jobs in this career, such as the skills and aptitudes they require.
- **Create** a document titled *Career Research* from your notes and file it in your Personal Career Portfolio.
- **Review** your *Inventory of Interests, Aptitudes, Skills, and Values* list.
- **Note** in your *Career Research* document how your career of interest makes use of the items you listed in your *Inventory of Interests, Aptitudes, Skills, and Values*.
- **Review** your *Goals to Accomplish* list.
- **Revise** your *Goals to Accomplish* list if the career you are interested in would require you to reconsider your goals.
- **List** your new portfolio entry on your Personal Career Portfolio contents page.

Chapter 4

Making Career Decisions

Lesson 4.1

Making Decisions

Lesson 4.2

Career Strategy

CAREER CLUSTER

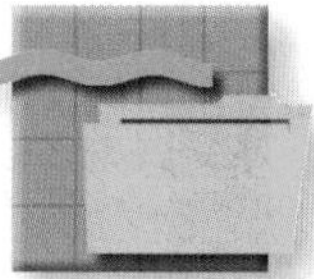

You will explore the Business, Management, and Administration career cluster.

What You'll Learn

- You will learn that decision making allows you to take charge of your future.
- You will learn how to make major decisions in seven steps.

Get Ready!

Rate Your Decisions

Record the decisions you make during one day. Label each decision with an *E* if it was easy to make or an *H* if it was hard to make. Then ask an adult friend or family member to list and label five recent decisions.

Apply Compare the lists. Which decisions were hard to make? Which were easy? Why are some decisions harder to make than others? What did you do to make the hard decisions?

Lesson 4.1

Making Decisions

Discover

- Why decision making is an important skill
- Steps you can follow to make decisions
- How to deal with things that stand in the way of decisions
- How to make better decisions

Why It's Important

Decisions are an important part of life. The stronger your decision-making skills, the wiser your decisions will be.

KEY TERMS

- **decision**
- **obstacle**
- **outcome**
- **adaptability**
- **attitude**

Should I go to the mall or study for the test? Should I try out for the school play or go out for a sport? Which movie should I see? Should I tell my friend what someone said about her? Should I do what everyone else is doing?

Every day you make hundreds of decisions. Each **decision** is a choice you make about what action to take. Some decisions are pretty routine, like deciding what to wear. Other decisions—such as what classes to take—require more time and thought.

Taking Charge of Your Future

Decision making is an important life skill. Decision-making skills will help you in your personal and professional life. When you make a decision, you have a say about some part of your life. You take action, instead of leaving your choices to others or to chance. You take control of where you are and where you're going.

What do you want to do with your life? Whatever you choose, you'll face important decisions along the way. Some decisions are harder to make than others. Try building on each decision you make. Making decisions will give you confidence and a sense of freedom from knowing you're taking charge of your future.

Making Routine and Major Decisions

In the world of work, you will want to make the best decisions possible—no matter if they are routine or major. You make routine decisions every day, like deciding what to have for lunch or whether to walk or take the bus home. Routine decisions like these can seem almost automatic. You barely have to think about them.

Take Control
You've been making decisions all your life. *What decisions have you made already today?*

Major decisions are something completely different, however. They often have a lasting effect on your life. Because of this, you want to take time to think about them carefully.

The Seven Steps of Effective Decision Making

The hardest part about making an important decision may be figuring out where to start. Making a decision is easier if you break the problem into smaller parts.

Figure 4.1 on pages 64–65 shows seven basic steps to follow in making major decisions. You can apply these steps to any important decision you face. With each decision, you'll become more familiar with the steps. Soon you'll see how these steps help you make important decisions.

Overcoming Problems

Of course, nothing is ever as simple as 1-2-3. That's as true of decision making as anything else. Even when you carefully follow the seven basic steps, you can run into obstacles. An **obstacle** is something that stands in your way.

Meeting Obstacles

Ishiro Nagata ran into several obstacles when he faced an important decision. His heart set on a career in journalism, he signed up to be on the school newspaper staff. He was surprised when his friends said the newspaper job sounded boring. He was surprised again when his parents weren't happy with the idea. They were worried he wouldn't have time for his homework.

Although Ishiro was offered a spot on the newspaper's staff, he wasn't so sure that he should take it. He worried that his friends or his parents were right, or that he wouldn't do a good job anyway.

Figure 4.1 **SEVEN STEPS TO A DECISION**

Seven steps can help you make informed decisions. *What decisions do you need to make? How can the seven steps help you?*

1 Define Your Needs or Wants

Identify the decision you must make. Be as specific as possible. Narrow your ideas so that you can focus on just one decision.

2 Analyze Your Resources

When you analyze something, you carefully study all its parts. You've already spent some time analyzing your personal resources. How will these resources help you make a decision? What other resources can you use?

3 Identify Your Options

Options are possible choices. There are usually at least two options whenever you face a decision. What are your choices in this situation?

4 Gather Information

Find out as much as you can about your options. What are the advantages and disadvantages of each? Think through all the possibilities.

Finding Answers to Obstacles

Ishiro took some time to look at what was standing in the way of his decision. He knew he couldn't change his friends' ideas. That was all right. Working on the newspaper was important to him. It made sense for his future plans.

Then he thought about his parents' concerns. Ishiro decided to talk to other newspaper staff about how they made time for homework. He realized that he could handle his homework by managing his time carefully. Ishiro made a plan and shared it with his parents. Ishiro's parents felt much better after he explained his time management strategy. They decided to support his decision.

5

Evaluate Your Options

When you evaluate your choices, you judge their value or importance to you. Review the information you've gathered. Compare your options. Which will best meet your needs or wants?

6

Make a Decision

This is the point where you actually decide. Now is the time to choose one of your options.

7

Plan How to Reach Your Goal

When you make a decision, you set a goal for yourself. A goal is something you want to achieve, or carry out. Once you've made a decision, make a plan of action. Figure out how you're going to carry out your decision and make it real.

Career Opportunities

Business, Management, and Administration

If you like business, numbers, and organizing things, then you might consider a career in business, management, and administration. This career cluster includes people who keep business moving.

TAX EXAMINER

State government seeks tax examiner to review individual and business tax returns. Examiners must be detail-oriented and have excellent math skills. The background of the final candidate will be checked.

Critical Thinking

Why do you think a tax examiner would need to undergo a background check?

Never Give in to Obstacles

Ishiro could have let others' ideas stand in his way. He would have given up something important to himself, though. He identified what stood in his way, and he was able to do something about it.

Figure 4.2 shows some common obstacles to decisions and how to handle them. You'll run into these and other obstacles as you face decisions. The important thing is not to give up. Look for a way around the obstacles.

Making Better Decisions

As you go through life, you'll get better and better at making decisions. If you learn something from each decision, you'll make a better choice next time.

Keep Practicing the Seven Steps

The more decisions you make using the seven basic steps, the more skilled you'll become. With practice, you'll feel more comfortable using the decision-making process.

Figure 4.2

WHAT STANDS IN YOUR WAY?

Obstacles	Answers
You think you can't do something. "I can't because I'm not old enough." "I can't because I'm a girl/I'm a boy." "I can't because of my race or background."	You may not be able to do everything. For example, your age may keep you from driving or getting a certain kind of job. Make sure that you aren't using who you are as an excuse, though. Don't let an excuse stand in the way of a decision that's right for you.
You expect too much of yourself. "If I can't do it perfectly, I won't do it at all."	It isn't always possible or necessary to do things perfectly. You can always do your best.
You expect too little of yourself. "I won't even try, because I know I can't do it."	If you never try, you'll never know what you can do. You might even discover that the task is easier than you think.
Your family expects too much of you. "What if I let them down?"	Talk to your family members. Ask for their help in making decisions and carrying them out.
Your family doesn't have the money to support what you want to do. "I can't afford it."	You can apply for money for training and education. Find out about scholarships, financial aid, and student loans. You can get a job to pay your expenses. You can find a way to do what you want if you want it badly enough.
Your friends or family make fun of what you want to do. "Maybe they're right. It is a stupid idea."	Talk with your friends or family members. Tell them you feel hurt when they make fun of your dreams. Ask them for their support. Give them specific ideas about how they can support you.
Your friends pressure you to do what they want you to do. "I should go along with them or they won't be my friends anymore."	Trust yourself. You know what is right or not right for you. Your friends aren't really friends if they pressure you into something.
You're afraid of failure. "What if I'm no good at this?"	You fail only if you don't make a decision or don't try.
You're afraid of change and new situations. "I don't know what it's going to be like." "I don't know how to act or what to say."	Change isn't easy, but don't let fear of a new situation keep you from making a decision. You can't know exactly what's going to happen, but with time and experience you'll feel more comfortable.
You put things off. "I'll do that later."	Don't wait around. Make a date with yourself and keep it. If you wait too long, the decision may be made for you.

Making Decisions We can all think of reasons not to make decisions. Do any of these sound familiar? *Why does it help to identify obstacles that get in your way?*

Attitude Counts

Self-Esteem

Maybe you feel a little awkward talking about activities in which you excel. Don't be! As you prepare to investigate possible careers, remember that no one knows your skills better than you do. Speak up and tell people what you're good at!

Cooperative Learning Activity

- Working in a small group, look up the definition of self-esteem.
- Discuss this definition, then write your group's description of self-esteem on a poster board.
- Surround your description with a collage of pictures showing the many things your group members are good at and enjoy.
- Hang your poster in the classroom.

Pay Attention to Everyday Decisions

Think carefully about everyday decisions, even routine decisions. This will help keep you on track to your career goal. If a decision doesn't turn out well, figure out what went wrong.

Recognize and Plan for Obstacles

Obstacles cause less damage if you recognize them early. If an obstacle presents itself, figure out how to work around it and strategize a backup plan. If something is important to you, make it happen.

Accept The Outcome of Each Decision

The **outcome** of your decision is its result or effect. Even if you made the best decision possible, things may not turn out the way you thought they would. A new decision may have a different outcome.

Be Willing to Change Your Decision

Decisions are not set in stone. Have a backup plan prepared. If circumstances change, be flexible and adaptable. **Adaptability** is being able or willing to change in order to suit different conditions. It is an essential quality in an ever-changing work environment.

Check Your Attitude

Your **attitude** is your basic outlook on life. Do you look for good things to happen, or do you expect the worst? Your attitude determines how you react to different situations. It also affects how you are perceived by others. If you have a positive attitude, you're already on your way to success on the job.

Forget About Luck

You don't need to depend on luck for your decision. If you gather information and make a plan for reaching your goal, you don't need to think about luck. Take control of your life and what happens to you. Get the facts, make plans, and take action—for yourself!

Lesson 4.1 Review and Activities

Key Terms Review

1. Write a one-page article on making decisions. Use the key terms below in your article. Ask a partner to review your article when you're finished writing.
   - **decision**
   - **obstacle**
   - **outcome**
   - **adaptability**
   - **attitude**

Check Your Understanding

Use complete sentences to answer the following questions. Write your answers on a separate sheet of paper.

2. The third step of the decision-making process is to ______.
   a. make a decision
   b. identify your options
   c. evaluate the information
3. One way to polish your decision-making skills is to ______.
   a. pay attention to the decisions you make every day
   b. identify your options
   c. count on luck

Critical Thinking

Use complete sentences to answer the following questions. Write your answers on a separate sheet of paper.

4. Do you think it is important to consider other people's opinions when making a career decision? Explain.
5. What kinds of obstacles have you faced while making a decision? How did you handle them?
6. How might your attitude make it difficult to learn from a decision?

Character Building

7. **Is It Just Luck?** Mira loves animals. Last summer she wanted to take an animal training class, but her family couldn't afford it. The local zoo has a teen volunteer program this summer. Applications are due tomorrow. Mira just found out about the program. She doesn't think she has enough time to fill out the application perfectly, so she isn't even going to bother applying. Mira thinks she just has plain bad luck. Is this true? Write a paragraph explaining your answer.

Teamwork

8. **Create a Skit** In a small group, brainstorm excuses people might give for not making decisions. Write down all the ideas you have. Then create a skit with some group members role-playing people making excuses and other team members convincing the excuse-makers that it's important to make decisions. Rehearse your skit and then share it with the class.

Lesson 4.2

Career Strategy

Discover

- How to make decisions about careers
- How to check your career decisions

Why It's Important

Career choices are important decisions. Before making a choice, you'll want to give time and thought to all the possibilities.

Key Terms

- **decision-making process**
- **backup plan**

Imagine that you want to take a hike through a park or the woods. There are several different paths that you can take depending on where you want to go.

A career path is like a hiking path. Your ultimate career goal will determine which career path you take.

Taking It Step by Step

Choosing a career is a big decision—one that takes time and thought. You can use the decision-making process to decide on a career path. The **decision-making process** is the series of steps that help you identify and evaluate choices. It will guide you toward your career goal.

You don't have to make a decision about a career right now. For now, use the decision-making process as you explore career paths. You'll have some fun, and it'll be good practice. When you're ready to decide on a career, you'll know the steps to follow.

Be an Explorer
Sometimes making a decision is the only way to do some exploring. *What can you learn from exploring a decision?*

Step 1. Understand What You Need and Want

The path to a career starts with your hopes and dreams. To begin, think about the lifestyle you want. Where do you want to live? Do you want a career that allows you to travel or to stay at home? How much money do you think you'll need or want to earn? How much time and energy will you want to give to your career? What kind of people do you want to work with? What career will give you what you need and want?

Step 2. Review Your Career Resources

Who are you? What do you have to offer? Get out those lists of interests, values, aptitudes, and skills. Review them and update them. Also consider your personality and learning style. What you know about yourself will help you decide on a career that is right for you.

Step 3. Decide What Careers Seem Interesting

List your top career options. What are some careers that match your personal goals and resources? If you're having a hard time thinking of a career you would enjoy, dream a little. Does someone you know have an interesting career? Do you have an idea for a career you're not sure exists? Did a career in one of the career clusters sound interesting? Perhaps a career interest area that describes you points to some careers. Explore your options.

Get Advice
Family members can help you with career decisions. *Who else can give you career advice?*

Step 4. Research Potential Careers

You know where to look for information about careers. Go to the library. Search the Internet. Talk to people. Get some experience on the job. Gather as much information as you can. You may discover other interesting career possibilities. Add them to your list of options, then research some more.

Step 5. Compare Your Choices

Now evaluate your choices. Study the information you've gathered. Consider your needs and wants. How does each career match your personal goals and resources? Compare your choices. Try to zero in on the career that best meets your needs and wants. List the second best, the third, and so on.

Step 6. Make Your Decision

Choose the career that seems best for you. If you're having trouble deciding, take a deep breath and relax. None of the choices may stand out as the right one. The differences between them may be very small. Just make the best decision you can. Use your research and what you know about yourself. Keep in mind that you can change your mind. No decision has to be final, but making a decision—even if you change it later—will give your life direction.

Step 7. Plan How to Reach Your Career Goal

You've made a decision. Now you have to see it through. Make a plan. Figure out how you're going to get from where you are to where you want to be. Refer to Chapter 5 for some help in developing a plan of action.

Make a List
Sometimes it helps to see how your options stack up against each other. *What else might you do when you're having trouble making a choice?*

Try This Activity

Follow the Steps

Imagine that you have been offered two jobs, and you have to decide which one to accept. Both jobs are your desired occupation. The first job pays $30,000 a year and is in the field you are most interested in. The second job pays $34,000 a year. It is in a related field that you find interesting and in which you will be able to develop transferable skills and experience relevant to your career goals. Assuming that everything else is equal, use the seven-step decision-making process to choose between the two jobs.

Report Your Decision Prepare an oral or written report describing the specific factors that you considered during your decision-making process. Make a chart of the seven steps with a column for the decisions you make at each step and a column for the reasons for your decisions. If you give an oral report to the class, prepare your chart on a poster board or large piece of paper. Display and explain your chart during the presentation.

Checking and Changing Direction

Making a decision and acting on it is not the end of the decision-making process. Once you've put your plan into action, you need to check your decision. Continue to evaluate your decision to make sure you really are on the right path. One way to ensure that you stay on a path that's right for you is to have a backup plan. A **backup plan** is an alternative course of action.

Evaluate, Evaluate!

To evaluate a decision, look at both its benefits and its drawbacks. Be objective. If your decision was the right decision, you should be able to see benefits. If the decision resulted in drawbacks, identify them and figure out a way to correct them.

Evaluation is an ongoing process. You do it all the time. At each point on your career path, you will want to stop and evaluate where you are. Right now, take a good look at the information you've gathered about your career choice. Ask yourself, "Is this really what I want to go after? Am I committed to achieving it?" If the answer is no, you should reconsider your decision and come up with a new plan.

Making Decisions

Q: I'm afraid that I'll make the wrong choice. How can I be 100 percent sure about my decisions?

A: Start by following the decision-making steps in this book. Once you've done that, it's always helpful to ask your friends and family members for advice. In the end, you can never be 100 percent sure about a decision until after you have made it. That's why making a decision can be so hard. Remember, decisions don't have to be final. You can check and adjust your decisions along the way.

Keep Asking Questions

One way to check your decision along the way is to ask questions. **Figure 4.3** shows some questions that will help you to decide if you have made the right career decision.

Starting Over

Your answers to these questions will give you direction. They will help you decide if you need to start over. You may decide to continue on your career path, or go back and choose a different career.

Never be afraid to start over. Life is about change. That's part of the fun—and the challenge—of being alive.

Figure 4.3

CAREER QUESTIONS

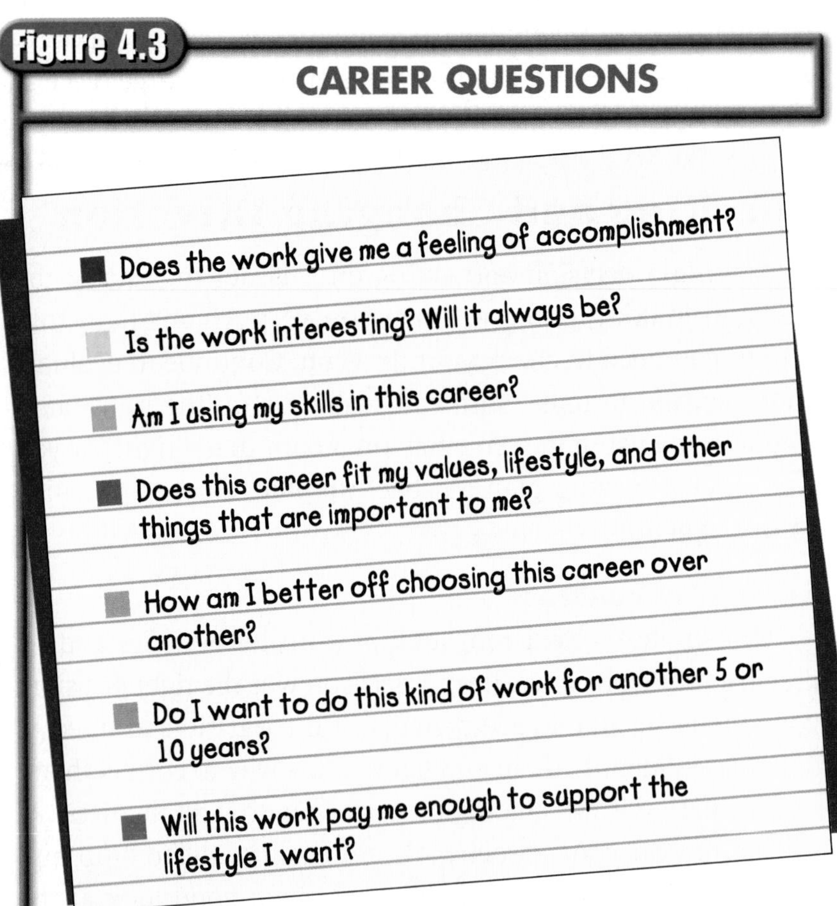

Interview Yourself Questions are a good way to check a career decision. Some questions will occur to you because of changes in your career field. Others may just show your changing feelings about a career choice. *What other questions might you ask about a career decision?*

The Global Workplace

How to Meet and Greet

It's polite to greet someone you have just met with a firm handshake, right? Not always! A handshake is the traditional way to greet a person in North America, but in other parts of the world greetings differ.

In Japan the proper way to greet a person is with a bow. To welcome another person in Southeast Asia, press together your palms as if praying. When meeting people in countries that do use the handshake as a greeting, know that you will still need to be careful. Others around the world consider the firm handshake used in the United States too aggressive. A lighter handshake is preferred in these countries.

Internet Activity

Use Internet resources to learn what the traditional greeting is in one other country. Is this greeting used in both business and social situations? Do men and women use the same greeting? Go to the *Exploring Careers* Web site at exploring.glencoe.com for a list of Web sites to help you complete this activity.

Martina Lewis of Titusville, Florida, thinks change can be wonderful. She started over when she was about your age. Her family moved to Florida when she was 12. She thought her life was over. She had grown up on a horse farm in Kentucky. All she wanted was to breed horses someday. Suddenly, there was more water around than grass. That move changed her life:

> "The more time I spent around the ocean, the more I loved it. It was a natural decision to become a marine botanist. I study ocean plants and how they keep the environment clean. If my family had stayed in Kentucky, I never would have discovered the ocean. I couldn't be happier."

Starting over can be scary and difficult. In the end, though, you may discover a path that you didn't even know existed.

Lesson 4.2 Review and Activities

Key Terms Review

1. On a separate sheet of paper, write a short paragraph on how to use the decision-making process. Explain how to use the decision-making process to choose and achieve a career goal. Use each key term at least once in your paragraph.
   - **decision-making process**
   - **backup plan**

Check Your Understanding

Tell whether each statement is true or false. Rewrite any false statement to make it true. Write your answers on a separate sheet of paper.

2. A career path is like a hiking path. To get to the career you want, you have to make a decision.
3. At each point on your career path, don't stop to evaluate where you are, or you will never make a decision.
4. Making a decision and acting on it is the end of the decision-making process.

Critical Thinking

Use complete sentences to answer the following questions. Write your answers on a separate sheet of paper.

5. Why is it important to use the seven decision-making steps when choosing a career?
6. When do you think you can stop evaluating a career decision? Explain your answer.

Connecting to the Workplace

7. **Career Check** Gaby has been a secretary for five years. She chose this career because it uses her word-processing and scheduling skills. She also loved working for only one executive. Her office just updated its computer system. This allows Gaby's boss to do most of her own typing and scheduling. Since Gaby has fewer duties, she now works for three executives. She's wondering if it's time to change careers. Make a list of some career questions Gaby should ask herself to check if her career path is still right for her.

Community Involvement

8. **Conduct an Interview** Interview a business owner in your community about the career path he or she chose. Ask the following questions during your interview. How did you decide to start a business? Did your original plans ever change? What decisions did you have to make to get the business going? Report your findings to the class.

Investigating Career Clusters

BUSINESS, MANAGEMENT, AND ADMINISTRATION

Business • Buying and selling goods and services

Management • The direction or control of a business

Administration • Maintaining the goals and rules of an organization

Job Title	Work Description
Auditor	Reviews business practices and financial records
Controller	Manages a company's finances
H.R. Manager	Recruits and interviews employees, or human resources (H.R.); gives advice on hiring and training; and runs employee programs
Management Analyst	Analyzes a company and suggests ways for it to do its work faster and better
Marketing Manager	Develops marketing plans to sell a company's products
Organizational Psychologist	Uses psychology to improve how well employees do their jobs and to improve the quality of life at work
Payroll Clerk	Makes sure that employees are paid on time and that their paychecks are correct
Secretary	Performs the administrative duties of an office

Exploration Activity

Business, Management, and Administration Use library and Internet resources to research a career in the Business, Management, and Administration career cluster. Write a report on the kinds of work, skills required, working conditions, training and education required, and career outlook.

Cooperative Learning Interview a classmate about the career he or she researched. Find out as much information about that career as you can during the interview. Then have your classmate interview you about the career you researched. Afterward, share what you learned with the class.

Chapter 4 Review and Activities

Chapter Highlights

Lesson 4.1 When you make a decision, you take charge of a part of your life.

Lesson 4.2 You can use the seven-step decision-making process to make career decisions.

Key Concept Review

Use complete sentences to answer the following questions. Write your answers on a separate sheet of paper.

1. List and explain the seven steps in the decision-making process.

2. What should you do if you run into obstacles while making a decision?

3. What can you learn from decisions you've made?

4. What important step follows the decision-making process?

5. How can you check a decision?

Critical Thinking

Use complete sentences to answer the following questions. Write your answers on a separate sheet of paper.

6. How is making no decision actually a decision?

7. Why is it bad to let others make your decisions?

8. What might happen if you skip steps in decision making?

9. What two steps in the decision-making process make luck unnecessary?

10. Why do you think some people are unhappy in their careers?

Skill Building

11. Thinking—Decision Making
Use the seven-step decision-making process to make a decision. Then evaluate the outcome of your decision. Make notes to help you with your next decision.

12. Interpersonal—Serves Clients/Customers
Carrie sells newspaper advertising space. She spends most of her time working with large stores because they buy the largest ads. The smaller advertisers say Carrie neglects them. Use the decision-making process to show how she can give all her customers the attention they need. Show the steps in a chart.

Personal Career Portfolio

Academic Applications

13. Mathematics

A cashier job pays $105.00 for 20 hours a week. A bike repair job pays $5.75 an hour for 16 hours a week. Which job pays more per hour? More each week? What besides money might affect your decision? Which job would you choose? Why?

14. Computer Science

In school, you use two kinds of software—one for word processing, and one for drawing. You'd like to buy some new software to try at home. You've got three choices, but you can't decide which to get. Where could you get the information you need to help you decide? Make a plan for gathering information. Share your plan with a partner.

Make a Career Plan

- **Use** the seven-step decision-making process to select a career.
- **List** the steps you will need to take to achieve your career goal. Describe each step in a sentence or two.
- **Summarize** the benefits of your plan in a short paragraph.
- **Write** a paragraph about the potential obstacles that could get in the way of your plan.
- **Write** backup plans to use in the case of each obstacle.
- **Title** the document *Career Plan* and file it in your Personal Career Portfolio.
- **Revise** the document if you discover new steps to your career goal as you continue to evaluate your career decisions.
- **List** your portfolio entry on your Personal Career Portfolio contents page.

Chapter 5

Planning Your Career

Lesson 5.1

How Planning Helps

Lesson 5.2

Designing a Plan

CAREER CLUSTER

You will explore careers in Education and Training.

What You'll Learn

- You will discover how planning can help you reach career goals in the future.
- You will learn what a career plan should include.
- You will set goals and make a plan for a career that interests you.

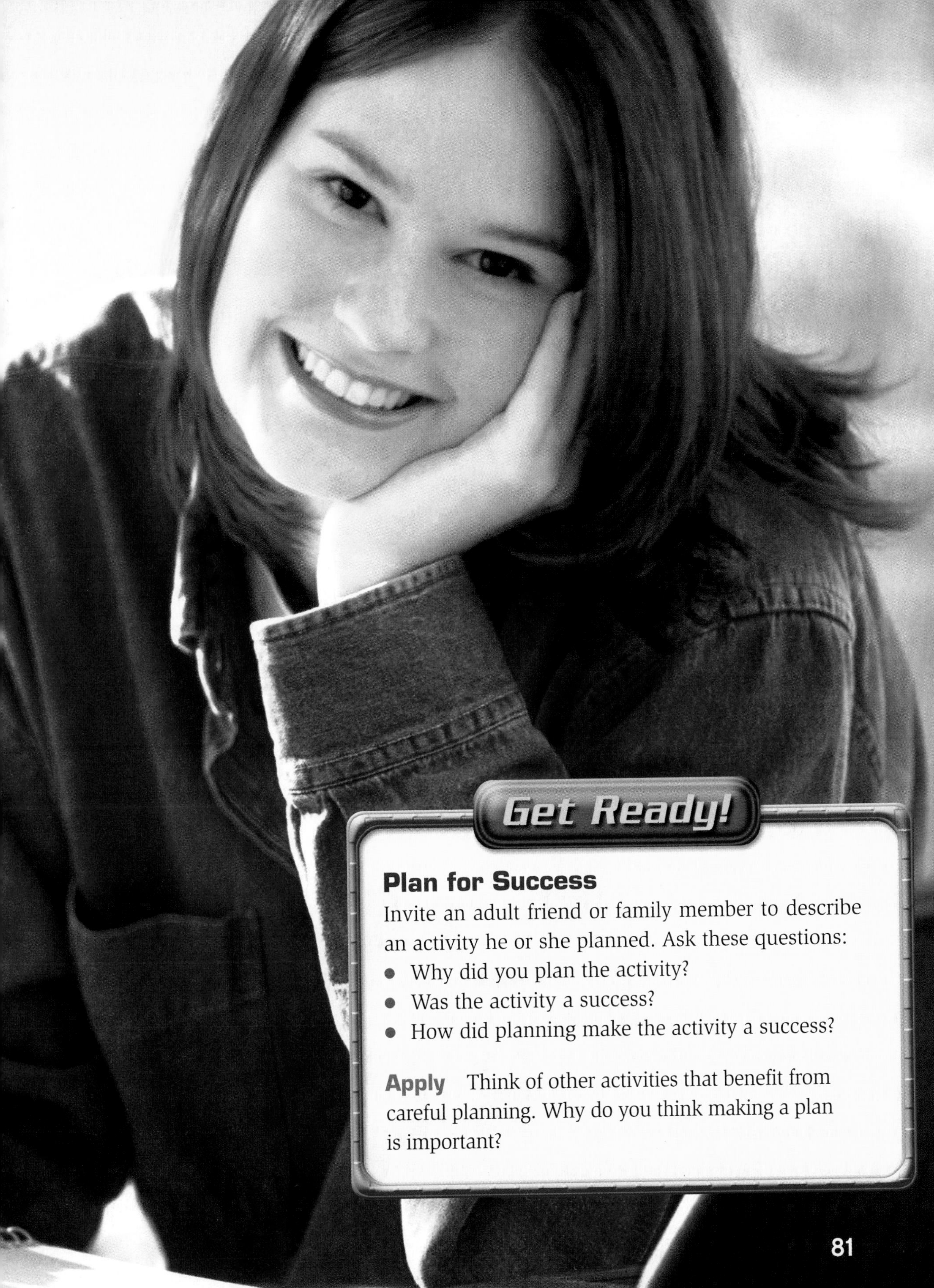

Get Ready!

Plan for Success

Invite an adult friend or family member to describe an activity he or she planned. Ask these questions:

- Why did you plan the activity?
- Was the activity a success?
- How did planning make the activity a success?

Apply Think of other activities that benefit from careful planning. Why do you think making a plan is important?

Lesson 5.1

How Planning Helps

Discover

- Why planning is important
- What a career plan should include

Why It's Important

Planning is the surest way to achieve your goals.

KEY TERMS

- **procrastinate**
- **prioritize**
- **part-time job**
- **temporary job**

"I've got a cool idea for . . . ." "Wouldn't it be great if I could . . . ." "If I had the money, I would . . . ." Everyone has ideas and dreams. Some people, though, go one step further. They make their ideas and dreams a reality. These people usually have something that other people don't. They have a plan of action. They plan how they are going to get what they want. Then they follow their plan.

Why Plan?

Have you ever made a plan? Have you ever set your sights on something and then carefully planned how to get it?

If you answered no, you're not alone. Many people live their entire lives without ever planning anything. They "play it by ear." They take things as they come. They say, "Why bother? No one knows what tomorrow will bring. Just live for today."

You *can* have some control over what tomorrow brings, though. As you learned in Chapter 4, there's a way to have a

Plan for Success
Planning helps make activities a success. *What kinds of activities have you planned?*

The Global Workplace

Foreign Language Basics

Many people around the world speak some English. This makes traveling easier for native English speakers. However, before going to a foreign country, learn a few basic phrases of that country's language to help in routine situations. Pocket-size phrase books are easy to carry and usually list many useful words. Learning *thank you* is a good place to start.

- **Italy** .... *grazie*
- **Germany** .... *danke*
- **Latin America, Spain** ..... *gracias*
- **South Korea** .... *kamsa hamnida*
- **Somalia** .... *mahadsanid*

Internet Activity

Use Internet resources to learn a few basic phrases in a language that interests you. Learn *hello, good-bye, please, thank you,* and four other terms you think would be helpful. Go to the *Exploring Careers* Web site at exploring.glencoe.com for a list of Web sites to help you complete this activity.

say about both today and tomorrow. You can take charge of your life by making decisions. Then you can plan how to reach the goals you've set.

Planning Helps You Manage Your Time

Planning is important for many reasons. For one, a plan helps you organize your activities and manage your time. That way you don't miss out on anything.

Alice Lonewolf is a seventh grader in Helena, Montana. She wants to be a sports coach someday. A typical school day for Alice includes classes and sports. "I want to be involved in as many sports as I can. Mondays, I play on an intramural basketball team after school. On Tuesdays and Thursdays, I swim at the YMCA. Friday night and Saturday morning, I have swim team practice. Wednesdays are free for biking or kicking a ball around the yard with my dad." Alice doesn't hesitate when asked about the benefits of having a plan:

> "If I didn't have a plan on paper, this schedule would be impossible. Besides all the sports, I need time to do my homework. With a plan, I have time for everything."

Planning Helps You Remember Events

A plan not only helps you do the things you need or want to do, it also helps you remember when they need to be done. When you have a plan, it's harder to procrastinate. When you **procrastinate,** you put off doing or deciding about something.

John Gikas, a computer student in Cambridge, Massachusetts, learned the importance of a plan the hard way. "I used to procrastinate all the time," John observes. "Last year I missed a chance to go to a once-a-year computer event in Boston. I didn't get my registration form in on time. A lot of my friends who are interested in computers did, though. They got to try out all kinds of new software and hardware. When I get the form this year, I'm going to make a note of the deadline. There's no way I'm going to miss out again."

Plan for Achievement You'll be amazed at what you can do when you have a plan. *What's the best way to do important projects well and on time?*

Planning Helps You Prioritize

Rachel Baum of Cleveland, Ohio, found another way planning is useful. She discovered that a plan helps you prioritize. When you **prioritize,** you put tasks in order. You order them from first to last or from most to least important.

Rachel is interested in acting. A family friend told her about a summer theater program for teens. It ran for six days a week, eight hours a day, six weeks of the summer. "Summer was my time for sleeping in, reading, and just having fun," Rachel explains. "Being in a serious theater production is part of my career plan, though. I couldn't pass it up. I figure I'll have plenty of chances to take a vacation later."

Planning Helps You Reach Goals

Last but not least, anyone who's ever made a plan and carried it out will tell you the same thing. A plan gives you a feeling of accomplishment. As you complete each part of your plan, you can cross it off. You can say, "I'm that much closer to my goal."

Tilly Ransom of Bedminster, New Jersey, can't remember ever wanting to be anything other than a doctor. When she was about 13, she made a plan. Her plan included science classes and volunteering at the local hospital. It also involved college and medical school. Then she did her residency, or advanced training in a special area, at a hospital.

"I still have that plan," Tilly notes. "It included all the important steps to being a doctor. As the years went by, I completed each one. Now here I am, head of surgery at a big city hospital."

Higher Education
Many careers require a college degree for even entry-level jobs. *What kind of jobs do you know of that require only a high school diploma?*

What Goes Into a Plan?

You can make a plan for a career that interests you, just as Tilly did when she was about your age. You'll want to include these important steps: education and training, jobs along the way, and career research.

The First Step: Education and Training

Most people think of education or training as a first step. **Figure 5.1** on page 86 lists some of your options for education and training. You can get started on this step right now. Work to strengthen your basic skills, such as reading, writing, and mathematics. As you'll learn in Chapter 10, basic skills count in all kinds of careers.

Classes you take now and in high school can help you prepare for a variety of careers. Mathematics classes will give you skills you might use as a city planner or a computer specialist. Science classes are good preparation for careers in natural resources, food, agriculture, and health science. In English, you will develop skills needed in many

Figure 5.1

EDUCATION AND TRAINING ALTERNATIVES

Options	Description
On-the-Job Training	Paid on-site instruction in how to perform a particular job. It may consist of a few days of orientation for new employees or more long-term instruction to help workers keep up with industry changes.
Apprenticeship	Learning how to do a job through hands-on experience in that job under the guidance of a skilled worker. Construction and manufacturing workers commonly train as apprentices.
Vocational-Technical Centers	Schools offering a variety of skills-training programs, such as courses in automotive or computer technology.
Trade Schools	Privately run schools that train students for a particular profession, such as chef or hairstylist. Trade schools are more expensive than vocational-technical centers.
Community and Technical Colleges	Colleges that offer two-year associate degree programs and certification programs in occupations such as accountant and desktop publisher. Credits can be transferred to a four-year college or university.
Four-Year Colleges and Universities	Schools that offer a bachelor's degree for four years of study. Careers such as teaching and physical therapy require bachelor's degrees. Postgraduate education is study after the completion of a bachelor's degree.
Military Service	Education and training offered by the U.S. government in exchange for service in a branch of the military, such as the Army. Training is given in more than 200 different jobs, including health technician and air traffic controller.
Continuing Education	Programs for adult students offered by high schools, colleges, and universities. These courses help adults complete education, brush up on old skills, and pursue new interests.
Distance Education	Online classes (sometimes called satellite classes) for specific training or for credit towards a degree. Offered by all types of education providers. Allows students more flexibility in geography and time.

Education and Training Alternatives You'll have different educational and training needs at different points in a career. *Why might you go back to school in the middle of a career?*

communications and media careers. Classes in music, art, and dance can lead to careers in the fine arts. Your work in social studies may inspire you to think about careers in travel, law, or government.

Following high school, you may choose to continue your education or get other training. As you think about your options, think about the value of a college education. **Figure 5.2** shows that jobs requiring college education are growing faster than all other jobs. They also will usually pay more. College is an important part of many people's career plans.

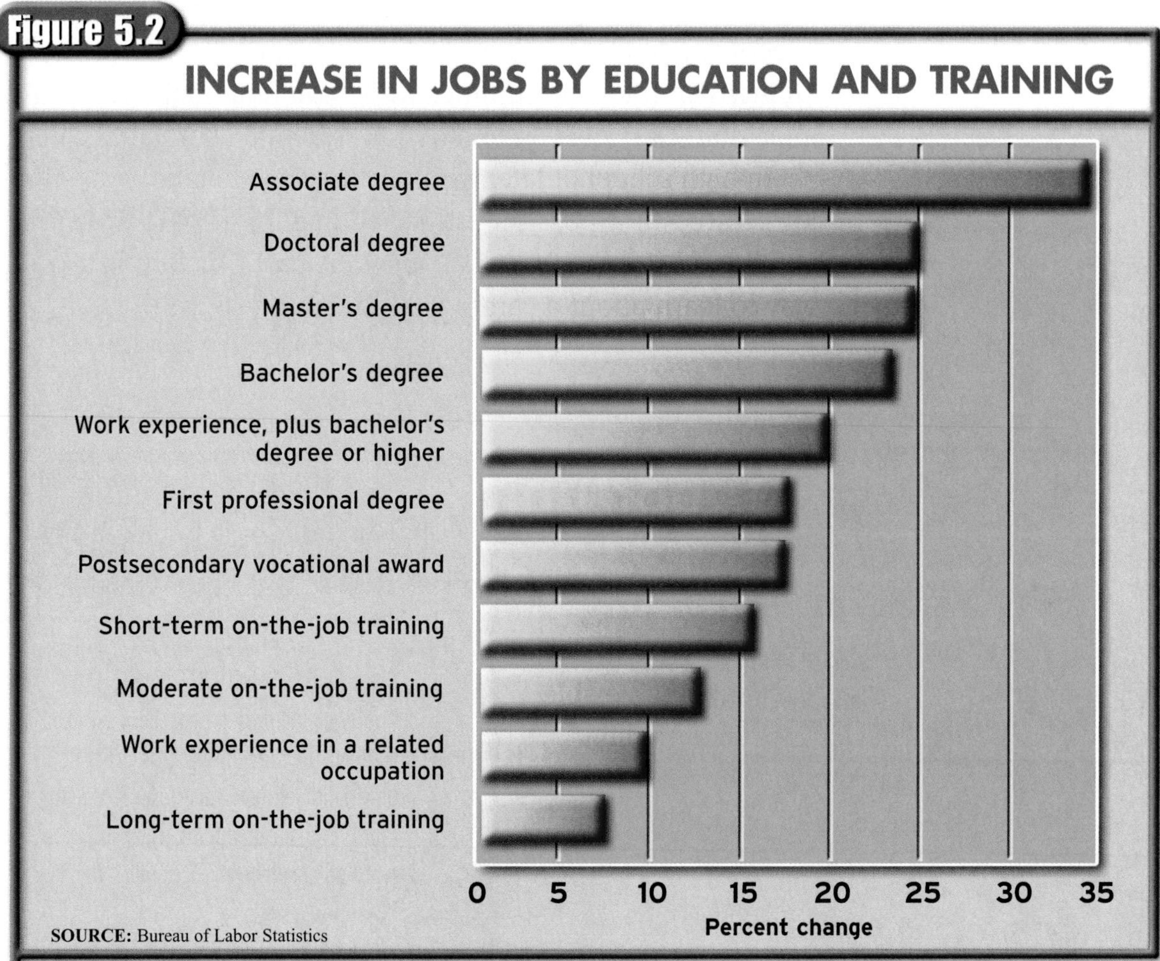

Learn to Earn This chart shows the percent change in number of jobs by source of education or training, projected 2000–2010. Jobs requiring college education are growing the fastest. *Why would it be wise to get a college degree in addition to work experience?*

Jobs Along the Way

Another important step in planning your career is planning the jobs you will hold along the way to your ultimate career goal. As you learned in Chapter 3, job shadowing and volunteering are great ways to explore careers. Both can also be an important part of a career plan.

An internship may also be part of your career plan. As you will recall, an internship is a temporary paid or unpaid position that provides valuable job skills in a particular career field. It is more formal than a volunteer job and usually requires a bigger commitment of time.

There are internships in many kinds of businesses. Many college students look for summer internships to get work experience in a career field. You might think about arranging an internship for the summer while you're in high school. An internship can help you find out more about a particular career.

In high school or later, you might decide to take a part-time job related to a possible career choice. In a **part-time job,** you'll work up to 30 hours a week. A part-time job is a good way to learn about a career field that interests you.

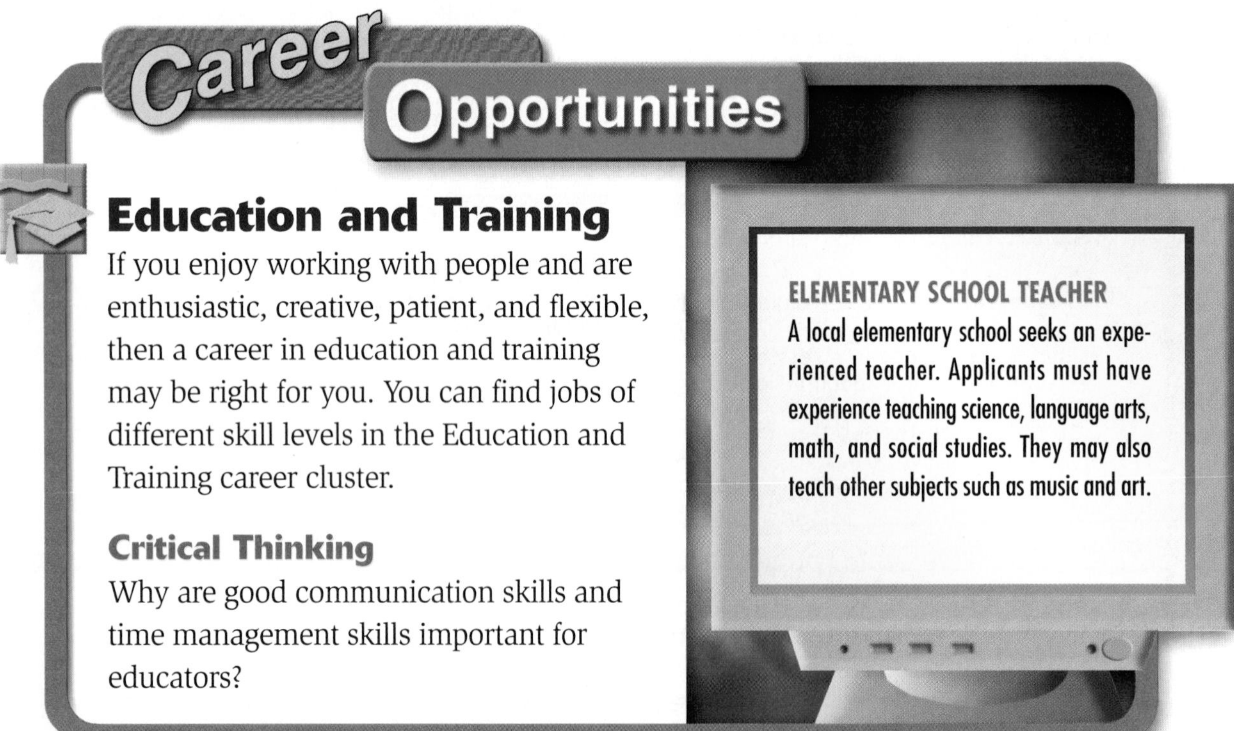

Education and Training

If you enjoy working with people and are enthusiastic, creative, patient, and flexible, then a career in education and training may be right for you. You can find jobs of different skill levels in the Education and Training career cluster.

ELEMENTARY SCHOOL TEACHER

A local elementary school seeks an experienced teacher. Applicants must have experience teaching science, language arts, math, and social studies. They may also teach other subjects such as music and art.

Critical Thinking

Why are good communication skills and time management skills important for educators?

A temporary job is another way to try a specific kind of work. It's also a good way to develop job skills you may need. Students and many other people find temporary jobs especially convenient. A **temporary job** usually lasts only a short while. Some temporary jobs are available just for a particular season, for instance. Lifeguarding, golf caddying, and catering (providing food and service for special events) are some examples of temporary jobs for young people.

Then, of course, there are full-time jobs. As you have learned, a full-time job amounts to about 40 hours a week. Like most people, you will probably work at several full-time jobs during your lifetime.

Plan of Action
Maria wants to become a pediatrician. She is working part-time in a day care center to gain experience working with children. *What other experiences might help Maria become a pediatrician?*

Career Research

Be sure to include career research as a step in your career plan. Career research does not end when you've identified interesting careers. It doesn't end when you choose a career either. You should continue to do career research as you explore careers. You should do career research as you work toward a career goal. You'll learn about new opportunities and changes in career fields. What you learn could affect your career plan.

Where can you look to find out what's going on? You can use the same resources you would use to research career options. You'll find current information at the library and on the Internet. You can also learn a great deal by talking to people. While you're still in school, discuss with your guidance counselor the job market for different careers. Once you begin working, listen to what you hear on the job about career developments.

Take this advice. Stay informed. That way you can adjust your career plan as needed. When you build research into your career plan, your plan will always be up-to-date.

Teamwork

Working in teams can improve productivity and creativity. The right attitude will make your team a success. A good tip for effective teamwork: Respect your teammates and you'll find they will do the same for you.

Cooperative Learning Activity

- Work with a small group of classmates to brainstorm three important rules for successful teamwork.
- Share your results with the class.

Covering All the Bases

Education and training, jobs, and career research are the basic steps included in most career plans. There are other things to keep in mind, though. Money can be an issue. Part of your career plan should focus on how you're going to pay for education or training, for instance. Will your family be able to help you? Can you get a scholarship? Maybe you'll have to earn the money yourself. You may need to explore ways to raise money and figure out how long it will take. You will learn more about financing your education in Chapter 14.

Be Prepared and Be Flexible

Personal responsibilities may also have an effect on your career plan. You might delay a step in your plan until your children go to school, or you may change your plan so you can work at home.

When you make a plan, you want to try to think of all the things that might affect it. Of course, you also need to be prepared for surprises. You can't know the future. You shouldn't let that stop you from making a plan, though. Once you've got a plan, you just need to keep your eye on your goal and be flexible.

Try This Activity

Education Equals Opportunity!

There are many different types of jobs with differing levels of responsibility in every career interest area. If you are interested in health science, for example, you might be interested in pursuing a career as a medical lab technician or as a pediatrician. These jobs have very different education and training requirements and dramatically different levels of pay. It is important that you understand the opportunities available to you based on your level of education and training.

Classify Employment Opportunities Select ten different careers in your career interest area. Research the education and training required for each career. Then, develop a chart classifying employment opportunities in your career interest area based on educational and training requirements.

Lesson 5.1 Review and Activities

Key Terms Review

1. Imagine you are a career counselor who leads career planning workshops. You begin each workshop with a brief speech. Write a speech that includes each of the following terms. Then give your speech to the class.
   - **procrastinate**
   - **prioritize**
   - **part-time job**
   - **temporary job**

Check Your Understanding

Choose the correct answer for each item. Write your answers on a separate sheet of paper.

2. To reach a career goal, you'll need to _______.
   a. know your friends' goals
   b. make and follow a plan of action
   c. have a job offer
3. A career plan includes _______.
   a. a comparison of the career plans of your peers
   b. education and training
   c. how much money you will make

Critical Thinking

Use complete sentences to answer the following questions. Write your answers on a separate sheet of paper.

4. What kinds of problems occur when you don't make a plan?
5. What do you think is the most important part of a career plan? Explain your answer.
6. Why are temporary jobs a good idea for young people?

Connecting to the Workplace

7. Career Decisions Karen planned to be a master plumber. It would take five years. Besides serving an apprenticeship, she had to take classes, pass some tests, and get a license. As a master plumber, she would make $25 an hour. Karen found a plumbing apprenticeship at $8 an hour. She later quit to take a factory job that paid her $10.50 an hour. Explain whether Karen made a wise decision.

Teamwork

8. Make a Group Presentation As a class, find names and addresses of the various types of educational options profiled in **Figure 5.1** on page 86. Then form teams of two or three students. Each team should research a different school and request information about the school. Then, as a class, create and give team presentations about training options.

Lesson 5.2

Designing a Plan

Discover

- How to set goals you can reach
- Different kinds of goals
- How to make your own career plan

Why It's Important

A plan will show the steps that will help you reach your career goal.

KEY TERMS

- **short-term goal**
- **medium-term goal**
- **long-term goal**
- **chronological order**

You already know the first step in creating any plan. You need to make a decision. Following the decision-making steps in Chapter 4, you must first set a career goal.

That's really the hardest part. What comes next? Next you need to figure out the steps you must take to reach your goal. You need to create a detailed plan of action.

How to Reach Your Goals

It will be up to you to set goals to reach your ultimate career goal. What are the secrets to success? Here are a few pointers:

Reach for the Stars Reaching goals now will help you achieve goals throughout your life. *What goals have you set for yourself lately?*

- ***Be as specific about each goal as you can.*** State exactly what you plan to do. Specific goals are easier to aim for and achieve.
- ***Put your goals in the order that you'll do them.*** That way you'll know which to work on first, second, and so on.
- ***Make realistic goals.*** Aim high, but aim at what's possible. If your goals are too easy, you may lose interest in them. If they're too hard, you may become discouraged.
- ***Change your goals as needed.*** Check your progress. Think about where you're headed. Don't be afraid to change your mind and take a new direction.

Make Your Goals Realistic

Q: If achieving my goals takes longer than I planned, does that mean my goals are unrealistic?

A: No, your goals can take longer than planned. It is important to be aware of what it will take to achieve your goals. If your goals are taking longer than you first estimated, then figure out why. Did you need more money? Did you forget to include the hours spent on chores? Periodically reevaluate your goals and adjust them to include the things you didn't consider.

Setting Goals

Right now, a career goal probably seems a long way off. That's partly because you're still thinking about your career options. It's also because a career goal is your ultimate, or final, goal. Before you reach your career goal, you must first set and reach other goals. Each goal will be a stepping stone to your ultimate goal.

Stepping Stones to a Career

The goals between you and a career goal are short-, medium-, and long-term goals. A **short-term goal** is something you might start right away. Sometimes you can complete it quickly. Let's say your ultimate goal is to be a landscape architect. A short-term goal might be to get a summer job at a greenhouse.

At the same time or later, you might work on a medium-term goal. A **medium-term goal** is usually more challenging than a short-term goal. It also takes longer to achieve. A medium-term goal might be to earn a master's degree in landscape architecture. Another medium-term goal might be to work as an apprentice to a licensed landscape architect.

Beyond your short-term and medium-term goals are long-term goals. A **long-term goal** may take a long time to reach. Short-term and medium-term goals can sometimes help you achieve a long-term goal. To become a landscape architect, you might set a long-term goal of working for the national park service. Such an opportunity might be open to you only if you already have some experience.

To get a clearer picture of the goals on the way to a career goal, look at **Figure 5.3**. Bill Mann followed these stepping stones to his ultimate career goal to become a landscape architect.

Figure 5.3 **STEPPING STONES TO A CAREER**

Short-, medium-, and long-term goals can help you reach your ultimate career goal in stages. *In what other areas could setting short-, medium-, and long-term goals help you?*

A

Set a Career Goal

Bill Mann's career decision began with a summer job as a landscaper. He mowed lawns and planted shrubs and trees. A neighbor suggested Bill think about becoming a landscape architect. Bill did some research and decided the career was made for him. **He listed the steps he would take to reach his career goal.**

B

Short-Term Goals

Bill determined his short-term goals. They were to

- Get a summer job at a greenhouse .
- Go to college and major in botany.
- Take drafting courses and learn to draw plans.
- Finish college with a bachelor's degree.

Make a Career Plan

As you can see, making a career plan is a big job. Why not give it a try right now? Design a plan for one of your career choices. It's a good way to prepare for future career decisions. You won't waste energy worrying later. You won't procrastinate either. You'll know what's involved, and you'll be able to sit down and do it.

C

Medium-Term Goals

Bill's medium-term goals were to

- Get a master's degree in landscape architecture.
- Work as an apprentice under a licensed landscape architect.
- Get a license as a landscape architect.

D

Long-Term Goal

Bill's long-term goal was to work as a landscape architect for the National Park Service. Working for the park service, he designed a new visitor center for a major Civil War battlefield. **Bill reached his long-term goal and saw his career goal become reality.**

Try This Activity

Plot Your Career Course

Now that you know the process of career planning, get started with your own career. First, write your ultimate goal at the top of a sheet of paper. Then use library and Internet resources to research and make three lists. Your teacher, guidance counselor, adult family members, and friends may also be able to give you helpful advice.

Graduation Plan In the first list, identify and select classes, activities, and experiences now and in high school that are related to the career goal. Think of this list as a graduation plan that could lead to a specific career choice.

Education and Training Plan In the second list, detail the education or training you'll need after high school. Be specific. List and explain your education and training alternatives, including courses you might take, and certifications and degrees you must earn.

Experience Plan In the third list, put experiences now, in high school, and after high school that will lead to your specific career choice. Include all kinds of work experience. Don't forget internships or apprenticeships and volunteer, part-time, and temporary jobs.

Set Your Goals Once your lists are complete, you're ready for the next step. Figure out whether each of the items you've listed is a short-, medium-, or long-term goal. Chart your goals in **chronological order,** or the order in which they will happen. Think about when you might start and complete each one. What can you do now? What will you do, say, one, three, and five years from now? How long will it take you to reach your ultimate goal?

Achieving Your Goals

The more specific and realistic your goals are, the more likely you will achieve them. For example, imagine that your ultimate career goal is to become an emergency room doctor. To get a job working in a hospital would not be a specific enough medium-term goal. A better goal would be to enter a medical school program to become a physician. The career plan in **Figure 5.4** shows a series of specific goals set in chronological order.

Remember, your plan is never set in stone. Your goals and the time you spend on them may change over time. You must face your future with an open mind. Think of it as an athletic contest. Your plans might change with every step of the game. That's what makes it exciting.

The motivation to achieve your goals comes from within. If you are not achieving your goals, don't allow yourself to lose motivation. Find out why you are stuck. As you review and revise your goals, you must also renew your motivation.

The most important thing is to have a plan. Without a plan, you've just got an idea or a dream. With a plan, you're moving toward your ultimate career goal, step by step. You'll keep moving forward until you find the career that's right for you.

Figure 5.4

A CAREER PLAN

Short-Term Goal	Medium-Term Goal	Long-Term Goal	Ultimate Goal
Work as an intern at a newspaper and get practical journalism experience. • Start now • Finish in 2 years from now	Earn a Bachelor of Arts degree in English from a college. • Start 2 years from now • Finish in 4 years after start	Work for a publishing company as an editor or writer. • Start 5 years from now • Finish in 6 years after start	Become an editorial director. • Start 10 years from now

Step by Step Chronological order makes it easy to see the steps to a career goal. *If you were pursuing this career plan, which goals would you need to work on at the same time for a while?*

Lesson 5.2 Review and Activities

Key Terms Review

1. Write a paragraph about the different kinds of goals that lead to meeting a career goal. Compare and contrast the goals. Use each of the key terms below.
- **short-term goal**
- **medium-term goal**
- **long-term goal**
- **chronological order**

Check Your Understanding

Tell whether each statement is true or false. Rewrite any false statement to make it true. Write your answers on a separate sheet of paper.

2. The first step in creating any plan is to make a decision.

3. The goals between you and your career goal include short-, medium-, and long-term goals.

Critical Thinking

Use complete sentences to answer the following questions. Write your answers on a separate sheet of paper.

4. How do short-, medium-, and long-term goals help you reach your ultimate career goal?

5. Why is it important to be specific when you set goals?

6. Why is it okay to change your goals as needed?

Character Building

7. **Human Relations** The skills that are necessary for good relations with others are the most important skills that anyone can learn in life. Human relations is the skill or ability to work effectively through and with other people. Practicing effective human relations means being yourself at your very best. Write two paragraphs about how good human relations skills help you in achieving your career goals.

Community Involvement

8. **Research Community Groups** Identify a group that is actively involved in bettering your community. Use the *Yellow Pages* or the Internet to get the group's address and phone number. Contact the group and ask to interview the group's leader or a member of the group about the group's mission and goals. Share your findings with the class in a brief oral report.

Investigating Career Clusters

EDUCATION AND TRAINING

Education • The process of teaching and learning

Training • Education in a specific skill or professional area

Job Title	Work Description
Athletic Coach	Leads and instructs a sports team
Corporate Trainer	Organizes and conducts training workshops for employees
Librarian	Assists people in finding library information and using it effectively
Professor	Instructs college students in a specialized area of study
Reading Specialist	Helps students with reading and helps teachers teach reading skills
School Administrator	Manages school activities and staff
School Counselor	Helps students deal with problems and think about their futures
Special Education Teacher	Instructs students with mental or physical impairments, behavioral disorders, or learning disabilities
Teacher	Teaches students in private or public schools

Exploration Activity

Education and Training Use library and Internet resources to research a career in the Education and Training career cluster. Write a report on your findings. Include information about the kinds of work, skills required, working conditions, training and education required, and career outlook.

Cooperative Learning Interview a classmate about the career he or she researched. Find out as much information about that career as you can during the interview. Then have your classmate interview you about the career you researched. Afterward, share what you learned with the class.

Chapter 5 Review and Activities

Chapter Highlights

Lesson 5.1 Planning helps you do what you need or want to do when it needs to be done. It helps you prioritize and gives you a feeling of accomplishment.

Lesson 5.2 You need to set realistic goals on the way to your career goal. It helps to be specific, put your goals in order, and make changes as needed.

Key Concept Review

Use complete sentences to answer the following questions. Write your answers on a separate sheet of paper.

1. Why is planning important? Give four reasons.
2. What basic steps are included in most career plans?
3. What three kinds of goals do you set and meet on the way to your ultimate career goal?
4. Why do you need a career plan?

Critical Thinking

Use complete sentences to answer the following questions. Write your answers on a separate sheet of paper.

5. Why is it important to plan time for rest and relaxation?
6. How might achieving an important goal affect your attitude toward other goals?
7. Why might you take a part-time job instead of a full-time job while you're a student?
8. How can you tell if your goals are realistic, or reachable?

Skill Building

9. **Basic—Listening**
   Invite a friend to share with you his or her goals and plans for achieving them. Then draw a picture that illustrates how your friend plans to reach his or her goal. Present the drawing to your friend, and ask whether it accurately represents the plan.
10. **Interpersonal—Participates as a Member of a Team**
    In a small group, decide on a project for your school. Plan the short-, medium-, and long-term goals needed to reach your goal. List steps to put your plan into action.

Personal Career Portfolio

Academic Applications

11. Mathematics

Karen gave up her career plan to become a master plumber to take a factory job. After five years, her wages rose from $10.50 to $12 an hour. She could have become a master plumber in five years and earned $25 an hour. Karen works 40 hours a week. How much does she earn a week at the factory? How much more would she have made each week as a master plumber?

12. Science

Imagine you make videos about the steps people can take to different careers. Your next video is about becoming an astronomer. Research the basic steps in reaching that career goal. Break them into short-, medium-, and long-term goals. Then explain the career plan, as if you were offering career counseling.

Prepare an Educational and Career Plan

- **Think** of a career that interests you.
- **Access** career information using print and online resources to complete an educational and/or training plan for a career pathway.
- **Prepare** an educational and career plan that begins with entry into high school and continues through a post-secondary educational and/or training program.
- **List** in chronological order the goals you would need to accomplish to achieve the career.
- **Categorize** the goals as short-, medium-, or long-term.
- **Title** the document *Educational and Career Plan* and file it in your Personal Career Portfolio.
- **List** your portfolio entry on your Personal Career Portfolio contents page.

Chapter 6

Finding a Job

Lesson 6.1

Gathering Leads

Lesson 6.2

Organizing Your Job Search

CAREER CLUSTER

You will explore careers in the Finance career cluster.

What You'll Learn

- You will learn how to go about finding a job.
- You will identify sources of information about job openings.
- You will discover how to use information you gather to get the job you want.

Get Ready!

Finding Jobs

Gather together a group of friends and have a "roundtable" discussion about finding jobs. As you go around the group, each person should name a job that sounds interesting to him or her.

Apply As a group, brainstorm ways to find out about openings for each job named. Keep a list of the methods mentioned. Which method of finding a job would you use first? Why?

Lesson 6.1

Gathering Leads

Discover

- What is involved in a job search
- How talking with people can turn up job leads
- Other ways to find out about job openings

Why It's Important

One day, you will be looking for a job. You'll want to know where to look for information about job openings.

KEY TERMS

- **work permit**
- **job lead**
- **networking**
- **career fair**
- **contact list**
- **referral**
- **classifieds**
- **school-to-work program**

You've got an idea for a job. Maybe you'd like to work as a party helper or a pet sitter. Maybe you want to do lawn or garden care. Perhaps you'd like to volunteer your time at your local hospital or recycling center.

Many part-time and volunteer job opportunities are open to you right now. By the time you reach high school, you'll have an even greater variety of job choices. To apply for some jobs, you'll need a work permit if you're under 16. In some states you'll need one if you're under 18. A **work permit** is a legal document that allows a minor to hold a job. It shows the number of hours you can work and the kinds of jobs you can hold.

Once you have an idea of what you want to do, you can take the next step and start your job search.

Talk and Listen
Talking to people is an important part of every job search. *What do you think you can learn by talking to people? What can they learn from you?*

Starting Your Job Search

A large part of a job search is detective work—tracking down leads, clues, and evidence. Your search for the right job will begin with a job lead. A **job lead** is information about a job opening.

Once you get a job lead, you'll follow it. You'll chase job leads until you land the job you want.

Networking

How do you go about finding job leads? One of the best ways is by networking. **Networking** is communicating with people you know or can get to know. When you network, you share information and advice with others.

You've probably already done some networking. Remember that summer art class or softball league you heard about? How about the after-school teen center that just opened? You talked with teachers, friends, neighbors—anyone who might know something about it. In the same way, networking can also lead to a job.

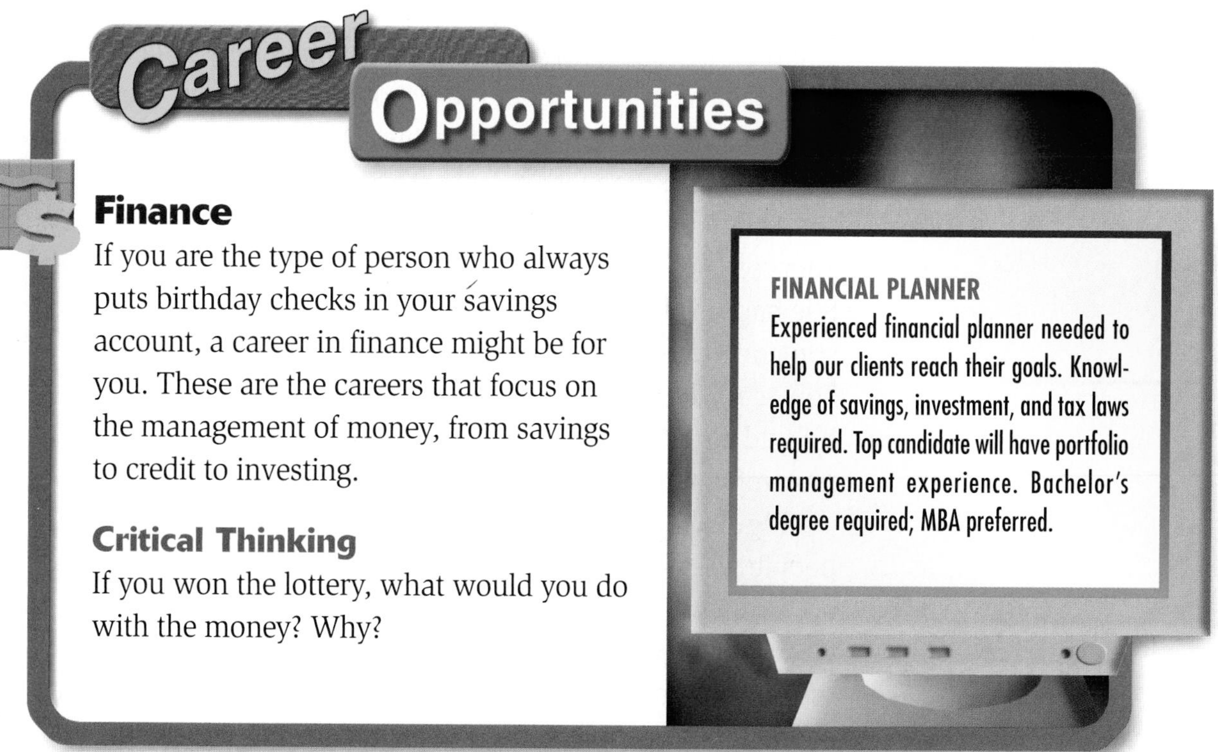

Finance

If you are the type of person who always puts birthday checks in your savings account, a career in finance might be for you. These are the careers that focus on the management of money, from savings to credit to investing.

Critical Thinking

If you won the lottery, what would you do with the money? Why?

Friends and Family
You can begin networking with anyone you know. *How might friends and family members be able to help you find a job?*

How Networking Works

It's easy to start networking to find job leads. You can begin by just talking with people about what you're interested in. Spread the word. Ask people you know to spread the word to others for you.

Your network will grow quickly. Someone you know will know someone else. That person will know someone else, who knows a person you need to talk to. To get the ball rolling, all you have to do is talk to people you know.

Tony Demetriou knows that networking works from experience. He used networking to find a job mowing lawns in the summer and shoveling snow in the winter. Tony talked to his next-door neighbors about lawn mowing and snow shoveling. One said he did the work himself. The other had older children who did the work.

Although neither neighbor had work for him, a few days later, one of the neighbors telephoned Tony with a job lead. She had several older friends in the neighborhood who needed someone to do their lawn mowing and snow shoveling work. Tony called them. They were happy to hear about the services he had to offer. Tony now has a busy schedule year-round mowing lawns and shoveling snow.

Figure 6.1 shows that networking works. In fact, more people get their jobs through networking than any other way.

Start Building Your Network

Start building your own network right now. It's never too soon. Talk to people about jobs and careers that interest you.

School clubs and events such as career fairs are great places to network. A **career fair** is an event where employers offer career and employment information. When you start looking for a job, your networking may bring you job leads.

The steps in networking are simple. First, it helps to make a contact list. A **contact list** is simply a list of people you know. For example, do you have any friends who have started new jobs recently? Write their names down on your list. Do any family members or friends own or manage their own businesses? Write their names down, too. They may need someone with your qualifications or may have a business contact who is looking for a good worker.

Figure 6.1

WAYS THAT PEOPLE GET JOBS

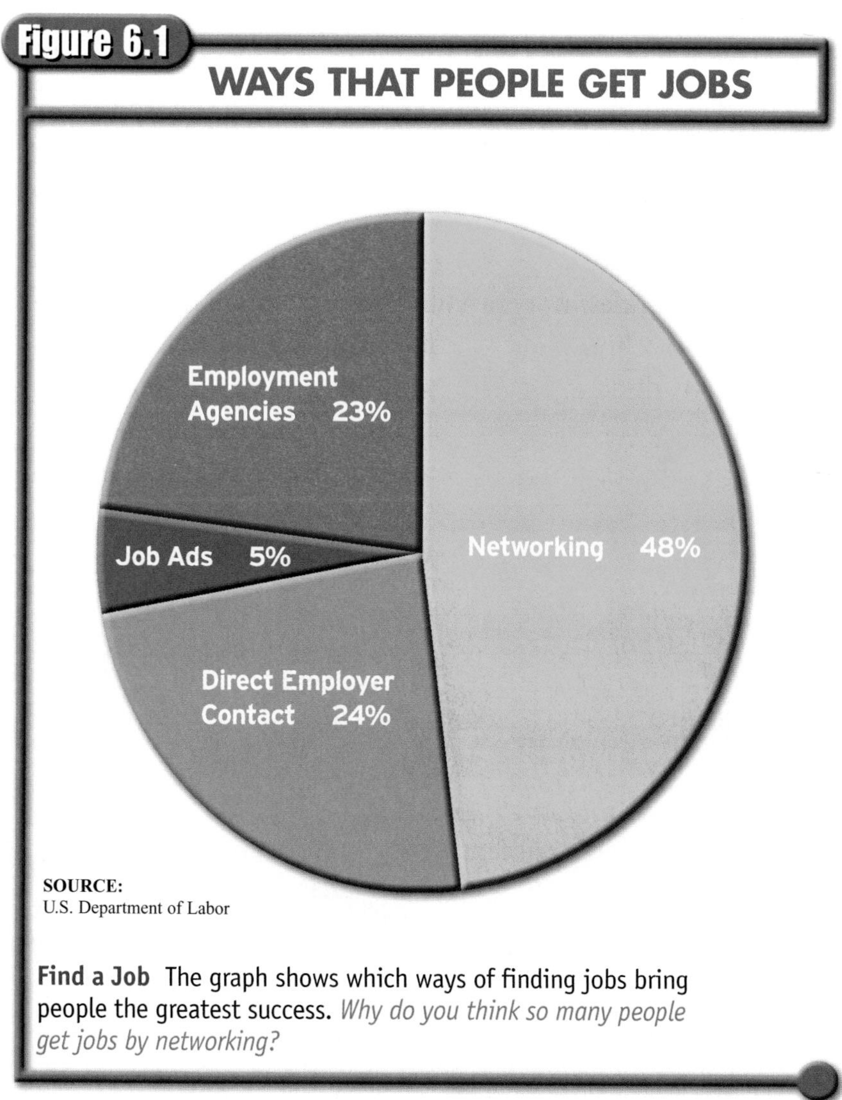

Find a Job The graph shows which ways of finding jobs bring people the greatest success. *Why do you think so many people get jobs by networking?*

Try This Activity

Get Started

Start a contact list. Include everyone—family members, family friends, neighbors, teachers, classmates, friends of friends. People who are just acquaintances also belong on your list. Keep your list up-to-date by adding new people you meet or get to know.

Take Another Step Think of a job you'd like. Make a contact list for that job. Write down the names of everyone you know who might give you a lead for the job.

Once you have a list, the next step is to contact the people listed. Talk to each person on your list about your job idea, even if you aren't quite ready to look for a job yet. Ask for any information that might lead to a job.

Some people on your list may not know anything about job openings. A neighbor or friend of theirs might, though. Don't cross people off your list. Ask contacts whether they know someone who works in the area you're interested in.

Grow Your Network With Referrals

Getting a referral from each person you talk to is the next step in networking. A **referral** is someone to whom you are referred, or directed. That person may have the information about a job or job opening that your contact did not. Your contact list will grow with each referral. By contacting referrals, you'll expand your network.

Make Contact
Contacts are anyone you know. *Who would be the first five people on your contact list?*

Networking will come in handy as you plan and build a career. By talking to people, you can learn a lot about your career field. You can also share what you know with other people. You never know where networking will lead. The networking you do today may lead to a job in the future.

Other Ways to Get Information

Although networking is one of the best ways to find a job, it isn't the only way. **Figure 6.1** on page 107 shows that people have success finding jobs in other ways.

Phone Businesses for Leads

One of the first things many job seekers do is call businesses they might like to work for. They ask for general information. They also ask about job openings and whom they can talk to about them. Calls like these are known as *cold calls*.

The secret to making successful cold calls is careful planning. Look at **Figure 6.2** for some tips on using the telephone to get job leads. The more calls you make, the more comfortable you'll feel on the phone. Just remember, the first cold call is often the hardest. You'll warm up in no time.

Figure 6.2

TELEPHONE TIPS

- Write a script for your call. A script will help you remember what you want to say and help you feel more relaxed. Jot down important questions.
- If possible, know the name of the person you are calling, his or her title, and the department in which he or she works. Learn how to pronounce the person's name before calling.
- If you don't know the name of the person you need to speak to, explain who you are and why you are calling. Then ask to speak with someone who can answer your questions.
- If you reach your party, greet him or her by the proper title, such as Professor, Dr., Mr., or Mrs., and his or her last name. Then introduce yourself and state the purpose of your call.
- Create a positive impression by how you speak. Be aware of what you sound like and avoid littering your speech with verbal clutter, such as *uh*, *um*, and *like*.
- Get the information you want. Ask about job openings. Don't forget to ask for referrals.
- *Always* remain pleasant and professional.

A Powerful Tool The telephone is a useful job-hunting tool. *How else can you contact businesses you'd like to work for? Why might a phone call be a better job-hunting tool than other methods?*

Check the Classifieds

Many job hunters go straight to newspaper classifieds. The **classifieds** are advertisements organized in classes, or groups. The classifieds section lists things for sale and places for rent. It also lists job openings, often in the region the newspaper serves.

The truth is, though, that only a small number of people find jobs through print ads. There are other ways, such as networking, that businesses fill jobs. Many businesses post "Help Wanted" signs when they have job openings. A local day care center may have a bulletin board on which parents post ads for baby-sitters and other jobs, for example. Keep your eyes open for job leads.

Search Internet Job Sites

The Internet is another place to look for job advertisements. On the Internet, you can find jobs far beyond your own community. You'll be looking at job openings in the worldwide community. When you begin a search one day for a full-time job, you'll probably check the Internet for listings.

Try This Activity

Find Online Job Listings

Just for fun, locate some job listings on the Internet. You can log on to the Internet on a computer at home, school, or your local library. Most public libraries have computers connected to the Internet.

Search Smart Use a search engine or Web directory to find links to job sites. Enter search keywords such as *careers* or *employment opportunities*. You might visit America's Job Bank, USAJobs, or the Monster job site, for example.

Read Company Job Listings You can also go to company Web sites. Use the name of a company whose products you like as the keyword for your search. When you reach the company's site, click on the link to employment opportunities.

Take Notes Take notes on three interesting job openings you find on the Internet. Record where you found the posting, what the job is, and why it interests you.

Ask for Help and Advice at School

You can also look for help or advice about jobs at your school. Most schools have a counselor or teacher who helps students with career plans. Some schools even have a placement office to help students find jobs.

Make your school counselor part of your network. Tell him or her about careers you'd like to explore. Ask your counselor about student organizations related to careers. Your counselor may be able to set up an appointment for you to do some job shadowing. He or she may also know about volunteering opportunities in your community and special events such as career fairs.

In high school, your school counselor may be able to help you get into a school-to-work program. A **school-to-work program** brings schools and businesses together. If you take part, you will gain work experience and training at a local business. When you graduate from high school, the business may even consider hiring you.

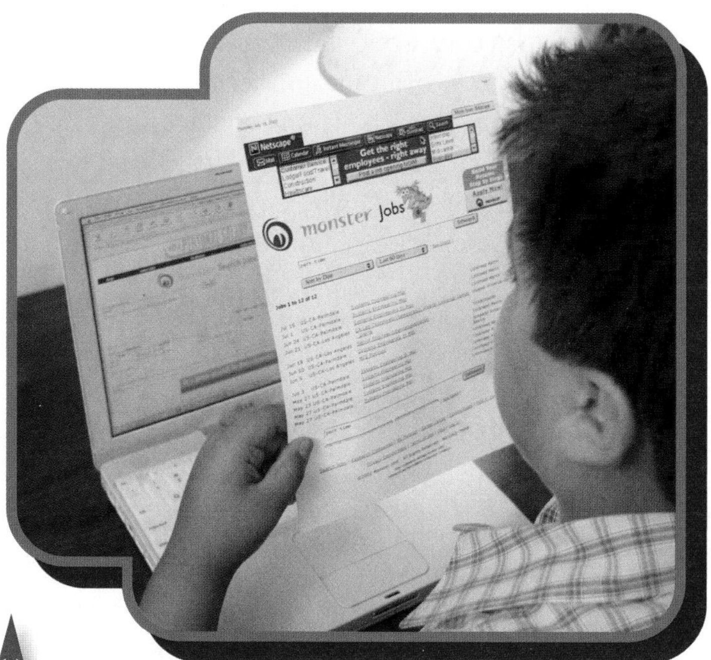

Opportunities Online
Thousands of jobs are posted on the Internet. *What keywords would you use to find job listings for careers of interest to you?*

Keeping Contact

Q: If a contact has no job leads or referrals for me, can I cross this person's name off my list?

A: No! You aren't finished with this person yet. First, you should thank your contact. It's very important to thank *everyone* you speak to—even those who don't have information for you. After all, they did give up their time to speak to you. Sending a note is one nice way to say thanks. It's also a good idea to keep in touch later on. Consider sending out a yearly card or a friendly e-mail letting your contacts know what's new with your career. They might have a job for you next time.

Lesson 6.1 Review and Activities

Key Terms Review

1. A friend has asked you for job-hunting advice. Write a letter to your friend explaining how to find a job. In your letter, use each of the key terms below.

- **work permit**
- **job lead**
- **networking**
- **career fair**
- **contact list**
- **referral**
- **classifieds**
- **school-to-work program**

Check Your Understanding

Choose the correct answer for each of the following items. Write your answers on a separate sheet of paper.

2. Your search for ______ will begin with a job lead.

- **a.** how to perform on the job
- **b.** the right job
- **c.** a network

3. You can build a network by ______.

- **a.** giving out your phone number
- **b.** making a contact list
- **c.** asking people to find jobs for you

Critical Thinking

Use complete sentences to answer the following questions. Write your answers on a separate sheet of paper.

4. Why is it important to know what kind of a job you want before you start looking for a job?

5. Why do you think most people get their jobs through networking?

6. Why is it important to use more than one way to find a job?

Character Building

7. **Sharing Information** You've found some great contacts and leads for possible baby-sitting jobs. A friend is also hoping to find some summer baby-sitting work, but has not had much success finding job leads. He's asked you if you have any contacts or leads he might follow. Should you share your information? Why or why not? Write a paragraph explaining your answer.

Teamwork

8. **Make a Group Presentation** Working in a small group, choose a job in the Finance career cluster. Research openings for the job. Each team member should use a different research method. Compare your results with your teammates' results. What information did each method produce? As a group, present your findings to the class.

Lesson 6.2

Organizing Your Job Search

You've got some good ideas about where to look for job leads. Now you need a way to keep track of the information you gather. Being organized is the key to a successful job search.

Discover

- How to keep track of job leads
- How to gather information about jobs and businesses

Why It's Important

When you're organized, it's easier to use the information to get the job you want.

KEY TERMS

- **database**
- **employer**
- **annual report**

Keeping Track

You'll talk to many people during a job search. You'll discover job leads in many places. It's easy to forget people's names and what they said. Don't rely on your memory. Don't make notes on scraps of paper. You need a well-organized system for remembering.

Setting Up a System

Organize your job search from the beginning. That way you'll know where you started, and you'll see where you're going.

A simple way to organize your job search is to record job leads on index cards or sheets of paper. Put each lead on its own card or sheet of paper.

Get Organized
Organizing your job search is a good idea. Think of some other projects or activities you have organized. *What kind of system did you use for each? How did it work? What could you have done differently?*

Starting a New Job

Starting a new job is hard for anyone. You may not know your coworkers' names, where to eat lunch, or even where to find the restroom. What's the best thing to do? Relax! Your employer doesn't expect you to know everything right away. If you're willing to learn and have a sense of humor, your first few weeks will not be too difficult.

Cooperative Learning Activity

- Team up with two or three classmates.
- Brainstorm a list of things you might need to do on the first day of a new job.
- Discuss ways to prepare for each situation.

If you prefer working with computers, you can organize your job leads in a database program. A **database** can store data, or information, in different ways. If you use a database, you will be able to search, sort, and reorganize the information you enter.

Getting the Details Down

Create an index card or a database entry for every person on your contact list. If there are any businesses you'd like to work for, create a card or database entry for each. You can also create cards or database entries for classified job listings you are interested in.

Whether you use cards or a database, you'll want to record the same information:

- name and title of person or business
- if it's a person, name of his or her department and company
- address, telephone number, and e-mail address
- additional information

Figure 6.3 shows how to list all of this information on a job-lead card.

Figure 6.3

A JOB-LEAD CARD

Mrs. Goldbaum

335 Prospect Street

(924) 555-0100

She needs someone to help with grocery shopping once a week. Aunt Elaine suggested I call her.

Write It Down You'll need to keep detailed information on your job-lead cards in order to make a contact. *How would you open a conversation with Mrs. Goldbaum, using this information?*

How the System Works

Now here's how to use your system. Let's say you have decided to use job-lead cards. After you've made a card for each contact or lead, make contact. After contacting the person or business, make notes on the card. Keep your cards handy. If someone you've talked to calls you, get out his or her card. Use it to refresh your memory. Update the card with new information.

The time you take to get organized and stay organized will be worth it. As **Figure 6.4** on pages 116–117 shows, a well-organized job search helped Jason Lee locate a job. Organization can work for you too.

Researching Jobs and Employers

Getting a job lead is exciting. Getting a job is even more so. In between, though, you have another job to do. You need to do some investigating.

The Benefits of Research

You can stand out in a job market full of qualified people if you do your research. A person who takes the time to do such preparation stands out among his or her competition.

You want to find out as much as you can about possible jobs and employers. An **employer** is a person or business that pays a person or group of people to work.

Researching employers will give you self-confidence, which will help you make a good impression. You will feel comfortable talking to your contact and be able to ask intelligent questions about a job opening. The person you talk to will notice that you took the time to do some research. He or she will know that you are serious and genuinely interested in the company.

What you learn will also help you decide whether a particular job is right for you. You will want to find out what kind of situation you'll be working in and who you'll be working with. You'll want to know as much as possible about the kind of work you'll do. Then you can match what you learn with what's important to you.

Questions to Ask

You can get basic facts about a business by asking these questions:

- What kinds of goods or services does the business offer?
- What kind of reputation does the business have?
- What types of work do people do there?
- Is the business growing and expanding?
- Is it possible to move up in the business?

Figure 6.4 **ORGANIZING JOB LEADS**

Jason Lee of Roanoke, Virginia, wants to be a veterinarian someday. After his first year of college, he took a summer job at a small animal clinic. Jason's job-lead cards show how networking got him the job he wanted. *If Jason had kept his job leads in a database instead of on cards, would the information be different?*

A

Liz Sherman, Neighbor
134 Dogwood Street
Roanoke
555-0198

Suggested I call:
• Winnie Scott, office manager
Vinton Pet Care, Vinton

While home on break, Jason talked to his neighbor Liz Sherman about her new puppy. He mentioned that he wanted to work with animals. Liz gave him the name of the office manager at an animal clinic. Jason made a card with Liz's name that included a referral to Winnie Scott.

Ways to Get Answers to Your Questions

How do you get answers to your questions? Here are a few suggestions. If you know someone who works at the business you're interested in, ask him or her about it. Talk to customers of the business. Ask why they use it and what they like about it.

Search for stories about the business in news databases at the library or online. News stories will give you information and leads to other sources of information.

B

Winnie Scott, Office Manager
Vinton Pet Care, 11 Elm St., Vinton
555-0176

• Called 2/23
Connected me with Dr. Ainsley, the vet at the clinic

Then Jason made a card for Liz's referral. He followed up by calling her. Winnie Scott connected Jason to Dr. Ainsley, the vet at the clinic. Dr. Ainsley said he was thinking of hiring someone. He promised to give Jason a call in a couple of months.

C

Jason made a card for Dr. Ainsley. On it, he made notes about their conversation. Dr. Ainsley called Jason back in the spring. Jason looked at his notes to recall their earlier conversation. Dr. Ainsley told Jason there was a job opening at the clinic for the summer. He invited Jason for an interview. A week later, he offered Jason the job.

Dr. Jim Ainsley, Veterinarian
Vinton Pet Care, 11 Elm St., Vinton 555-0176
• Spoke on 2/23. May be hiring for summer. Won't decide for a couple of months. Took my phone number and promised to call me
• Called me 4/15 and set up an interview for 4/20 at 1:30 PM
• Interview on 4/20 went well, will call me by 4/30 at the latest
–4/27 GOT THE JOB!

You might even visit the business. Judy Johnson thought that would be a good idea. She had her eye on a part-time job at a bakery in town. Before calling about the job, she stopped by the bakery to check it out. "My best friend came with me," Judy explains.

> "We bought a few cookies to see what the baked goods were like. There were lots of other customers. The woman behind the counter was very friendly and helpful. It looked like a great place to work to me."

Do what Judy did if you can. Visit before you make contact. Pay attention to what you see. Does the business have a good atmosphere? Does it look like a safe place to work? Do the people who work there look happy? Are they courteous and ready to help? Are the customers happy? Ask yourself, "Is this a place I'd like to work?"

Other Paths to Information

One way to find out about a public business is to call, write, or e-mail and ask for its annual report. An **annual report** is a summary of a company's business for the year. It will tell you a lot about a business.

Get the Facts
There are many ways to gather information about places where you might work. *Where would you get information about a business or organization for which you'd like to work?*

You might also check out the Web site of the business. There you'll find a lot of general information. You'll get up-to-the-minute news about the business. You'll learn about its latest products or projects.

Gather Your Facts

You won't be the only one asking questions. A possible employer will want to know about you. Employers want to know about your education, skills, and interests. They're also interested in other jobs you've held, including both part-time and volunteer work.

The next step is to gather the facts about yourself. Presenting yourself is an important part of your job search. You'll learn about this important step in Chapter 7.

The Global Workplace

Dining Around the World

Mealtime in America means breakfast, lunch, or dinner; but you may have to eat your way through a few other meals while traveling on business to a foreign country. In Spain, save room for appetizers called "tapas" eaten at around 5 P.M. Don't worry about spoiling your appetite. Dinner in Spain is not eaten until much later, after 9 P.M. In England, you might have "high tea" between 4 and 6 P.M. instead of dinner. During high tea you'll be served tea along with finger sandwiches and desserts. In Chile, you can take a small break at 5 P.M. called "onces" and eat bite-sized sandwiches, pastries, and tea. *Bon Appétit*!

Internet Activity

Using the Internet and library resources, find out what the traditional foods are in one other country. How are these dishes prepared? When are they served? Go to the *Exploring Careers* Web site at exploring.glencoe.com for a list of Web sites to help you complete this activity.

Lesson 6.2 Review and Activities

Key Terms Review

1. Write a glossary definition for each of the key terms below. Compare your entries with those of your classmates.
   - **database**
   - **annual report**
   - **employer**

Check Your Understanding

Tell whether each statement is true or false. Rewrite any false statement to make it true. Write your answers on a separate sheet of paper.

2. The best way to keep track of job leads is to memorize the company information you uncover.
3. The place to begin organizing your job search is your contact list.

Critical Thinking

Use complete sentences to answer the following questions. Write your answers on a separate sheet of paper.

4. Why do you think it's important to organize your job search from the beginning?
5. What would you especially want to know about a business you might work for? Explain your answer.
6. What would be convenient about using a database instead of cards to organize job leads? How might a database not be practical?

Connecting to the Workplace

7. **Develop a Contact List and Card System** Think of a part-time or volunteer job you'd like to have, such as tutoring, baby-sitting, dog walking, newspaper delivery, or helping older people shop. Put together a contact list that will help you get the job. Use a card system to organize your search for work. Arrange your card system on a poster board to show how your network developed from one contact to several. Share your poster with the class. Use it to explain your card system and search results.

Community Involvement

8. **Prepare a Group Report** Team up with two or three classmates. Together, select a business in your community that offers financial services. List questions your group has about the business. Then gather information to answer these questions. Ask friends and family members what they know about the business. Do some networking to get more information. If it's possible, visit the business. Then prepare a brief report on the business, based on your group's research. Share your group report with the class.

Investigating Career Clusters

FINANCE

Finance • Acquiring, investing, and managing money

Job Title	Work Description
Accountant	Prepares and analyzes financial information for managers of businesses
Bank Examiner	Makes sure that banks operate according to the law
Bank Teller	Cashes checks, accepts deposits and loan payments, and processes withdrawals
Budget Analyst	Researches, analyzes, and develops budgets
Economist	Studies and analyzes economics and economic conditions
Financial Planner	Helps clients establish and accomplish their financial goals
Insurance Agent	Sells insurance policies to individuals or businesses
Loan Officer	Works in a bank and helps people apply and get approved for loans
Stockbroker	Buys and sells stocks, bonds, and commodities for clients
Tax Preparer	Prepares tax returns for clients

Exploration Activity

Finance Use library and Internet resources to research a career in the Finance career cluster. Write a report on your findings. Include information about the kinds of work, the skills required, the working conditions, the training and education required, and the career outlook.

Cooperative Learning Interview a classmate about the career he or she researched. Find out as much information about that career as you can during the interview. Then have your classmate interview you about the career you researched. Afterward, share what you learned with the class.

Chapter 6 Review and Activities

Chapter Highlights

Lesson 6.1 Networking is one of the best ways to get job leads.

Lesson 6.2 Being organized is the key to a successful job search.

Key Concept Review

Use complete sentences to answer the following questions. Write your answers on a separate sheet of paper.

1. What is networking?
2. How is networking useful in developing job leads?
3. What are some other sources of job leads besides networking?
4. What are two ways you can keep track of job leads?
5. How can you gather information about jobs and businesses?

Critical Thinking

Use complete sentences to answer the following questions. Write your answers on a separate sheet of paper.

6. Why might employers like to hire people referred to them through a network?
7. Which source for job leads would you use first in job hunting? Why?
8. Which source for job leads would give you the most control over your job search? Explain.

Skill Building

9. **Basic—Speaking**
   Role-play telephone conversations with a partner. Pose as someone looking for a job. Explain what you are looking for and why. Your partner should give you a referral. Role-play a second conversation in which your partner poses as the referral. Then switch roles with your partner. Afterward, discuss how you could improve your telephone skills.
10. **Information—Use Computers to Process Information**
    Explore job listings on the Internet. Then create a Web page for people to read before job hunting online. In the page, give advice for conducting an online job search. Suggest keywords other than *careers* and *employment opportunities* to use for a job search. List Web sites that provide job listings. Include other advice.

Academic Applications

11. Mathematics

Steve has 20 people on his first contact list. Each person refers him to 2 more people. Each of those people refers him to 1 more person. How many people will be on Steve's list after these referrals?

12. Language Arts

Review the classifieds for job openings. Make a list of abbreviations used in the ads. Then create a glossary of all the abbreviations you found and the phrase or term that each stands for. Share your glossary with your classmates.

Personal Career Portfolio

Create a Networking List

- **Create** a table, list, or database that contains information on at least ten contacts who may be valuable members of your personal network.
- **Include** columns for relevant contact information (name, address, phone number, and e–mail) as well as contact attempts and contact results.
- **Describe** what type of assistance you expect each contact to be able to provide.
- **Contact** each person on your networking list and ask for any information that might lead to a job.
- **Document** the results of the contact and any planned follow-up.
- **Title** the document *Network* and file it in your Personal Career Portfolio.
- **Update** the document when you make new contacts.
- **List** your portfolio entry on your Personal Career Portfolio contents page.

Chapter 7

Applying for a Job

Lesson 7.1

Presenting Yourself

Lesson 7.2

Putting Your Best Foot Forward

CAREER CLUSTER

You will explore careers in the Government and Public Administration career cluster.

What You'll Learn

- You will find out what is involved in applying for a job.
- You will discover ways to present and market yourself to an employer.
- You will learn what to do before, during, and after an interview.

Get Ready!

Applying for a First Job

Interview three adult friends or family members about their first job. Ask questions such as these:

- What was your first job?
- How did you apply for the job?
- How did you show that you were qualified?
- Do you have advice about applying for a job?

Apply What do the answers tell you about applying for a job? Which piece of advice mentioned seems most important to you?

Lesson 7.1

Presenting Yourself

Discover

- How to organize information about yourself in a résumé
- What a cover letter is and why it is important
- Tips for filling out job applications

Why It's Important

One day, you'll apply for a job. Whether or not you get the job may depend on how you present yourself to the employer.

KEY TERMS

- **résumé**
- **format**
- **personal fact sheet**
- **cover letter**
- **personal career portfolio**
- **job application**
- **references**
- **letter of recommendation**

Life is full of wonderful surprises. You finally read that book with the boring cover. To your surprise, it turns out to be your all-time favorite. You take time to get to know someone who seems different than you. You're surprised later to find how much you have in common.

Many of life's surprises are pleasant. Even so, people don't always welcome surprises. Employers, as a rule, aren't looking for surprises. They don't have time. In the world of work, first impressions count.

Make an Impression
First impressions can be powerful. *What were your first impressions of some of your close friends? Of middle school? What do you think of both now?*

Putting a Résumé Together

Employers want to find the best person to fill a job. Whether it is a part-time job after school or a full-time job, most job openings attract many applicants. Employers have to pick and choose among them. They don't have time to get to know people well. They can't take time to talk to everyone. Instead, employers look at personal summaries. They choose people who make good impressions in their summaries.

In the work world, a summary of personal information is known as a résumé. A **résumé** describes your education, skills, work experience, activities, and interests. It introduces you to potential employers.

Get the Job
Having good manners and exhibiting ease in social situations can make the difference in whether or not you leave a good first impression and get the job. *How can good social skills translate into success at job interviews and on the job?*

Résumé Formats

There are two basic kinds of résumés—a chronological résumé and a skills résumé. A chronological résumé presents information in order of time—reverse time order, to be exact. For an example of a chronological résumé, look at **Figure 7.1** on page 128. Kira Franklin has listed her work experience in reverse time order. Her current job appears first, then the job before that, and so on.

The skills résumé in **Figure 7.2** on page 129, shows the same information about Kira in a different **format,** or arrangement. A skills résumé highlights skills and accomplishments. Each heading identifies a skill or strength. After each heading is a description of the skill and the experience related to it.

Which Format Is Better?

The kind of résumé you choose may depend on the job you're looking for. It can also depend on what you want to emphasize: work experience or skills. People who've had a series of jobs in one career field often use a chronological résumé. Time order is an excellent way to show growth from job to job. A skills résumé is often a good choice for first-timers in the job market. That's because it focuses on strengths instead of work experience.

CHRONOLOGICAL RÉSUMÉ

1 Name and Address
Give your name, full address, and telephone number (with area code). Include your e-mail address, if you have one.

2 Job Objective
State the job you are applying for. You can change your job objective for different jobs.

3 Work Experience
List your work experience, beginning with your most recent job. Include volunteer work.

4 Education
List the schools you have attended or are currently attending. Also include any subjects or programs in which you specialized.

5 Honors and Activities
List any honors or awards you have received. Name activities you have participated in that relate to the job you want.

6 Special Skills and Abilities
List any skills and abilities you have.

Kira Franklin
87 Southwest Eighth Avenue
Morgantown, OR 93072
(503) 555-0171
kfranklin@school.edu

JOB OBJECTIVE A challenging full-time summer position working with children and ecology.

EXPERIENCE

August 2002 — **Camp Counselor, WISTEC Science Camp, McKenzie River, Oregon**
- Responsible for 12 campers ages 8 to 10 during three one-week sessions.
- Helped plan science activities and outdoor projects having to do with the environment and ecology issues.

June-July 2002 — **Science Club Teaching Assistant, WISTEC Science Center, Morgantown, Oregon**
Organized and taught weekly science activity classes for children ages 5 to 7.

Summer 2001 — **Experiment Tester, Franklin Publishing Group, Eugene, Oregon**
Tested science experiments for students ages 8 to 10.

Summer 2000 — **Volunteer, Parks Conservation Project, Eugene, Oregon**
- Helped care for recreation walkways throughout the city by picking up litter, pruning shrubs, and installing benches.
- Led group of young volunteer workers.

2000-2002 — **Flute instructor to beginning and intermediate students.**

EDUCATION Currently a senior, Morgantown High School, Morgantown, Oregon

HONORS AND ACTIVITIES Dean's Honor List, Biology Award, student delegate to Morgantown's "Science in the City Project," Most Valuable Musician Award 2002, Food Rescue volunteer

SPECIAL SKILLS AND ABILITIES Experience with Macintosh and Windows operating systems, Microsoft Office software applications, and Internet searches. Creative thinker. Like to solve problems. Work well with people and as a member of a team.

Show Your Experience There are different formats for organizing information in a résumé. Most résumés, however, include the same basic information. Headings and spacing indicate major categories of information. *How do the headings in the chronological résumé compare with those in the skills résumé?*

Whatever format you finally use, make yourself look good! Remember, your résumé is a personal introduction. It should shine a positive light on your experience, skills, and interests. When creating your résumé, keep the following suggestions in mind:

- Keep your résumé short. One page is usually plenty.
- Make sure your résumé is neat and easy to read.
- Check for typing, spelling, and grammar errors.

Figure 7.2

SKILLS RÉSUMÉ

Kira Franklin
87 Southwest Eighth Avenue
Morgantown, OR 93072
(503) 555-0171
kfranklin@school.edu

JOB OBJECTIVE Seeking a challenging full-time summer position working with children and ecology.

SKILLS AND ABILITIES

Science Work With Children
Worked with children as a teacher aide and camp counselor in two WISTEC summer science programs in the summer of 2002. Responsible for creating and carrying out science projects and outdoor ecology experiences for children ages 5 to 10 in classroom and camp environments. Also taught flute lessons, which involved scientific explanations of breathing.

Computer Skills
Experience with Macintosh and Windows operating systems as well as Microsoft Office software applications. Used knowledge of computers and the Internet to gather information for science experiments in the summer of 2001.

Teamwork
All my experience has involved working with other people to create and carry out activities, projects, and programs. I am an enthusiastic team player. On the Parks Conservation Project in 2000, I was leader of a group of young volunteers.

Responsible Worker
I take the quality of my work very seriously. I can be counted on to do more than is required and to meet all deadlines. I particularly like the challenge of organizing complex tasks.

EDUCATION Currently a senior, Morgantown High School, Morgantown, Oregon

HONORS AND ACTIVITIES Dean's Honor List, Biology award, student delegate to Morgantown's "Science in the City Project," Most Valuable Musician Award 2002, Food Rescue volunteer

Show Your Skills A skills résumé lets you highlight your areas of strength. *What skills has Kira Franklin listed? Under what heading can you find information about Kira's work experience?*

Try This Activity

Develop a Personal Fact Sheet and Résumé

By the time you apply for a job, you've gathered some information about the employer or business. Gathering information about yourself is also an important part of your job search. Take steps now to create a personal fact sheet with the information you will need to create a résumé. A **personal fact sheet** contains basic information about you and your education, experience, qualifications, and skills.

Make a List List your education and experience in chronological order. Include all of the work experiences you have had, whether paid or unpaid. Then list your other qualifications for employment, including your skills and how you have used them. Include transferable skills as well as job-specific skills. Think of skills you've learned at home or at school.

Develop a Résumé Use your personal fact sheet to develop a résumé for an employment opportunity in your career interest area. Your résumé can be chronological or skills-based, and it can be formatted for print or electronic submission.

Electronic Résumés

A popular way to send résumés to employers is via the Internet. Therefore, it's a good idea to have an electronic résumé ready. An electronic résumé is a résumé that is created on a computer and formatted so it can be sent electronically.

Many companies today scan paper résumés into their computers and store them electronically. Then when they need to hire someone, they do a computerized search of the résumés in the database. They search for keywords describing the skills or work experiences they are seeking. Typical keywords include *creative thinker*, *computer skills*, and *team worker*. The keywords quickly locate applicants who might be right for a job.

Smart job seekers today know it's important to create a résumé that's computer-friendly. They keep paper résumés and electronic résumés simple. They use black ink on white paper. They avoid boldface, italic, and other formatting. They type headings in capital letters. Most important of all, they include keywords that describe their skills and experience so that a computer search will find their résumé.

Writing Cover Letters

No résumé should go anywhere without a cover letter. A **cover letter** is a one-page letter telling who you are and why you're sending a résumé. It is the first thing a potential employer sees, and it can make a powerful impact. **Figure 7.3** on page 132 shows a sample cover letter.

A cover letter is another opportunity to make a good impression on an employer. Let your personality come through. Think of a cover letter as an introduction: a piece of paper that conveys a smile, a confident hello, and a nice, firm handshake. You want to catch the employer's interest. A cover letter is a good place to highlight interesting details about yourself that do not appear in your résumé. For example, this is where you can mention that someone in the company referred you to the job. Don't include personal information that is not related to the job you're applying for. You may be a great cookie baker, but unless you are applying for a job in a bakery, this information doesn't belong in your cover letter. What you say in a cover letter will persuade the reader to turn to your résumé. It may even get you the job.

Applying by E-Mail

Q: I saw a job ad on the Internet. The ad says to e-mail résumés. Do I need to send a cover letter?

A: You don't need to mail a *paper* cover letter, but you do need to send a cover e-mail with your résumé. Include the same information you would in a regular cover letter. Note your home address, telephone number, and e-mail address below your name at the end of the e-mail. Include the title of the job in the subject line of the e-mail. Then attach your résumé to this e-mail or paste your résumé at the bottom of the e-mail. Before you hit the send button, make sure you've checked your spelling and grammar.

Marketing Yourself With a Personal Career Portfolio

A great way to showcase your accomplishments and personal growth is to create a personal career portfolio. A **personal career portfolio** is a collection of information about you. It includes projects and work samples that show your skills and qualifications to employers. It includes information about your interests, goals, and accomplishments as well as the documents and correspondence you will need to start your job search.

You can use a personal career portfolio throughout your career. Use it to market yourself and to set you apart from other job applicants. You can even use a portfolio to help you get a promotion. The Personal Career Portfolio activity in each chapter review will help you to develop your own portfolio. You can continue to refine and improve your personal career portfolio over the course of your career.

Filling Out Job Applications

Many businesses will have you fill out a job application. A **job application** is a form that asks questions about your skills, work experience, education, and interests.

When you visit a business to apply for a position, be prepared to fill out an application. Have your personal fact sheet with you. That will assure that you have all the information you need to fill out the application. You may be able to take the application home, but some businesses prefer that you don't. Whichever you do, remember that a job application deserves just as much attention as a résumé and a cover letter.

Figure 7.3

COVER LETTER

1 Opening Introduce yourself. State the job you are applying for and how you found out about it.

2 Body Sell yourself. Describe the skills and experience you have that make you right for the job. Mention that you are sending a résumé. Include information that is not in your résumé.

3 Closing Ask for an interview. Thank the person for his or her time and interest.

Kira Franklin
87 Southwest Eighth Avenue
Morgantown, OR 93072
(503) 555-0171

April 3, 2002

Dr. Derek McDermott
Director
Oregon State Department of Science Education
Salem, OR 97310

Dear Dr. McDermott,

Ms. Gina Alvarez, my biology teacher at Morgantown High School, suggested that I contact you about a full-time summer intern position in your Summer Science Institute program for children. Please consider me as an applicant for an intern position.

As my résumé shows, I have a great deal of science experience. I learned a lot working with WISTEC for two summer projects. I also discovered how much I like working with children. It was fun coming up with interesting science activities for all of us to do together.

With my science skills and experience working with children, I think I would have a lot to offer to the Summer Science Institute. I am very interested in pursuing a career in environmental education.

I would be happy to meet with you for an interview at your convenience. My phone number is (503) 555-0171. Thank you for your consideration. I look forward to meeting with you.

Sincerely,

Kira Franklin

Kira Franklin

Introduce Yourself Every good cover letter has three parts. Each part has a specific purpose. *What part of the letter is the best place to let your personality come through?*

Complete a Job Application

Try This Activity

Complete a job application form for a job in your career interest area. You can acquire an application form from a real business, or your teacher or career counselor can supply one.

Check Your Work Read the entire application before you begin filling it out. Follow directions. Be truthful, neat, and complete. If a question doesn't apply to you, write *NA* for *Not Applicable*. Double-check all of your answers.

Supplying References

You should also be prepared to supply references on a job application. **References** are people who will recommend you to an employer. Choose references carefully. Ask people who know you well and who think highly of you to be your references. Teachers, neighbors, and anyone you've worked for make good references. Always ask permission to use someone as a reference. You usually have to supply names, addresses, and phone numbers for all your references. Some references will supply you with a written letter of recommendation. A **letter of recommendation** is a letter in support of you from a reference. It provides insight into your background, skills, work ethic, and character.

A Good Reference References are people who know your character and work ethic and will recommend you to an employer. References can include teachers, coaches, business professionals, and former employers. *If you were applying for a job, who would you ask to serve as a reference?*

Lesson 7.1 Review and Activities

Key Terms Review

1. Make a poster that uses both captions and images to explain the following terms. Display your poster in class.
   - **résumé**
   - **format**
   - **personal fact sheet**
   - **cover letter**
   - **personal career portfolio**
   - **job application**
   - **references**
   - **letter of recommendation**

Check Your Understanding

Choose the correct answer for each item. Write your answers on a separate sheet of paper.

2. Two types of résumés include chronological résumés and ______.
   a. name résumés
   b. skills résumés
   c. job résumés
3. A form that asks questions about your skills, work experience, education, and interests is a ______.
   a. résumé
   b. cover letter
   c. job application

Critical Thinking

Use complete sentences to answer the following questions. Write your answers on a separate sheet of paper.

4. What skills and abilities do you have that you would include in a chronological résumé? Why?
5. Why should you always send a cover letter with a résumé?
6. What can an employer learn about someone from his or her application?

Character Building

7. **Qualifying for a Job** Suki wants to apply for a job as a part-time computer-lab aide, but she doesn't have all of the qualifications required. Should Suki apply for the job? Are her chances of getting the job better if she's honest on the application or if she stretches the truth about her qualifications? Explain your answer.

Teamwork

8. **Create a Job Application Guide** Work with a small group to create a guide for teens that tells how to apply for a job. Explain how to put together a résumé, write a cover letter, and fill out a job application. Include an example of a résumé and cover letter that you create as a group. Gear all the information to part-time or volunteer work. Compare your guide with those of other groups.

Lesson 7.2

Putting Your Best Foot Forward

What happens next? When you send a résumé or complete an application, your goal is to get an interview. An **interview** is a formal meeting about a possible job between a job seeker and an employer. It is the employer's chance to meet you and decide if you're right for the job. It is your chance to convince an employer that you are the right person for the job and to decide if the job is right for you.

Getting Ready for an Interview

What you do before an interview is as important as what you do during the interview. Would it surprise you to know that you're already preparing for your first job interview? Have you ever tried out for a team, a play, or the school orchestra or band? Have you ever run for school office? In each case, you had to show that you were ready and able to do the job.

Prepare Yourself
Many everyday situations will help prepare you for a job interview. *What kinds of everyday skills can you bring to an interview?*

Discover

- How to prepare for an interview
- What happens in an interview
- How to follow up after an interview

Why It's Important

Interviews are an important part of applying for a job. The more practice you get, the more confident you'll be in future interviews.

Key Terms

- **interview**
- **pre-employment tests**
- **body language**

Maybe you've tried to persuade your parents to give you more responsibility or independence. Maybe you stopped by to meet your new neighbors and found out they sometimes need someone to walk their dog. You spent some more time talking and patting the dog. Before you knew it, you were hired.

These situations help build your confidence. They also involve skills that you'll use one day in a job interview.

Be Prepared

When you finally get an interview, you've got some work to do. You need to be prepared to answer questions about your interests, skills, work experience, education, and career goals. You also need to be prepared for any pre-employment tests. **Pre-employment tests** are tests given to a job seeker by an employer to find out if the job seeker fits the job. They tell how successful the job seeker would be in the job. Pre-employment tests can evaluate your personality and your skills.

Know the Job and the Company

To succeed in an interview, you need to know as much as possible about the job you want. If you saw the job in an ad, study the ad carefully. If you got the job lead by networking, talk to your contact. Find out as much as you can about the job before the interview. Then you will be better able to sell yourself as the best possible candidate.

Practice Makes Perfect Rehearsing before an interview will help you be more relaxed. *What should you practice?*

Also get to know the business or organization where you are interviewing. Review all the information you gathered before you applied for the job and be prepared to ask questions about the job and the employer.

Practice Makes a Difference

You can't know exactly how an interview will go. You can imagine what it might be like, though, and you can practice. One way to practice is to ask a friend or family member to role-play an interview with you. The more practice you have, the more comfortable you'll feel during a real interview.

Career Opportunities

Government and Public Administration

People in the Government and Public Administration career cluster collect taxes, build infrastructure, protect the nation's borders, and make laws. Workers in this cluster often have excellent job security and benefits.

Critical Thinking

What do you think is the most important skill for an urban planner to have? Why?

URBAN PLANNER

Growing city seeks urban planner to help plan for future development. Experience with environmentally-friendly construction a plus. Applicants must have ideas for creating a friendly community that serves the needs of residents and businesses.

Try This Activity

Role-Play

Role-play appropriate interviewing techniques with a partner. Pretend that you are interviewing for an employment opportunity in your career interest area. Research what types of interview questions might be typically asked in an interview for the job you are interested in. Write out answers to the questions. Practice them by yourself, then have your partner ask you typical questions. Practice answering them. Ask an adult to critique your answers.

Practice, Practice, Practice! Tape-record or videotape the interview if you can. If you don't have access to a video recorder, role-play interviews in front of a large mirror. This will help you become more aware of your body language. Dress as you would for a real interview. Look your best.

Review Your Performance Listen to yourself. Look at yourself. Are you speaking clearly? Do you sound confident? Are you sitting up straight? Do you look interested and relaxed? Do you look directly at the interviewer? Keep practicing until you get it right.

There are other ways you can practice, in addition to role-playing. Make a list of general questions you might be asked about yourself or your career goals. Prepare answers to them. Questions such as "Why are you the best person for this job?" can be challenging to answer on the spot. They will be easier to answer if you've thought about them ahead of time. Also, make a list of questions you want to ask about the job.

Dress the Part

Don't forget to give some thought to what you are going to wear. Remember, first impressions count. The first thing an employer will notice when you meet is your appearance.

A good rule to follow when dressing for an interview is to dress as others in the same job would dress. It's a good idea, though, to dress a bit better than you would on a normal day on the job. Make sure you're neat, clean, and well-groomed from head to toe. Let your skills and personality stand out—not your clothes, jewelry, perfume, or makeup.

Dress for Success An interviewer will notice the details of your appearance. *Which person do you think will make a better first impression? Which would you hire?*

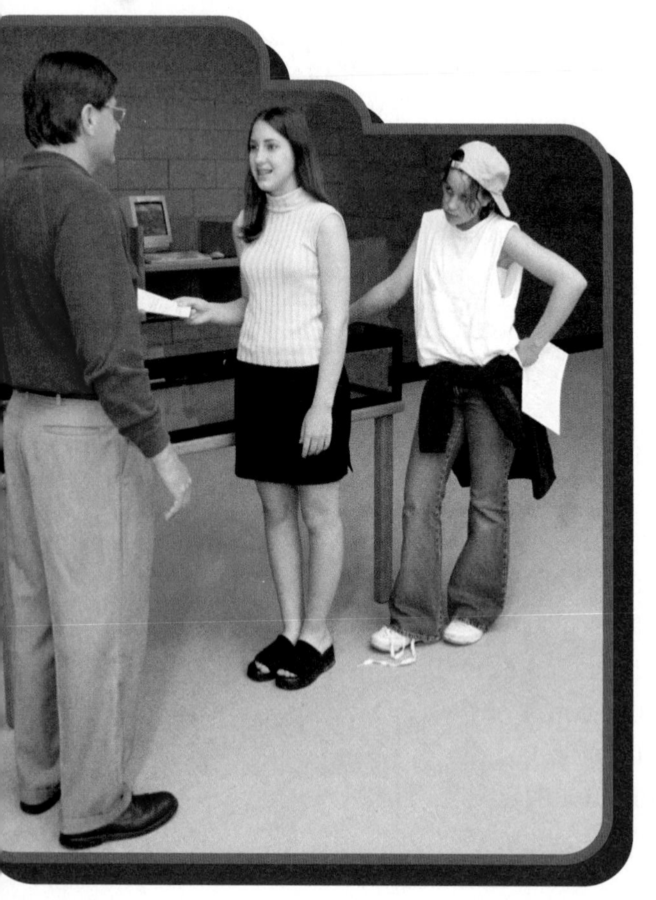

The Interview Itself

In many ways an interview is no different from a big test or a big game. If you've put effort into preparing, it's likely to go well for you. Knowing you've done all you can to get ready is reassuring. You'll feel confident and relaxed.

A Winning Attitude

The biggest boost you can have going into an interview is a positive attitude. Let your friendly smile and enthusiasm project your positive attitude. If you feel positive, you'll have just the attitude employers are looking for. When you have a positive attitude, you feel good about yourself. You're also excited about the job. According to Bev Curtis of Environment First in Portland, Maine,

> "Attitude is everything."

Environment First educates the public about protecting the environment. Bev runs its volunteer program. "What I'm looking for," Bev explains, "is more than interest in the environment. I'm looking for energetic people. We need people whose enthusiasm will rub off on others. If the person I interview is enthusiastic, the job is theirs."

So go ahead. Communicate your positive attitude to an employer! You'll show you can be counted on to do your best.

A Good Conversation

There are many ways to communicate a positive attitude during an interview. An employer will listen carefully to how you answer questions. Your answers will show whether you are hardworking, dependable, and skilled. They'll also show how you feel about the job and yourself. Be ready to answer questions like the following:

- What can you tell me about yourself?
- What are your greatest strengths?
- What are your greatest weaknesses?
- Do you prefer to work with others or on your own?
- Why do you want this job?
- What are your career goals?

Your answers should be honest and specific. Even if you think your answer isn't what the interviewer wants to hear, answer truthfully. The response you get may surprise you.

A good interview is like a good conversation. Each person should have a chance to speak and ask questions. Each should listen carefully and pay attention to the other. You'll have a turn to ask questions. The questions you ask should focus on the business and job, not yourself. They should show your enthusiasm and interest.

Watch Your Body Language

What you do and how you act in an interview can also say a lot. In fact, sometimes your actions can speak louder than your words. For example, eye contact shows that you are paying attention. A firm handshake signals self-confidence. Nodding your head shows that you're thinking.

Stress

Do you ever feel as if you have too much to do? Does this feeling make you tense and maybe keep you awake at night? If you have experienced this feeling, you know what stress is.

Coping with stress is an important part of having a good attitude. Remember to rest, exercise, and eat well. Break large tasks into smaller parts and find someone to help you. Discussing your feelings with someone you trust can also do wonders to lessen stress.

Cooperative Learning Activity

- Work with a small group of classmates to create a "commercial" that advertises positive ways to cope with stress.
- Rehearse your commercial and share it with the rest of the class.

Body language communicates many things. **Body language** is the gestures, posture, and eye contact you use to express yourself. For better or worse, body language plays an important part in an interview. **Figure 7.4** below shows some of the positive messages you can send with body language. In what everyday situations might you practice positive body language?

Figure 7.4

BODY LANGUAGE

Make sure your body language sends the right message at an interview. Your gestures, posture, and eye contact should say you're a positive, confident person. *What actions are not appropriate at an interview?*

A

Introduce Yourself

Make eye contact right away. Be sure to smile as you introduce yourself to the interviewer. Extend your hand, and shake hands firmly. Try practicing your handshake with others before the interview. Your handshake shouldn't be limp or crushing.

B

Maintain Good Posture

Sit when the interviewer invites you to sit down. Then check your posture. Don't slouch. Sit up straight, leaning forward slightly in your chair. Look directly at the interviewer. Then the interviewer will know you're interested in what he or she has to say. Nod your head occasionally as you listen to show you're paying attention.

After You Say Good-Bye

At the end of the interview, you may be offered the job on the spot. More often than not, however, you'll have to wait. Don't just sit by the telephone, though. There are some important things you should do following an interview: follow up and say thanks, and then reflect on and learn from the experience.

C

Think About Body Language

Think about your hands whether you're listening or speaking. Don't clench your fists or bite your nails. Don't play with your hair or clothing. These are all signs that you're nervous or unsure of yourself. When speaking, use your hands in a relaxed, confident way.

D

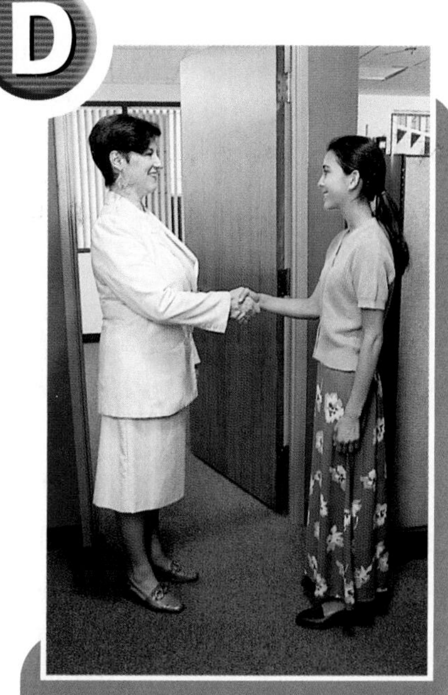

Leave a Positive Impression

Be friendly as the interview comes to an end. Stand up straight. Shake the interviewer's hand. Smile and make eye contact as you do.

Figure 7.5

THANK-YOU LETTER

3827 Elmdale Drive
Sumner, Pennsylvania 19327

April 21, 2003

Mr. Emilio Alvarez
Editorial Director
Jarod Publishing Company
Sumner, Pennsylvania 19327

Dear Mr. Alvarez:

Thank you for meeting with me yesterday to talk about a summer internship at Jarod Publishing.

The internship sounds interesting and challenging. It would also make good use of the skills I have developed working on my school newspaper. As noted in my résumé, I have served as a reporter and editor for the school paper for the past two years.

I hope that you will consider me for an internship this summer. As I mentioned to you yesterday, I am very interested in a career in communications. I know that I could learn a great deal at Jarod Publishing. With my experience on the school newspaper, I think I could contribute a great deal, too.

Thank you again for taking the time to meet with me. I look forward to hearing from you.

Sincerely,

Amy Bloomfield

Amy Bloomfield

Don't Wait to Say Thanks Everyone likes to be thanked. Write a thank-you letter right after your interview. *What might you mention about the interview in your letter?*

Take Time to Say Thanks

Send a short thank-you letter to the person who interviewed you no later than the day after the interview. **Figure 7.5** shows an example of a thank-you letter.

In your letter, thank the interviewer for his or her time. Express your enthusiasm for the job and stress the experience and skills you have that match the job. Mention something you discussed in the interview. If you forgot to tell or ask the interviewer something, include that in your letter.

Write a letter of thanks no matter how the interview went. The interviewer is a new contact. He or she may give you a referral or consider you for a different job.

The Global Workplace

I'm So Angry I Could Smile!

A smile is usually a sign of pleasure and approval around the world. Sometimes, a smile in the wrong place can cause some confusion, though. In Thailand, Singapore, Japan, and the Philippines, people often use a smile or nervous laughter to cover up embarrassment, anger, confusion, or an awkward situation. In these cultures publicly showing certain emotions is usually considered bad manners.

So how can you interpret a smile? Look at the eyes. A genuine smile will cause other changes in facial expression, such as crinkled skin in the corners of the eyes.

Internet Activity

Using the Internet and library resources, research Thailand, Singapore, the Philippines, or Japan. Find out what other common American signs can have totally different meanings in one of these countries. Go to the *Exploring Careers* Web site at exploring.glencoe.com for a list of Web sites to help you complete this activity.

Take Stock

You should also make some notes for yourself while the interview is still fresh in your mind. Write a summary of the interview. What went well? What could you improve? Note questions that you had trouble answering. Jot down anything you'd do differently next time.

Take It in Stride

You may get the job. You may not. If you don't, don't give up. Rejection is part of life and part of the learning process.

If you don't get the job, contact the employer and ask why, if it's convenient for the employer. Use that information to prepare for your next application and interview.

Above all, don't put yourself down. The right job is out there waiting for you. You just have to keep moving toward your goals.

Lesson 7.2 Review and Activities

Key Terms Review

1. Write a one-page report about interviewing. Use all of the key terms in your report.
   - **interview**
   - **pre-employment test**
   - **body language**

Check Your Understanding

Tell whether each statement is true or false. Rewrite any false statement to make it true. Write your answers on a separate sheet of paper.

2. What you do before an interview is not as important as what you do during the interview.
3. At an interview, attitude and body language count as much as what you say.
4. It is important to follow up after an interview.

Critical Thinking

Use complete sentences to answer the following questions. Write your answers on a separate sheet of paper.

5. What questions would you ask an employer at a job interview? How would you learn what questions to ask?
6. What would you do if you did not hear from an employer after an interview?

Connecting to the Workplace

7. **Interview Practice** Research the job of an adult you know. Then put yourself in the place of the adult's employer. Interview the adult for the job he or she currently holds. Ask the adult typical interview questions like those listed in the lesson. Listen carefully to the person's answers. Also allow time for him or her to ask questions. Afterward, discuss the questions and answers and other aspects of the interview. Note what you learned about interviewing from this activity.

Community Involvement

8. **Go on an Informational Interview** Select a volunteer job in your community. Call to set up an informational interview to find out more about it. Use what you have learned in this lesson to prepare for, carry out, and follow up an informational interview. Describe to the class how the interview for the volunteer job went. Share some of the questions you were asked at the interview and the responses you gave. Explain what you did right, and what you would do differently in a future interview.

Investigating Career Clusters

GOVERNMENT AND PUBLIC ADMINISTRATION

Government
- The institution through which the state keeps order in society, provides services, and enforces laws

Public Administration
- The administrative management of government and nonprofit organizations

Job Title	Work Description
Army Officer	Supervises soldiers in the Army
CIA Agent	Performs secret operations on behalf of the United States
City Manager	Runs a city government
Foreign Service Officer	Represents the United States and its policies abroad
Legislator	Researches, writes, endorses, and votes on laws
Postal Worker	Sorts, distributes, and delivers the mail
Tax Examiner	Examines tax returns and accounting records
Urban Planner	Develops land use plans for the growth of cities

Exploration Activity

Government and Public Administration Use library and Internet resources to research a career in the Government and Public Administration career cluster. Write a report on the kinds of work, skills required, working conditions, training and education required, and career outlook.

Cooperative Learning Interview a classmate about the career he or she researched. Find out as much information about that career as you can during the interview. Then have your classmate interview you about the career you researched. Afterward, share what you learned with the class.

Chapter 7 Review and Activities

Chapter Highlights

Lesson 7.1 Résumés, cover letters, and job applications are ways of applying for a job. They are also opportunities for making a good impression on an employer.

Lesson 7.2 Preparation helps you do well in an interview. Know yourself, the business or organization, and the job you are applying for. Practice. Dress appropriately.

Key Concept Review

Use complete sentences to answer the following questions. Write your answers on a separate sheet of paper.

1. How do you decide which résumé format to use?
2. What are the three main parts of a cover letter?
3. Why do you need to line up references before filling out a job application?
4. What does your attitude tell an employer?
5. Why should you make notes about an interview afterward?

Critical Thinking

Use complete sentences to answer the following questions. Write your answers on a separate sheet of paper.

6. What skills do you have that might be included in a résumé?
7. Who might you ask to be a reference?
8. Why should you ask questions that focus on the business and the job in an interview?
9. What might an interviewer think if you do not make eye contact?

Skill Building

10. **Personal Qualities—Integrity/Honesty**
    Your friend has never held a job before. She is thinking about making up some work experience to include on her résumé. What would you advise her to do?
11. **Technology—Applies Technology to the Task**
    With a partner, create a computer-friendly résumé. Use either the chronological or the skills format. Include keywords. Print it and scan it into a computer using character-reading software. Discuss what needs to be corrected.

Academic Applications

12. Mathematics

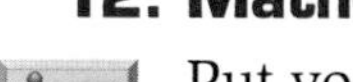

Put your work experience in time order for a chronological résumé. Arrange the following dates in correct reverse time order: June–August 2000, June–August 2002, December 2001–January 2002, July–September 2001, September 2002–present, January–June 2001, October–December 2000.

13. Social Studies

Create a time line of personal growth. Plot events that have contributed to your career skills or work experience. Include classes, assignments, activities, hobbies, and projects. Also include part-time, weekend, volunteer, and summer jobs. Write the date for each event. Share the time line with your family and classmates.

Personal Career Portfolio

Create a Personal Fact Sheet and Résumé

- **Create** a personal fact sheet. You can use the one you developed in the Try This Activity on page 130.
- **Title** the document *Personal Fact Sheet* and file it in your Personal Career Portfolio.
- **Use** your personal fact sheet to create a résumé. You can start with the résumé you created in the Try This Activity on page 130.
- **Customize** the résumé for a job for which you would like to apply. Be sure to customize the job objective.
- **Title** the document *Résumé* and file it in your Personal Career Portfolio.
- **Update** your personal fact sheet and résumé as you gain new skills and accomplishments and as you identify other jobs you would like to pursue. File updated versions in your Personal Career Portfolio.
- **List** your portfolio entry on your Personal Career Portfolio contents page.

Chapter 8

On the Job

Lesson 8.1

Workplace Expectations

Lesson 8.2

What an Employer Expects of You

CAREER CLUSTER

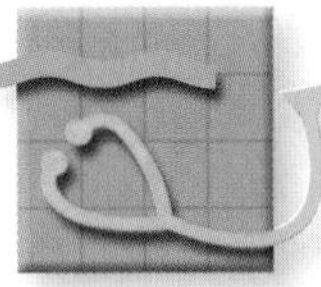

You will explore careers in the Health Science career cluster.

What You'll Learn

- You will find out more about life in the workplace.
- You will learn what to expect on your first day at a new job.
- You will discover what an employer will expect of you.

Get Ready!

Try Something New

Gather together with a group of friends. Share your experiences of how you felt when you did something totally new for the first time, such as going to a new school or traveling alone. Write three words that describe those feelings on a piece of paper. Each person should add words to the paper after sharing.

Apply Review the words. What kinds of feelings might you have on the first day at a new job?

Lesson 8.1

Workplace Expectations

Discover

- How to handle your first day at a job
- Ways you may be paid and benefits you may receive
- How you can expect to be treated at work

Why It's Important

What you learn about the workplace will help you prepare for your first full-time job.

KEY TERMS

- employee
- orientation
- supervisor
- coworkers
- mentor
- Form I-9
- W-4 Form
- corporate culture
- wages
- entry-level
- overtime
- salary
- commission
- benefits
- minimum wage

Where do you imagine yourself working someday? Do you picture yourself indoors or outdoors? Are you in an office building or a home office? Perhaps you work in a studio, a theater, or a lab. Maybe your work involves a lot of traveling. What you do, where you do it, how you do it—your options are as big as your imagination.

You may wonder, though, what being in the workplace will really be like. What can you expect as an **employee,** someone who works for a person or business for pay?

Your First Day on the Job

Remember that first day in a new class? How about the day you moved to a new home or neighborhood? As with anything new, you probably had mixed feelings. You may have felt excited, unsure, and nervous at the same time. You may have been very happy to be there one moment and scared or sad the next moment.

Jump on Board When you go to work at a company, you become part of a team. *Why is it important to get to know people at work?*

On your first day at a job, you'll have many of the same feelings. Beginning a new job is an adventure like other new experiences. It can be stressful, but you can enjoy it—especially if you're prepared.

Getting Ready

There are several things you can do to make sure you have a good first day. Start by calling your employer a day or two before you begin work. Ask when you should arrive and where you should go first. If you're uncertain about how to dress, ask what you should wear. Find out if you need to bring any tools, supplies, or special equipment. Also ask what personal information you may need to supply the first day.

Decide what you're going to wear, and take some time to figure out how long it will take to get ready and get to work. On the big day, allow plenty of time so you won't have to hurry.

What to Expect From Orientation

While you're preparing to report to work, your employer will also be preparing—for you. Many companies provide orientation for new employees. An **orientation** introduces you to a company. It explains the company's policies and procedures, or ways of doing things.

As part of an orientation, you often get a tour of your new work environment. At a large company, you may receive an employee handbook at orientation. At a smaller company, your supervisor may meet with you and give you the information you need. Your **supervisor** is the person who assigns, checks, and evaluates your work. You also meet many of your **coworkers,** the people you will work with. Some companies assign a mentor to each new worker during orientation. A **mentor** is an experienced coworker who can answer your questions and offer you guidance.

You may also be required to fill out paperwork during your orientation. Employers usually ask new employees to bring their Social Security card and driver's license with them on the first day of work. The employer will make copies of each and keep them on record. If you are under 16, or under 18 in some states, you will also need to present a work permit.

Personal Information

Q: What kind of personal information will my employer want me to bring on my first day?

A: Your employer might want to see some of these items again on your first day:

- Photo ID
- Work permit
- Social Security card
- Emergency contact information

Remember though, it's a good idea to just call your employer and ask what information you need to bring on your first day.

Other forms that you will have to complete include the employment eligibility verification form (Form I-9) and the W-4 form. **Form I-9** is a form that verifies that you are legally qualified to work in the United States. On a **W-4 Form,** you tell your employer the amount of money to deduct from your paycheck for taxes.

For a part-time job such as baby-sitting, house-sitting, or doing yardwork, the orientation may be more informal. The person who hired you may quickly explain what you need to do. Then he or she may show you where to find keys, tools, and other supplies.

Whatever introduction you receive at a new job, pay close attention. Listen carefully, make notes, and take materials home to read.

Getting Accustomed to a New Job

The first few days on a new job may seem overwhelming. The secret is to be patient. Take things one step at a time. For instance, don't worry if you forget people's names. You can't be expected to remember everyone's name at first. Just ask again. Repeat the name out loud as you're introduced. Then use the name again when talking to the person.

If you don't understand an employer's policies, ask your supervisor to explain them. If you're not sure what to do or how to do something, your supervisor or mentor can help.

Ask and Learn
Don't be afraid to ask questions when you're new to a job. *What should you do if you still do not understand something after receiving an answer?*

The Global Workplace

Vacation Time

Workers in the United States get about two weeks of paid vacation a year. If two weeks just isn't enough vacation time for you, then you might consider working in Europe, where workers enjoy the longest vacations in the world. Workers in Spain get 30 days of paid vacation per year. In France, employees get five weeks of vacation. Italian workers get 42 days of vacation.

Most Europeans take their vacations during July or August. In fact, so many workers in the cities of Rome and Paris go on vacation during August that both of these cities practically shut down. Visitors during this month will find many shops and businesses closed.

Internet Activity

Use Internet or library resources to find out how much vacation time workers have in Asia, South America, or the Middle East. At what times of the year do these workers take vacation? Go to the *Exploring Careers* Web site at exploring.glencoe.com for a list of Web sites to help you complete this activity.

Use your first few days on the job to get a clear idea of your job responsibilities. Ask your supervisor to explain exactly what is involved in your job. Just be friendly, and don't be afraid to ask questions.

Soon you'll feel like part of the group, and you'll know what you're doing. You'll also have a good sense of your company's corporate culture. **Corporate culture** is the characteristics and customs that make a company unique.

Forms of Payment

As you read in Chapter 2, one of the main reasons most people work is to earn money. Being paid for your hard work is a big part of having a job. The money you earn is called *wages*, *salary*, or *commission*.

Hourly Wages

Wages are a fixed amount of money paid for each hour worked. Many people with part-time jobs earn wages. If you baby-sit, for example, you probably receive wages. Say your wages for baby-sitting are $7 an hour. If you work four hours, you earn $28.

Wages are the form of payment for many **entry-level,** or lower-level, full-time jobs. At the end of each week, your employer will figure the number of hours you've worked. That number will be multiplied by the hourly wage rate for your job to determine your pay for the week.

Obviously, with hourly wages, the more hours you work, the more money you make. Many people who earn wages are also paid overtime. They receive **overtime** when they work more than 40 hours a week. Overtime pay is usually one and one-half times regular pay for each hour worked beyond the 40 scheduled hours. For example, if your regular wage is $10 an hour, you would be paid $15 an hour for overtime.

Try This Activity

Calculate Wage Earnings

Practice your math skills by calculating the answers to the following two wage scenarios:

Weekly Wage Earnings Jim Moore has a full-time job at a guitar shop in Lubbock, Texas. He works 40 hours a week and is paid $6 an hour. How much does Jim earn each week?

Wages Plus Overtime One week a month, Jim Moore also works 4 hours on Saturdays for a total of 44 hours. That week he receives his regular pay for the first 40 hours. In addition, he earns $36 for 4 hours of overtime. How does his employer arrive at $36 for Jim's overtime pay? What are Jim's total earnings for the week?

Fixed Salaries

Unlike wage earners, most people on salary do not get paid overtime. They receive the same amount of pay no matter how many hours they work. A **salary** is a fixed amount of money paid for a certain period of time. Salaries are usually figured

Clock In, Clock Out
Many workers who earn wages must "clock in" at a time clock. *Why is it important for these workers to keep track of their work time?*

by the year and paid each month or every two weeks. For example, if your salary is $52,000 a year, you earn $1,000 a week, even if you work 60 hours a week.

Commissions

Some workers are paid a commission. The earnings of people who make a **commission** are based on how much they sell. Tamara Peterson is a salesperson in a clothing store. She receives a 10 percent commission on the clothing she sells. In other words, for every $10 of clothing she sells, she earns $1. "The more I sell," Tamara explains, "the more I make."

> "There's no limit to what I can earn on commission. That inspires me to get out there and make one sale after another."

Kinds of Benefits

Whatever the job, whatever the form of payment, everyone looks forward to payday. The rewards for working aren't limited to a paycheck, however. Many jobs come with benefits. **Benefits** are the "extras" an employer provides in addition to pay.

Can you think of any benefits you have at your part-time job? If you do yardwork for the family next door, maybe you get to swim in their pool. If you work in a store, you might get a discount, or money off, what you buy there. As a baby-sitter, you may get to watch as much TV as you want after you've put the children to bed.

The kinds and value of benefits for full-time workers vary from employer to employer. **Figure 8.1** shows benefits many employers offer.

Figure 8.1 **BENEFITS**

For many people, benefits are an important reason for working. *Which benefits do you think will be most important to you in your first full-time job?*

A

Health Insurance

Many workers consider health insurance the most valuable benefit. Health insurance helps pay doctor and hospital expenses. Workers often share the cost of health insurance with their employer.

B

Paid Time Off

A company may name holidays on which workers do not have to work. At many businesses, workers receive pay for these holidays. Employees may also receive pay for time off for illness and vacation.

C

Retirement Plan

To help workers save for when they no longer work, some employers set up a retirement fund. Usually workers contribute some of their pay to the fund. Employers may also contribute to the fund.

Your Workplace Rights

A paycheck, benefits—what more could you ask for? The answer is "much more." You have rights in the workplace, too. Under the law, your employer must respect these rights.

You have a right to expect your employer to be honest. You should be paid the agreed wage or salary regularly and on time.

D

Child Care

Some people with families are lucky enough to work for companies that offer child care. Such child care is usually low-cost and convenient. Workers drop off their children at a company-run day-care center when they arrive for work. They may visit their children during lunch or break. At the end of the workday, they stop in to pick up their children.

E

Education Assistance

Your employer may be willing to help you pay for further education. Some employers, for instance, cover all or part of college or technical school costs if you are working toward a degree. Others cover the cost of classes or workshops that will help you learn to do your job better.

You must be paid at least the **minimum wage**—the lowest hourly wage an employer can legally pay for a worker's services. You should receive all the benefits that were promised when you got the job. If your work situation changes, you should be told as soon as possible.

Fair Treatment

You also have a right to be treated fairly by your employer. Under the law, your employer cannot discriminate against you. That is, you cannot be treated unfairly because of your race or age. Your gender—whether you are male or female—cannot be used as a reason for unfair treatment. You must be treated the same as others—no matter what your religious beliefs or nationality (where you were born).

Your employer cannot treat you unfairly because of your physical appearance or disability. A *disability* is a condition such as a physical, mental, or behavioral impairment. The Americans With Disabilities Act requires employers to provide reasonable accommodation or adjustments to the workplace that allow qualified employees to do the basic functions of their job. Reasonable accommodation allows employees with disabilities to enjoy the same benefits and privileges of employment that employees without disabilities enjoy.

A Diverse Workforce Workplaces include individuals from different backgrounds. *What advantages does this bring to business?*

Many state and federal laws protect workers against unfair treatment and an intimidating, hostile, or offensive work environment. If you feel you have been treated unfairly, discuss it with your supervisor. Try to resolve the problem. If the company does not correct the problem, the next step is talk to the person above your supervisor or to file a complaint. To do that, you would contact the government agency that carries out the law. There are many organizations dedicated to helping employees resolve workplace problems.

Lesson 8.1 Review and Activities

Key Terms Review

1. Write a two-page employee handbook that tells new employees what to expect on the job. Use each of the following terms in your handbook.

- **employee**
- **orientation**
- **supervisor**
- **coworkers**
- **mentor**
- **Form I-9**
- **W-4 Form**
- **corporate culture**
- **wages**
- **entry-level**
- **overtime**
- **salary**
- **commission**
- **benefits**
- **minimum wage**

Check Your Understanding

Choose the correct answer for each item. Write your answers on a separate sheet of paper.

2. To make the first day on the job easier, you can ______.
  - **a.** bring a friend with you
  - **b.** prepare for it by calling ahead
  - **c.** show up a little late

3. Employees have a right to ______.
  - **a.** honest and fair treatment
  - **b.** determine the hours they work
  - **c.** create job tasks

Critical Thinking

Use complete sentences to answer the following questions. Write your answers on a separate sheet of paper.

4. Why is it a good idea to ask questions when you're new to a job?

5. What kind of person might do well at a job that earns a commission?

6. Why do you think laws to prevent discrimination have been passed?

Connecting to the Workplace

7. Beginning a New Job Tomorrow is your first day on the job as the weekend receptionist at an animal shelter. As the receptionist you will greet visitors, give them animal adoption forms, and answer their questions. You will also answer telephone calls. Make a list of the things you think your employer should go over with you during your orientation tomorrow. Compare your list with your classmates' lists.

Teamwork

8. Prepare an Orientation Presentation Team up with several classmates. Together, make up your own company. Then prepare an orientation program for your company's new employees. Your presentation should describe your company, tell about the benefits it offers, and explain its payment policies. Hold an orientation for your classmates.

Lesson 8.2

What an Employer Expects of You

Discover

- Qualities employers look for in employees
- How to behave in the workplace
- How your work will be evaluated

Why It's Important

When you start working full-time, you'll want to fit in and do well. You can get ready now by developing certain qualities and learning the right ways to behave.

KEY TERMS

- **cooperate**
- **social skills**
- **business etiquette**
- **discretion**
- **initiative**
- **self-motivation**
- **adaptability skills**
- **ethics**
- **performance reviews**
- **human resources**

Do your teachers discuss their expectations of students at the beginning of the year? If so, listen carefully. You may pick up pointers that will help you be successful when you have a job. Many employers expect the same things of employees that teachers expect of students in the classroom.

What Employers Want

These days, employers have great expectations of their employees. It used to be that employers looked for workers with specific skills. As you know, though, the workplace is changing rapidly. Employers today aren't just looking for people with skills to do a particular job. They want people who can do many things well. They also want people who fit in and adapt to the changing workplace.

What can you do now to be the kind of employee employers are looking for? You can strengthen your basic skills—reading, writing, mathematics, speaking, and listening. You'll learn more about how to do that in Chapter 10. You can work on your thinking skills—reasoning, making decisions, and solving problems. You can also develop the personal qualities that employers value most.

Cooperate
You can show your willingness to cooperate by doing whatever task you're assigned. *What should you do if the task is boring?*

Cooperating

Employers prize employees who know how to cooperate. When you **cooperate,** you work with others on the job to reach a common goal. Cooperation skills are the key to successful teamwork.

You have many opportunities right now to learn how to cooperate with others. Here are just a few ways.

- Do tasks you don't like without complaining or trying to avoid them.
- Do your fair share of a job when working with others.
- Pitch in to help someone who has a tough job or has fallen behind.
- Volunteer to help others meet a deadline or reach a goal.

Getting Along With Others

Social skills are one of the top qualities employers look for in a job candidate. **Social skills** are the skills people use to interact with others. Workers with good social skills often become successful leaders.

Employers also value employees who have good business etiquette. **Business etiquette** is the rules of good workplace manners. Knowing the rules of etiquette will help you create a good impression. It will also help you avoid making embarrassing mistakes at work. An important part of business etiquette is **discretion,** or good judgment. People with discretion use good judgment when they act or when they speak so as not to offend others.

Following Directions

Think about it. How many times a day do you get directions for doing something? Almost every assignment at school comes with its own set of directions.

What is your strategy for or approach to following directions? Do you stop everything you're doing and listen carefully? Do you take notes? Do you ask questions when you don't understand what you're supposed to do? These are all excellent ways to make sure you get the directions right.

On the job, you'll be asked to do many things. To complete each task, you must first follow directions.

I Think I Can

You would probably choose teammates for school projects who are enthusiastic and have a positive attitude. Employers are the same. They want "can-do" people to work for them. Can-do people are usually able to come up with new ideas to complete a project. They're upbeat even when their projects are difficult or not so enjoyable. They work well in groups and ask for help when they need it.

Cooperative Learning Activity

- Working in a small group, brainstorm a list of fresh ways to improve one aspect of your school.
- Share your list of ideas with the class.

Doing What Needs to Be Done

Doing what you are told is important. Why stop there, though? Employers also value employees who show initiative. When you show **initiative,** you do what needs to be done without being told to do it. Self-motivated people show initiative. Your **self-motivation** is your drive to do something simply for the reward of feeling good and satisfied once you accomplish it.

Jolene Anderson showed initiative and self-motivation at her after-school job as a supermarket cashier. When she saw a customer accidentally drop a jar, she alerted the manager. Someone was able to clean up the broken glass and wet floor before anyone was hurt. "The manager said that I've got what it takes to be an assistant manager someday. What it takes is a lot of initiative," explains Jolene.

Taking on More Responsibility

Responsibility is the willingness to accept a task, carry it out, and be accountable for it. Employers are on the lookout for people who are willing to take on more responsibility. Employees with this quality help make better products and provide better services.

How do you react to more responsibility? Would you rather stick with what's familiar and easy? The next time your teacher asks for volunteers, raise your hand. It may seem scary at first, but then you'll be pleasantly surprised. The more responsibility you take on, the more confident you'll feel. The more confident you are, the better job you'll do.

Above and Beyond People with initiative look for work that needs to be done. *How have you shown initiative this week?*

Continuing to Learn and Adapt

Have you ever heard someone say, "You learn something new every day." Do you? If you don't, start to right now. Learning makes all of life more interesting. Be curious and look to learn something from everything you do.

No matter what your job is, your duties won't stay the same. Your duties will change as new procedures and technologies are developed. That's why it's important to have **adaptability skills,** or the ability to change when you need to fit new circumstances. Adaptability skills are especially important with technology because it changes so quickly.

Employees who have good learning skills are valuable in today's changing workplace. Survey after survey has shown that employers want one thing more than anything else. They want employees who are willing to learn.

Working by the Rules

It's not enough to have skills and personal qualities. Employers also expect their employees to have ethics. **Ethics** are the rules of behavior that govern a group or society.

Right Ways to Behave

Employees who behave ethically do not lie, cheat, or steal. They are honest and fair in their dealings with others. They can be trusted. **Figure 8.2** on page 164 shows different areas and examples of ethical and unethical behavior on the job.

The Importance of Ethics

Employees who act ethically build a good reputation, or name, for themselves. They are known to be dependable and trustworthy. They also contribute to their employer's or company's reputation.

A single unethical act can do a lot of damage. Here's just one example. Jill baby-sat all day on weekends for a young boy across the street. She was paid the usual hourly wages for babysitters in her neighborhood. The boy's mother also left $20 spending money for expenses during the day. She trusted Jill to use it wisely.

After a few weekends, Jill felt that she was not paid enough for taking care of the little boy. She was afraid to ask for higher wages, though. Her neighbor might get a different baby-sitter. Instead, Jill began to take $10 a week for herself from the spending money. After all, her employer never asked how she used the money.

Figure 8.2

WORKPLACE ETHICS

Area of Concern	Ethical Behavior	Unethical Behavior
Time	Arriving to work on time and working the hours you say you will	Taking longer breaks than allowed, coming to work late or leaving early, talking on the telephone with friends and family members while at work, doing personal business during company time
Money	Using company money wisely and only for company business	Taking money from a cash register, taking goods from a store without paying for them, using company money to pay for personal items or entertainment on a business trip
Company Property	Using company property carefully and only for company business	Taking office supplies home, copying company software for your own use, using the company copy machine to make photocopies for personal use, making personal long-distance phone calls on office telephones
Information	Keeping company information secret from people outside the company	Giving people who do not work for the company confidential information about new products or services, expansion plans, and ongoing projects; sharing private information about employees and customers with people outside the company
Treatment of Others	Treating your employer, coworkers and customers fairly, openly, and with honesty	Having a negative attitude toward people of different backgrounds, calling people names, making racist or sexist comments, making generalizations about groups of people

The Right Actions When you behave ethically, you do the right thing in every situation. *How do you learn ethical behavior?*

Jill's employer did notice that the spending money was being used, though. She asked her son where Jill and he had gone during the day. He told her they never left the house. Then the boy's mother asked Jill how she used the money. Jill lied to cover up what she had done. Her employer knew she was lying. She told Jill she was going to look for another baby-sitter. She also told other parents in the neighborhood what had happened. No one would hire Jill because she had been dishonest.

Ethics and You

How will you know the right way to behave on a job? Even if you haven't held a job yet, you've got experience with ethical problems. Like everyone else, you face ethical decisions every day. You decide how to behave in many difficult situations.

You may also observe ethical problems that do not involve you. Even if you are not directly involved in an unethical situation, you still have an ethical choice to make. Acting ethically also means that you do not ignore unethical behavior. Many times ethical problems can by cleared up by a calm and open discussion with those involved.

You don't have to wait until you have a job. You have many opportunities to behave ethically every day. Do the right thing when faced with a decision or when you witness ethical problems. The ethics you practice in areas of your life now will carry over to the workplace.

Try This Activity

Interview Employers About Ethics

Interview two or more employers about the importance of ethics in the workplace. Ask permission to tape record the interviews, or take notes during the interviews. Ask each employer about the importance of ethical behaviors such as honesty, confidentiality, dependability, promptness, getting along with others, and respecting other people's property.

Write a Report Write a report explaining the importance of productive work habits and attitudes. In your report, summarize the employers' opinions on the importance of various types of ethical behavior in the workplace.

Performance Reviews

Progress reports, report cards, test scores, conferences—all tell you how you are doing in school. Each is a way of evaluating your work. Your work at a job will also be evaluated. Many companies schedule performance reviews on a regular basis. **Performance reviews** are meetings between you and your supervisor to evaluate how well you're doing your job.

Reviews are important to both you and your employer. They let you know how you're doing and help you become better at what you do. They also help you build your career. Performance reviews also help employers keep track of workers' growth and progress. Your company's human resources department will keep your performance reviews in your permanent employee file. **Human resources** is the department that recruits employees, administers company policies, develops employee training programs, and manages employee records.

A performance review is a good time for you and your employer to set goals. Your employer may set some for you. You should also set some for yourself. You may discuss your future with the company. Your review may lead to a pay increase and new responsibilities.

Career Opportunities

Health Science

If you are interested in helping people feel better, the Health Science career cluster may be for you. Workers in this cluster include doctors, dentists, nurses, technicians, and even the workers who keep hospitals clean and functional.

HEALTH EDUCATOR

HMO seeks educator to plan, organize, and lead classes on how to quit smoking, weight loss, and diabetes management. Must be knowledgeable about health issues and comfortable speaking in front of groups.

Critical Thinking

Why do you think a health maintenance organization (HMO) would employ a health educator?

Prepare for a Performance Review

Try This Activity

Imagine that your performance review for your part-time cashier's job is scheduled for tomorrow. Make a list of your accomplishments. What could you do better? What are your goals?

Plan a Positive Response Write down responses to two potential constructive criticisms. Plan how you will respond positively. Explain how you can take your supervisor's criticism as an opportunity to advance in your career.

How should you get feedback if you work for a company that does not hold performance reviews? Your work at a part-time or volunteer job may not be evaluated. Your teachers may give you nothing more than a grade. If that's the case, schedule a meeting to discuss your performance. There's nothing wrong with asking how you're doing. It will show that you take an interest in your work. In addition, you'll get useful ideas that will help you improve your performance.

It's also a good idea to take time now and then to evaluate yourself. Evaluate yourself as a member of your family. Evaluate yourself as a friend. Look at your performance at school and in other activities. What do you do well? What could you do better? What would you like to do that you're not doing?

Before you know it, self-evaluation will be a habit. It will be a good habit, too. Why? Evaluation by yourself and others will help you grow—whether you're at home, at school, or on the job.

Performance Evaluation Some employers evaluate workers informally. *Which type of evaluation—formal or informal—do you think you would prefer? Why?*

Lesson 8.2 Review and Activities

Key Terms Review

1. Pretend you own a company. You want to write a welcome letter for new employees that describes the qualities you seek in employees. Use each of the key terms below.
   - **cooperate**
   - **social skills**
   - **business etiquette**
   - **discretion**
   - **initiative**
   - **self-motivation**
   - **adaptability skills**
   - **ethics**
   - **performance reviews**
   - **human resources**

Check Your Understanding

Tell whether each statement is true or false. Rewrite any false statement to make it true. Write your answers on a separate sheet of paper.

2. Employers want employees who can cooperate and follow directions.
3. Employers don't have the right to expect employees to act ethically.

Critical Thinking

Use complete sentences to answer the following questions. Write your answers on a separate sheet of paper.

4. What are two ways you can show initiative at home? At school?
5. Why are performance reviews as important to workers as to their employers?
6. How can self-evaluation help you grow?

Character Building

7. **Ethics** You work at Lots-a-Flavors ice cream parlor. Lots-a-Flavors employees can eat as much free ice cream as they want during their breaks. They also get a 50 percent discount on any ice cream they take home. Payments for take home purchases are taken out of weekly paychecks. Last week you took home an ice cream cake for your friend's birthday party, however, your weekly paycheck didn't show a deduction for this cake. What should you do?

Community Involvement

8. **Community Service Project** With a group of friends, identify something that you can do to improve or help your community. Together, figure out how you can provide this service. You might want to volunteer at an existing organization or create your own project, such as removing litter around your school. Report what you did to the class. Tell about the qualities you needed for the project. Explain how these qualities are similar to those that employers look for in employees.

Investigating Career Clusters

HEALTH SCIENCE

Health Science • The science of maintaining and improving human health

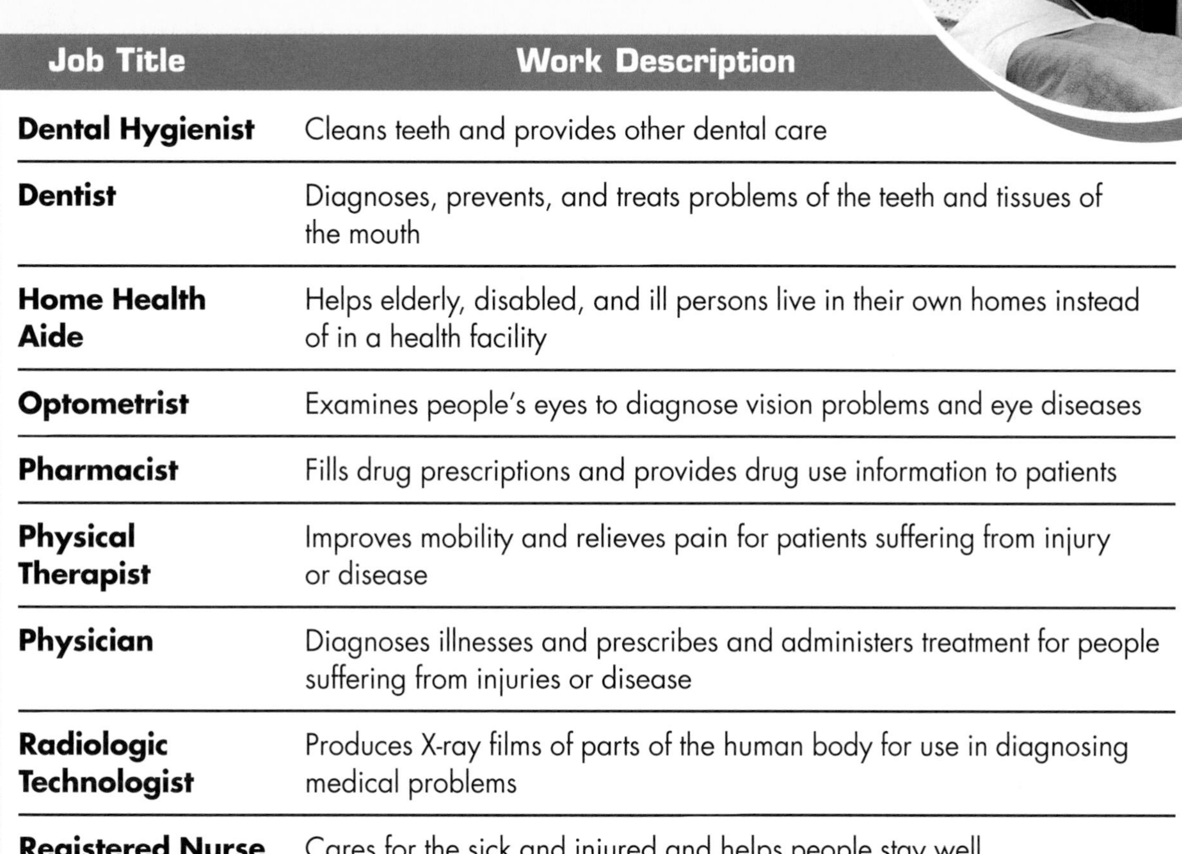

Job Title	Work Description
Dental Hygienist	Cleans teeth and provides other dental care
Dentist	Diagnoses, prevents, and treats problems of the teeth and tissues of the mouth
Home Health Aide	Helps elderly, disabled, and ill persons live in their own homes instead of in a health facility
Optometrist	Examines people's eyes to diagnose vision problems and eye diseases
Pharmacist	Fills drug prescriptions and provides drug use information to patients
Physical Therapist	Improves mobility and relieves pain for patients suffering from injury or disease
Physician	Diagnoses illnesses and prescribes and administers treatment for people suffering from injuries or disease
Radiologic Technologist	Produces X-ray films of parts of the human body for use in diagnosing medical problems
Registered Nurse	Cares for the sick and injured and helps people stay well

Exploration Activity

Health Science Use library and Internet resources to research a career in the Health Science career cluster. Write a report on your findings. Include information about the kinds of work, the skills required, the working conditions, the training and education required, and the career outlook.

Cooperative Learning Interview a classmate about the career he or she researched. Find out as much information about that career as you can during the interview. Then have your classmate interview you about the career you researched. Afterward, share what you learned with the class.

Chapter 8 Review and Activities

Chapter Highlights

Lesson 8.1 Many companies provide new employees with an orientation on the company's policies. Employees are paid wages, salary, or commission. They may also receive benefits, such as health insurance and paid time off.

Lesson 8.2 Employers want employees who cooperate, get along with others, follow directions, show initiative, take on responsibility, continue learning, and act ethically. Employers evaluate employee performance on a regular basis.

Key Concept Review

Use complete sentences to answer the following questions. Write your answers on a separate sheet of paper.

1. Why do companies provide orientation for new employees?
2. How do wages differ from a salary?
3. What is initiative?
4. What are three areas of ethical behavior in the workplace?
5. What is the purpose of a performance review?

Critical Thinking

Use complete sentences to answer the following questions. Write your answers on a separate sheet of paper.

6. What do you think will be the main thing on your mind the first day at a new job? Explain.
7. Why do you think benefits are important to many workers?
8. Why are honesty and fairness important in the workplace?

Skill Building

9. **Thinking—Knowing How to Learn**
   Think of a part-time job you'd like to have. With a partner, role-play a phone conversation in which the employer has called to answer questions you have about your first day. What questions would you ask? Switch roles, and role-play a second conversation.
10. **Personal—Sociability**
    Make a list of ways to get to know coworkers. Keep writing until you've run out of ideas. Compare lists with a classmate. How many ways of getting acquainted have the two of you identified?

Academic Applications

11. Health Science

Make a collage with words and pictures that celebrates the services that at least three health science careers provide. Review "Investigating Career Clusters" on page 169 for ideas of careers to include. Cut pictures and words out of magazines or newspapers. You can also make your own drawings and labels. Display your collage in class.

12. Mathematics

Tamika has just completed her first month in television advertising sales. The monthly base salary is $2,400. In addition to the salary, Tamika makes a commission of 15 percent on what she sells. Tamika worked hard and sold $8,000 worth of advertising this month. How much is her commission? What are her total earnings for the month?

Personal Career Portfolio

Create Job Search Correspondence

- **Use** library and Internet resources to research various forms of job search correspondence.
- **Write** a cover letter tailored to a job for which you would like to apply. Review **Figure 7.3** on page 132 for an example of a cover letter.
- **Title** the document *Cover Letter* and file it in your Personal Career Portfolio.
- **Write** a thank-you letter that you can customize for each interview you have. Review **Figure 7.5** on page 142 for an example of a thank-you letter.
- **Title** the document *Thank-You Letter* and file it in your Personal Career Portfolio.
- **Update** your job search correspondence as you identify other jobs you would like to pursue. File updated versions in your Personal Career Portfolio.
- **List** your portfolio entries on your Personal Career Portfolio contents page.

Chapter 9

Working With Others

Lesson 9.1

Building Relationships

Lesson 9.2

Teamwork

CAREER CLUSTER

You will explore careers in the Hospitality and Tourism career cluster.

What You'll Learn

- You will learn the basics of working well with others.
- You will find out how to build relationships and deal with conflicts when they arise.
- You will discover why being able to work as part of a team is important.
- You will take a look at how teams work.

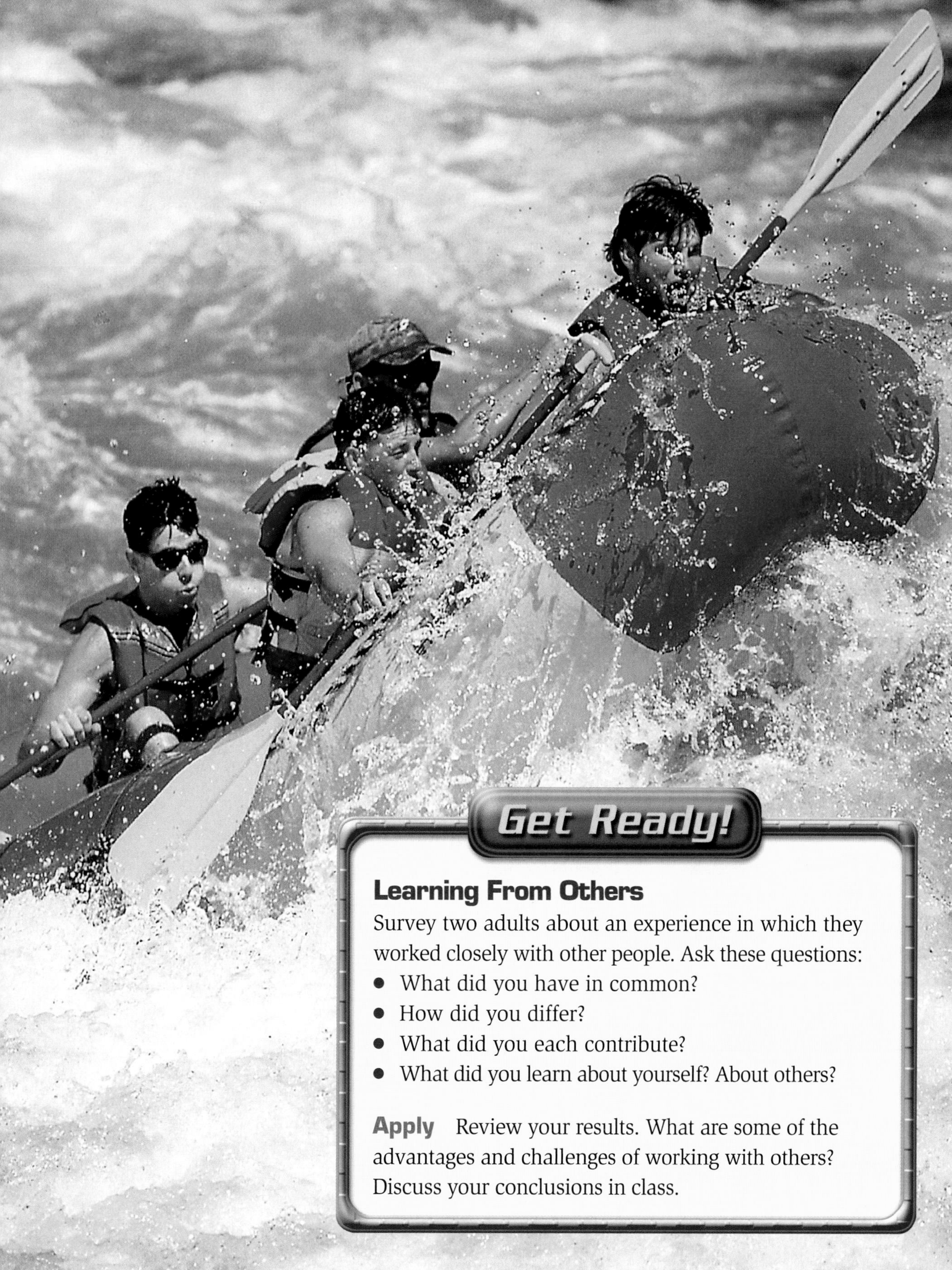

Get Ready!

Learning From Others

Survey two adults about an experience in which they worked closely with other people. Ask these questions:

- What did you have in common?
- How did you differ?
- What did you each contribute?
- What did you learn about yourself? About others?

Apply Review your results. What are some of the advantages and challenges of working with others? Discuss your conclusions in class.

Lesson 9.1

Building Relationships

Discover

- The key to getting along with others
- How to build relationships with other people
- The part self-esteem plays in relationships
- How to deal with conflicts between people

Why It's Important

Getting along with others will help you at home, at school, and on the job.

KEY TERMS

- relationships
- respect
- empathize
- self-esteem
- conflict
- prejudice
- mediator
- compromise
- conflict resolution

How well do you get along with others? Think about all your **relationships**—your connections or dealings with people. You have relationships with your friends and family. You also have relationships with teachers and others each day at school. Then there are the people in your community, such as neighbors and shopkeepers. How do you treat all of these people? How do you behave toward them?

You may act differently with different people, depending on how well you know them. You don't have to know people well to get along with them, though. The key to getting along with people is quite simple. It's the same no matter who's involved. The key is **respect,** or consideration, for others.

Respect Is the Key

Remember your report cards in elementary school? In addition to grading your schoolwork, your teacher also commented on your social

Connect With Others
Learning how to build strong relationships is a skill that will help you throughout your life. *Why do you think that this is so?*

skills. Maybe your teacher wrote, "Works well with others." Maybe he or she made these notes: "Respects other people's opinions" or "Always willing to help others."

All of these skills showed how well you got along with others. These skills are important on the playground and in the classroom. Employers take these skills seriously. They know that employees who have social skills have the key to good relationships in the workplace.

Getting Along With Others

Show other people respect. It sounds easy, but it can be hard work sometimes. As you know from experience, it's impossible to get along with everyone all the time.

We've all known someone who made our surroundings at home or school unpleasant or difficult. The workplace is no different. There will be people you don't like. Not everyone will like you. Some people will just be easier to be with than others.

You'll want to do everything you can to build and keep good relationships with people at work. When you get along with your coworkers and others at work, you will do a better job. You will also enjoy your work more.

Be Considerate
You can show respect, or consideration, for others in many ways.
How is this person being considerate?

Ways to Build Relationships

Here are some pointers for getting along with others.

- ***Treat people as you would like to be treated.*** Be thoughtful and considerate.
- ***Try to understand the other person's side.*** Be open-minded. **Empathize**—try to see things from the other person's point of view and understand his or her situation.
- ***Speak carefully.*** Think of the way others will feel when they hear what you have to say. Share information clearly and thoughtfully so that others understand you.

- ***Listen when others talk.*** Let other people know you're interested in them. Pay attention to what they say. Ask for and listen to their opinions and ideas.
- ***Help others.*** Lend a hand if you see someone having trouble doing something. If you finish what you have to do, help someone else.
- ***Be friendly.*** Be pleasant and smile. Greet people. Invite newcomers to join you.
- ***Have a sense of humor.*** Find ways to see the light side of a situation. Let your sense of humor carry you and others through difficult times.

Try This Activity

Understand Productive Work Habits and Attitudes

Write job scenarios demonstrating positive relations among employees and between employees and customers. Then write job scenarios demonstrating negative relations among employees and between employees and customers.

Analyze Your Scenarios Compare and contrast the scenarios you wrote. What are the similarities and differences among the positive scenarios? The negative scenarios?

Getting Along With Yourself

Think about this. You treat other people the way you treat yourself. If you respect and like yourself, chances are you will feel the same way about others.

Help From Your Family When family members help each other, they build strong relationships. *In what ways do you help members of your family? In what ways do members of your family help you?*

Believe in Yourself Learning a new skill or reaching a goal you've set can boost your self-esteem. *What activities do you do well? What activities would you like to try?*

Here's an example. Say you make a mistake. Do you put yourself down? Do you think to yourself, "I'm really stupid" or "I never do anything right"? If you do, you may put others down when they make mistakes.

On the other hand, you might say, "I made a mistake, but I'll get it right next time." When you do, you give yourself a break. You're realistic about your expectations for yourself. You understand that nobody's perfect. You will probably forgive others when they make mistakes.

How you feel about yourself—your self-esteem—affects how you get along with others. **Self-esteem** is your recognition and regard for yourself and your abilities. When you have high self-esteem, you are confident about yourself and what you can do. When you are positive about yourself, you are likely to have positive feelings toward other people.

Dealing With Conflict

Even when people do their best to get along, conflicts can arise. A **conflict** is a strong disagreement. It often occurs when people have different needs or wishes. Conflicts can occur in families and among friends and neighbors. Employees, employers, and customers may also have conflicts with each other from time to time.

Causes of Conflicts

People disagree for many reasons. Think about the last time you had a disagreement. Can you remember the cause? Maybe you felt that someone wasn't respecting your feelings. Maybe you and another person wanted two different things.

Conflicts have a variety of causes. Some are based on misunderstandings. These misunderstandings often occur when people don't communicate clearly. Other conflicts come about because people have different beliefs or opinions, or because of gossip and teasing, or jealousy.

Prejudice is another cause of conflict. **Prejudice** is a negative attitude toward a person or group that is not based on facts or reason. Prejudice causes people to judge others without taking the time to get to know them. When you see someone as a stereotype, instead of as an individual, it will inevitably lead to conflict.

Resolving Conflicts

No matter what its cause, a conflict is like any other problem. To deal with a conflict, you need good problem-solving skills. Some conflicts can be solved by the people involved. You may disagree with your brother or sister about what television program to watch, for instance. After talking it over, though, you may be able to agree on a solution.

Stay Calm
Everyone experiences conflicts with others. *How have you handled recent conflicts? What would you do differently?*

Career Opportunities

Hospitality and Tourism

Does the idea of visiting far-off lands sound exciting to you? Perhaps you would enjoy a career in hospitality and tourism. You could work in a resort, for a tour company or an airline, or even on a cruise ship.

CRUISE DIRECTOR
Major cruise line seeks energetic, organized, creative, outgoing cruise director. Responsibilities include planning and organizing all on-board activities, supervising staff, acting as emcee during evening events, and acting as host of the ship.

Critical Thinking

Why do you think a cruise director needs to be energetic and outgoing?

If you can't agree, you may need to ask a family member to act as a mediator. A **mediator** is someone who helps opposing people or groups compromise or reach an agreement. When opposing sides **compromise,** they each give up something to settle a disagreement.

Disagreements at work can be handled in a similar way as conflicts at home and school. At work, a process called **conflict resolution** may be used to settle disagreements. Figure 9.1 on pages 180–181 shows how conflict resolution works.

Preventing Conflicts

To prepare yourself for dealing with conflicts in the workplace, practice your problem-solving and communication skills and learn to control your anger. When you feel yourself getting angry, try these ways of cooling off.

- Take a deep breath and count to 10.
- Go for a walk or do something else that is physical.
- Laugh it off and walk away.
- Take a few minutes to have a "talk" with yourself.
- Remind yourself why you don't want to act angry.

Remember though, it's always best to head off conflicts before they even start. The best way to prevent conflicts from ever starting is to pay attention to your own behavior toward others. By exploring your actions, you may find qualities in yourself that you can improve. Perhaps you need to work on accepting other people as they are. Maybe you need to try looking at situations from another person's point of view.

Figure 9.1 **STEPS IN CONFLICT RESOLUTION**

Conflict resolution is a way to work out a solution to a problem. The people involved in a disagreement work together to bring the conflict to an end. *Where besides work might you use these steps to resolve a conflict?*

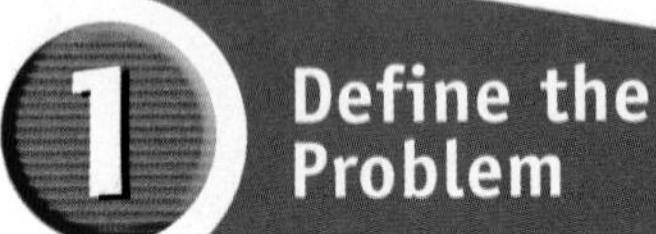

1 Define the Problem

Take turns describing the problem from your point of view. As you speak and listen, show respect for each other.

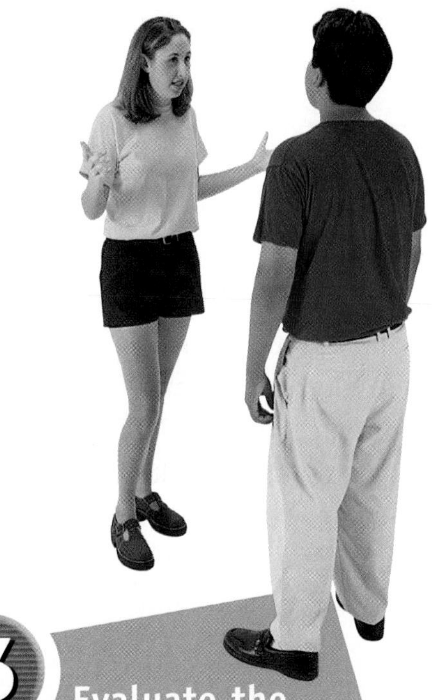

2 Suggest Solutions

Offer solutions to the problem.

3 Evaluate the Solutions

Discuss the suggested solutions. Explain the part of each suggestion that you agree with. Also explain the part you cannot accept. Listen carefully as the other person does the same.

Everyone has his or her own style of managing conflicts. The style you use will have a big impact on the outcome of the conflict. Your way of handling conflicts will also determine whether the conflict has positive or negative results.

Go back to the pointers for getting along with others listed on pages 175 and 176. See what you can improve. After all, your relationships with others begin with you.

4a Compromise

If you are close to agreeing, compromise. In other words, give up something to settle the disagreement.

4b Think Creatively

If you can't compromise, brainstorm solutions. Think of as many ways as you can to approach the problem. Then try again to compromise.

5 Get Another Point of View

If you can't reach a solution, invite a third person to help. Ask that person to listen and make suggestions for a solution.

6 Ask Someone Else to Decide

You both may want a solution but cannot agree on what it should be. Your only choice may be to hand the conflict over to a mediator. Agree that you will go along with the decision that person makes. Then ask the mediator to make the final decision.

Lesson 9.1 Review and Activities

Key Terms Review

1. Write an essay describing experiences you have had getting along with or not getting along with others. Use each term below in your essay.

- **relationships**
- **respect**
- **empathize**
- **self-esteem**
- **conflict**
- **prejudice**
- **mediator**
- **compromise**
- **conflict resolution**

Check Your Understanding

Choose the correct answer for each item. Write your answers on a separate sheet of paper.

2. When you are positive about yourself, you are likely to ______.

a. lose the respect of others
b. gain control of others
c. get along with other people

3. The first step to resolve a conflict is to ______.

a. explain your solution
b. define the problem
c. ask the other person to listen

Critical Thinking

Use complete sentences to answer the following questions. Write your answers on a separate sheet of paper.

4. Can you have good relationships with other people if you have low self-esteem? Explain.

5. How does learning to do something new help increase your self-esteem?

6. What can you do to avoid conflict with others?

Character Building

7. People Skills On the Internet or in a newspaper, look for a classified ad for a job in the Hospitality and Tourism career cluster. Print out or copy the ad. Write a summary and description of the job. Identify the people skills needed for the job. Which of these skills do you have? Which skills could you improve upon or develop? Name one thing you can do to begin developing one of these skills.

Teamwork

8. Design a Mediation Program Many schools use peer mediation to deal with student conflicts. In peer mediation, specially trained students help resolve conflicts among their peers, or people their age. Work with a group of classmates to research peer mediation programs. Use library or Internet resources to find out the details of how these programs work. Share your information with the class. Consider starting a peer mediation program at your school.

Lesson 9.2

Teamwork

Think of all the ways you work with others at home and at school to get things done. Perhaps you pitch in at home to help your family do chores. Maybe you and your classmates have put on a performance or held a fund-raiser. You might be a member of the student council, making decisions with others about school activities. Don't forget all the projects you've completed in cooperative learning groups. Working as a team member will continue to be important when you enter the world of work.

The Importance of Teamwork

What do wolves, the organs in your body, musicians, and soccer players all have in common? They all work as a team! Wolves live in packs because they have a better chance of surviving if they band together. They may also feel a need to be

Discover

- Why teamwork is important
- The steps involved in teamwork
- Problems teams face and how to handle them

Why It's Important

People work together to complete all kinds of projects. You'll use team skills in school and in the work you do someday.

KEY TERMS

- **collaboration**
- **empowerment**
- **brainstorming**
- **team planning**
- **assess**

Work Together
Sharing goals and responsibilities as part of a team is an experience that is valuable to everyone. *What goals have you shared with others on a team? How did you contribute to meeting your team's goals?*

The Global Workplace

The Politics of Personal Space

Next time you're talking with someone, stop and take a look at how far apart you're standing. You're probably at arm's length, about 30 inches. This is the average amount of personal space Americans are comfortable with. You might notice a shift in this space when you travel outside the United States. In Asia, people will stand farther away from you during a conversation. In South America and the Middle East, expect people to stand much closer to you during a business conversation. They might even touch your arms, hands, or shoulders while they speak.

Until you know a culture's rules though, it is best that you not touch others—especially women—while in conversation.

Internet Activity

Using the Internet or library resources, find out what topics of conversation are considered polite in one other country. Which topics are impolite in this country? Go to the *Exploring Careers* Web site at exploring.glencoe.com for a list of Web sites to help you complete this activity.

part of a group, just as we do. The human body functions smoothly, with each organ doing a different task. It takes all the organs working together, though, to keep us alive and healthy.

Musicians work together when they practice and perform. Each musician plays an integral part in the musical group's performance. As for soccer players, a good team offense and defense require good teamwork.

Teams in the Work World

Businesses today rely more and more on teams of workers to get jobs done. There are hospital surgical teams, software design teams, and book sales teams, to name only a few. In each case, the members of the group collaborate. **Collaboration** means working with others for a common purpose. The team's purpose may be to plan and complete a difficult operation. It may be to create a new computer game. It may be to break the record for the number of books sold in a year. Members of teams share the responsibilities and rewards of their efforts.

"Two heads are better than one." That's what they say. More people on a particular job or problem means more chances for creative solutions.

The Benefits of Teamwork

Businesses find that teams can get more done than the same number of people working separately. The goods teams make and the services they offer are of higher quality. Fewer supervisors are needed when people work in teams.

Team players also benefit. They tend to feel good about their work because they are empowered. **Empowerment** is the feeling of power and satisfaction that comes from being directly responsible for your work decisions.

Team members are empowered to share their ideas in order to find solutions to problems. Brainstorming is a creative method that teams use to come up with ideas to solve problems.

Attitude Counts

Perfection

It's got to be perfect! Although it's good practice to approach tasks with energy, always expecting perfection can cause problems. Remember, everyone is human. If you try to do everything perfectly, you will probably be disappointed and become stressed. Focus on doing your personal best at the moment, and you are sure to be a success.

Cooperative Learning Activity

Team up with several classmates and finish these sentences:

- Perfectionism is . . . .
- Perfectionism can cause . . . .

Share your team's completed sentences with the class.

A Diverse Team
People working together on a team may come from a variety of backgrounds. *How might their different backgrounds benefit the team and its work?*

Brainstorming is a method of shared problem solving in which all members of a group contribute ideas.

Team members often get to perform varied tasks, which makes work interesting. They may also share skills, expertise, and ideas. If you want to learn more about computer graphic design, for instance, another team member may be able to teach you. Then you could help that person with his or her tasks. That makes both of you more productive and more interested in your work.

Try This Activity

Pool Your Ideas

Test it out for yourself. Think of a problem at school. Write down as many ways to solve the problem as you can in one minute. Then ask three friends to do the same. Put all of your ideas together. Is the list longer than when you started it?

Evaluate the Ideas What ideas did your friends have that you didn't think of? Did any of your friends' ideas give you new ideas? A variety of ideas and points of view is one of the best reasons for working as a team.

High self-esteem is common among team players. Teams are usually in charge of their own work, and team members often help make and carry out decisions. Because all team members contribute to the result, they all feel good about themselves and what they can do.

As an extra bonus, people who work on teams usually learn to get along well with each other. That's because they have a chance to get to know each other's behaviors, attitudes, and ways of thinking, so they aren't so quick to judge one another. That means cooperation instead of conflict in the workplace.

Team Planning

Imagine that you and your friends have decided to throw a surprise birthday party. What will happen if you each go ahead and do what you think should be done? You may take care of some things, but you may forget others.

Learn as a Group
Think of a group project you've worked on. *What did you learn from the experience that might help you in a future career?*

If you plan the party together, you will have much better results. One person can send invitations. Another can decorate. One can be in charge of music, and another can buy the food. The end result will be a great party.

The same goes for running any successful team project. Before you start, you should make a plan. Since you will be working as a team, plan as a team. **Team planning** involves working with other team members to set goals, assign tasks, and assess results.

Setting Goals

Taking time to set goals helps everyone understand the purpose of the group. When you set goals as a team, you will all be moving in the same direction.

Take it from Nate, who found out the hard way what happens when people on a team have different goals. Nate thought it would be fun to form a basketball team and join the summer league. "Most of us just wanted to shoot some hoops and have fun," Nate explains. "There were a couple of guys, though, who were out to win the city championship. I figured that out pretty quickly. They got really angry every time we lost a game. After a few losses, it was no fun playing together anymore."

Can you think of times when you've been in a group in which people had different goals? It probably was not a good team experience.

Sometimes the best way to approach a large project is to use "stepping-stone goals." Short-term, medium-term, and long-term goals can be stepping stones to your final goal. These in-between goals, which you read about in Chapter 5, work as well for groups as for individuals.

Assigning Roles and Tasks

It's important for each team member to have a role, or part to play. Sometimes a person's role is a task, such as "buy the food." More often, your role as a team member will take advantage of your interests and skills.

Remember that party you were planning? You might choose the person with the best computer skills to create party invitations. The artist in the group might be in charge of decorations. The one who always has the latest music would probably do a good job handling the music. On a team, no one has to be good at everything. You all can take advantage of each other's interests and skills.

No matter what your role, the other members of the team will count on you. If you do not do your job, everyone loses. Say you're planning that surprise birthday party with three other friends. Since there are four team members, you divide the work into four tasks: invitations, decorations, music, and food.

Try a New Role
You probably have many opportunities in group projects at school to play a role that's new to you. *What new role would you like to have in your next group project? Why?*

Team Roles
In order for a team to be successful, each member needs to have a role, or part to play. *How should a team decide what role to assign to each team member?*

If all four team members do their part, the party will be a great success. What happens if the person in charge of bringing the food doesn't do his or her job? No one gets a slice of birthday cake, that's what happens!

Try This Activity

Team Characteristics

Make a list of the characteristics of an effective team member. Next to each characteristic, explain how such a characteristic could be developed.

Develop Your Strengths Write a report explaining which characteristics of an effective team member you have and why. Explain how you have used each characteristic in the past during team projects. Which characteristics of an effective team member do you need to develop? How do you plan to develop those characteristics?

Assessing Results

No birthday cake at a birthday party is a problem. Problems are less likely to crop up if team members meet from time to time to **assess,** or judge, their progress. Team members should meet on a regular basis—daily, weekly, or monthly—as the project demands.

Sharing Leadership Roles

Q: I'm good at being a team leader, but my teammates just think I'm bossy. What should I do?

A: It's good to develop and use your leadership skills, but everyone in a team needs to feel that his or her skills are also valued and used. Share the role of leader. You might find that you excel in the role of a cooperative team member. When you are in the role of team leader, remember to encourage and support teammates. No matter what your role, listening and communicating are always the keys to working well with teammates.

Meet and Talk
Team members need to meet and talk about how they're doing and where they're headed. *How often do you think a team should meet to assess its progress?*

Communication is important. When team members gather regularly, they can assess their progress and share any difficulties they are having. If necessary, the team can reassign roles and tasks. Sometimes the team may even decide to rethink its goals.

It's also a good idea to assess a project when it is over. Frequently, someone "higher up" will evaluate the outcome of a project. That person may be a parent, a teacher, or a supervisor.

Customers and other observers can also help assess a team's work. They point out strengths and weaknesses. Listen carefully to their comments.

"The design team was very creative, but the people were not easy to work with."

"We couldn't have asked for better service and food at our party."

"My hospital stay went so smoothly. I had great care, from the admitting nurse to the surgeon to the young volunteers."

The team itself should also assess what it has accomplished. Self-assessment can make each group experience better than the last. The team as a whole and individual team members might check their work by asking questions such as:

- How well did I do my job?
- How well did other members of the team do their jobs?
- How well did we work together?
- What could we do differently next time?

Dealing With Problems

Teams face their share of problems no matter how well organized they are. Think of the groups in which you've participated. If you've had a bad experience working in a group, don't give up. Groups differ, just as individuals do.

Figure 9.2 shows some common problems teams face. Most of these problems can be avoided. How? Team members must set clear goals, take action promptly, and most important, keep communicating. By doing this, teams can more easily come to a consensus, or agreement, about any issues that do arise.

Teamwork is challenging, but it can also be fun. As with many other skills, the secret is practice. Practice now while you're in school. Put your team skills to work wherever you can. Today's workplace needs people who can be part of a team. If you practice, you'll have what it takes.

Figure 9.2

PROBLEMS TEAMS FACE

- Unclear goals
- Misunderstandings about decision making and leadership
- Competitiveness among team members
- Team members not doing their share of the work
- Bad feelings because an individual's efforts are not recognized

Avoid Trouble Working on a team can be hard work. *What solution can you suggest for one of the problems teams face?*

Lesson 9.2 Review and Activities

Key Terms Review

1. Make a poster that tells about teamwork and the three main steps of team planning. Explain your poster to the class in an oral presentation. Use each of the key terms in your presentation.
   - **collaboration**
   - **empowerment**
   - **brainstorming**
   - **team planning**
   - **assess**

Check Your Understanding

Tell whether each statement is true or false. Rewrite any false statement to make it true. Write your answers on a separate sheet of paper.

2. Team planning involves setting goals, assigning tasks, and making sure you are in charge.
3. Setting goals as a team helps everyone move in different directions.
4. Team members need to keep communicating to avoid problems.

Critical Thinking

Use complete sentences to answer the following questions. Write your answers on a separate sheet of paper.

5. Why is teamwork important in school? How will knowing how to work on a team be important to you in the future?
6. What might happen if you do not assess your progress when working as part of a team?

Connecting to the Workplace

7. **Teamwork in Hospitality and Tourism Careers** Choose a hospitality and tourism career that sounds interesting to you. Investigate the use of teams in this career. Use library resources and the Internet to gather information. If you have time, interview someone with a job in this career, in person or by telephone. Write a one-page report that summarizes what you have discovered about teamwork in this career.

Community Involvement

8. **Plan a Drive** Make a contribution to a local charity by planning a clothing drive, a food drive, or a book drive. Team up with several classmates and select the type of items you will collect and the charity to which you will donate the items. As a team, set your goals. How many donations? How quickly will you collect them? Decide your team member roles and tasks. Present your team's plan to the class.

Investigating Career Clusters

HOSPITALITY AND TOURISM

Hospitality • Lodging and food and beverage management and service

Tourism • Services involving travel planning, tourist information, guided tours, entertainment, recreation, and meeting planning

Job Title	Work Description
Athlete	Participates in professional competitive athletic events to entertain audiences
Chef	Prepares meals, plans menus, sets prices, designs food presentation, manages food costs, educates service staff, and oversees kitchen staff
Fitness Trainer	Evaluates and advises people on achieving physical fitness
Hotel Clerk	Provides services to hotel, motel, and other lodging establishments
Lifeguard	Monitors activities in swimming areas to prevent accidents, rescues swimmers, and administers first aid
Recreation Worker	Organizes and leads programs in recreational facilities
Tour Conductor	Points out interesting locations to tourists and answers their questions
Travel Agent	Gives advice on destinations and makes arrangements for travelers

Exploration Activity

Hospitality and Tourism Use library and Internet resources to research a career in the Hospitality and Tourism career cluster. Write a report on your findings. Include information about the kinds of work, the skills required, the working conditions, the training and education required, and the career outlook.

Cooperative Learning Interview a classmate about the career he or she researched. Find out as much information about that career as you can during the interview. Then have your classmate interview you about the career you researched. Afterward, share what you learned with the class.

Chapter 9 Review and Activities

Chapter Highlights

Lesson 9.1 Respect for others and a positive attitude about yourself are keys to getting along with others.

Lesson 9.2 People who work on teams generally get along well with each other. On a team, they have a chance to get to know each other.

Key Concept Review

Use complete sentences to answer the following questions. Write your answers on a separate sheet of paper.

1. What is respect?
2. What are five causes of conflict?
3. When might you ask a third party to make a decision to end a conflict?
4. What is involved in team planning?
5. What kinds of problems do teams often face?

Critical Thinking

Use complete sentences to answer the following questions. Write your answers on a separate sheet of paper.

6. Why is a sense of humor helpful in getting along with others?
7. Do you think you have a positive attitude toward yourself? Why or why not? How could you develop one?
8. Why might close friends have conflicts?
9. What kinds of things have you done with a team that you could not have done alone?
10. What would you do if someone on your team wouldn't do work?

Skill Building

11. **Thinking—Problem Solving**
    Matt shares a bedroom with his brother, Josh. Josh never finishes his homework early enough for Matt to listen to music before bed. Matt's light bothers Josh when he is trying to sleep. List two solutions that are fair to both Matt and Josh.
12. **Interpersonal—Participates as a Member of a Team**
    Work together with five or six other students to prepare a newscast. Cover recent events at school and in your community. Choose a director, writers, researchers, reporters, and an anchorperson. Rehearse, then present your newscast to the class.

Academic Applications

13. Social Studies

Read a daily newspaper for one week. Collect examples of conflicts. Look in all the sections of the paper: front page, sports, features, even the comics and advice columns. In each case, identify the conflict, the people involved, and its outcome. Choose one example. Write a letter to the people involved. Tell them what you recommend and why.

14. The Arts

Look at the light side of getting along with others. Draw a comic strip about building relationships. Paste it at the top of a sheet of paper. Circulate your comic strip among your classmates. Ask them to comment on your comic. How did they interpret it? Did they find it funny? What did it teach them?

Personal Career Portfolio

Get References

- **Develop** a list of references.
- **Consider** asking current and former teachers, counselors, coaches, club leaders, employers, and internship and volunteer supervisors.
- **Send** potential references a letter requesting a reference.
- **Secure** permission from at least five people to use as references.
- **Organize** your list of references by noting each person's job title, relationship to you, address, phone number, and e-mail address.
- **Title** the document *References* and file it in your Personal Career Portfolio.
- **Update** the document as you find new people who agree to be a reference.
- **List** your portfolio entry on your Personal Career Portfolio contents page.

Chapter 10

Basic Skills Count

Lesson 10.1

Getting Your Message Across

Lesson 10.2

Applying Other Skills

CAREER CLUSTER

You will explore careers in the Human Services career cluster.

What You'll Learn

- You will discover why basic skills are important.
- You will gather tips for improving your communication skills.
- You will learn how to build your math, science, and computer skills.

Get Ready!

Learn About Basic Skills

Prepare a questionnaire that lists these skills: Speaking, Listening, Reading, Writing, Math, Science, Computer Technology. Make three copies. Select three adults with different jobs. Give each a copy of your questionnaire. Ask them to answer how they use each skill listed at work.

Apply Study the responses. What do they tell you about the importance of basic skills?

Lesson 10.1

Getting Your Message Across

Discover

- How to apply the basics of speaking
- How to listen effectively
- How to improve your reading and writing skills
- How to use images, or pictures, to present ideas

Why It's Important

Basic skills are tools for getting information and sharing ideas.

KEY TERMS

- communication
- purpose
- audience
- subject
- active listening
- previewing
- skimming
- context clues
- images

Let's play telephone. Do you remember that game? To play, one person whispers a message in another person's ear. That person whispers it to the next person and so on. By the time it reaches the last person, the message is usually very different from what it was at the start. Why? People along the way may not have heard or repeated the message correctly. That may be because they didn't speak or listen carefully.

You may laugh when you hear a garbled message at the end of a game of telephone. It's no laughing matter, though, when a real message you are sending or receiving is confused. The exchange of information between senders and receivers is called **communication.** Communication skills—speaking, listening, reading, and writing—are among the most important basic skills you can have. They will play a big part in your success at school and in the world of work.

Make Yourself Understood Being able to communicate is a basic skill. *In what ways do you communicate each day?*

Speaking

What do you like to do with your friends? Chances are that you like to spend most of your time together just talking. You talk with each other at school. You talk on the telephone after school. You get together on the weekend and just talk.

Talking is an important part of relationships. It is also an important part of nearly every kind of work. In the work world, speaking is one of the most important ways of sharing information.

Having a Purpose

Whether you're speaking to one person or to a group, you want your listeners to get your point. To make a point, you need to have a clear idea of your purpose, audience, and subject.

Most people have a **purpose,** or overall goal or reason, for speaking. Think of the last time you spoke to someone. What was your reason for speaking? You may have needed help or information. Perhaps you wanted to share an idea, a point of view, or your feelings about something. Maybe you just wanted to say hello. You may have had more than one purpose for speaking.

It is important to have a clear purpose in mind when speaking. After all, when you know what your goal is, you are more likely to reach it.

Know Your Audience

Knowing your audience can help you achieve your purpose in speaking. When you think of an audience, you may imagine people seated in a theater or stadium. An **audience** is anyone who receives information. When you speak, your listeners are your audience.

It helps to know who your listeners are. Then you can choose the best way to reach them with your words and ideas. You wouldn't talk to a teacher in the same way you talk to your best friend. You wouldn't use the same tone of voice with a baby as you would with your teacher. You use different ways of speaking with different audiences.

Learning From Mistakes

It's easy to learn from successes, but what about mistakes? Part of becoming a successful worker is learning how to have a sense of humor about your own mistakes. Put your mistakes to work for you! Just ask, "What have I learned from this experience, and what can I do differently next time?"

Cooperative Learning Activity

- With a small group of classmates, share a mistake you have made.
- Explain what you learned from the mistake and what you'll do differently next time.
- As a group, create a poster that illustrates the many ways your mistakes made you wiser.

Know Your Subject

It also helps to know your **subject**—your main topic or key idea—when speaking. Getting to know your subject may require some preparation. It's well worth the time, though.

Think of a speaker who completely captured your attention. That speaker probably knew his or her subject very well. He or she probably shared specific facts and examples that made the subject come alive for you.

Planning Ahead

To know your purpose, audience, and subject, you need to plan ahead. Think about what you're going to say before you speak. You won't need a plan every time you talk to someone, but planning can be useful in many situations. Planning can improve your oral reports. Planning can also make talking to someone or leaving a clear phone message easier.

Ramesh Mahabir knows the importance of planning. He often makes a plan before talking to his mother. "When I want to ask my mom something important, I think about what I'm going to say," Ramesh explains.

> "I also try to figure out in advance how she will react. My mom is much more open to my ideas when I've planned ahead. That's because I know what I want to say and why I want to say it. All it takes is a little preparation."

Good Speaking Habits

Of course, what you have to say doesn't matter if no one can understand you. No matter what the situation, *how* you say something will be just as important as *what* you have to say. For some tips on improving your speaking skills, look at **Figure 10.1**.

Listening

The other side of speaking is listening. Like speaking, listening takes practice. Listening is not just being quiet when someone talks. It's not the same as hearing. Listening is a conscious action. When you listen, you use your brain to interpret, or make sense of, what you hear.

Figure 10.1

GOOD SPEAKING HABITS

- **Connect With Your Audience** Make eye contact with your listeners. Address people by name if possible.
- **Match Your Body Language to Your Message** Check your posture and facial expressions. Use appropriate gestures.
- **Avoid Nonwords** Avoid nonwords such as *uh* and *um* and "empty" words such as *well, sort of, like,* and *kind of.*
- **Stress Key Ideas With Inflection** Inflection is the pitch or loudness of your voice.
- **Use Correct Pronunciation** Pronunciation is how you say the sounds and stresses of a word.
- **Practice Enunciation** Enunciation is speaking each syllable clearly and separately.
- **Be Enthusiastic and Positive** Remember, attitude counts!

More Than Words Your delivery is as important as your message. *Why?*

Active Listening

Many people don't know the first thing about listening. They think about other things while you're talking to them. They plan what they're going to say. They look away instead of making eye contact. They interrupt. They may even finish your sentences. Talking to a poor listener can be frustrating, even aggravating.

Name some people you like talking with. The people who come to mind are probably good listeners. Good listeners show that they care about what someone is saying. They practice active listening. **Active listening** is listening and responding with full attention to what's being said.

Active listeners focus on the main ideas a speaker is communicating. They use body language and facial expressions to respond. They might sit up straight, lean forward, smile, or nod, for example, to show their interest. Active listeners also react by making comments and asking questions. They encourage whoever's speaking to tell more.

Try This Activity

Practice Active Listening

Try active listening with your friends, family members, and teachers. Don't tell them that you are practicing your active listening skills. Just practice being an active listener whenever you talk together.

Note Reactions Note how people react when you pay attention to what they're saying. Think about how much more you learn by being a good listener. Also identify ways you can continue to improve your listening skills. As **Figure 10.2** shows, listening will be one of your main activities in the workplace.

Taking Notes

Active listening can be a very useful tool in class. In some cases, you will want to go a step further and take notes as you listen. Taking notes helps you remember facts and keeps your attention focused. When you take notes, both your mind and your body are involved in listening.

Communicate The average employee spends more than half the workday listening. Speaking takes up nearly a quarter of the workday. *What do you suppose the other activities in an average workday include?*

Practice these skills as you take notes in class. You will also find these same skills useful in the workplace and in many other situations.

- Jot down summaries in your own words. Focus on key words and main ideas. Don't try to write down everything a speaker says.
- Note actions you need to take.
- Use bullets (•), asterisks (*), and arrows (→) to show how ideas are related or connected.
- Review your notes fairly soon after you take them to be sure you understand the information.
- If you can't take written notes, make mental notes of important points.

Reading and Writing

Reading, writing—not a day in school goes by without them. Schools spend a lot of time teaching students how to read and write well. They do this for a very good reason. It's hard to get along in the world today without these basic skills.

Right now, you need strong reading and writing skills to do well in school. In the near future, you may use these skills to get a driver's license and complete applications for college. You'll also need reading and writing skills to apply for a job.

Reading and writing are also important on the job. Can you name a job that doesn't involve reading and writing? There aren't many. Employers value employees who can read and write well. Employees with these skills can take in, process, and exchange large amounts of information. Your success in a career will depend in part on your reading and writing skills.

The Importance of Reading
There are many things you cannot do if you do not know how to read. *How is this teen using basic reading skills?*

Key Reading Skills

It's probably hard to remember the time in your life when you didn't know how to read. You have years of experience by now. You're well on your way to having the strong reading skills you'll need in the workplace.

Think about some of the reading skills you use in social studies, science, and English classes. You have probably used previewing before. **Previewing** is reading only the parts of a written work that outline or summarize its content. You can find these parts in a book by looking at the table of contents or flipping through the pages. The chapter titles and headings will tell you what's in the book. Previewing saves time when you need a general idea of what the content is.

Skimming is another timesaving reading skill. You are **skimming** when you read through a book or document quickly, picking out main ideas and key points. To skim, look at the first sentence of each paragraph. Also try to identify key words and phrases. Skimming is very helpful when you're doing research. It's a good way to pinpoint information quickly.

When you read for information, you often read quickly. What do you do when you come across an unfamiliar word or phrase? It takes time to stop to look in a dictionary. There's another way to figure out the meaning. Try looking for context clues. **Context clues** are hints about the meaning of unfamiliar words or phrases provided by the words surrounding them. You can use context clues to understand the meaning of words you don't know.

As you recall, taking notes is a useful listening skill. It is also an extremely important reading skill. As you read, jot down main ideas, useful quotes, new vocabulary, and your own summaries of information. Note taking can be especially helpful when you're reading technical information. Notes will help you understand and recall what you read.

Reading on the Job

The reading skills you use in school will be just as important on the job. You'll use many of the same skills on the job to gather, evaluate, and interpret information. In the workplace, you'll read directions, letters, bulletins, and reports. You'll need reading skills to do research for projects. Sometimes you'll want to read quickly for general information. At other times, you'll want to read carefully for specific facts. Keep polishing your reading skills. You'll need them just as much in the future as you do now.

Writing Basics

Much of the advice for speaking well also applies to writing well. Whether you're speaking or writing, you need to know your purpose, audience, and subject. Writing is a way to communicate. You can communicate better when you know *why* you're writing, to *whom* you're writing, and *what* you're writing about. Here are some other guidelines for writing:

Take Careful Notes Follow the same tips for taking notes while reading as you would while listening. *Why is taking notes in your own words better than copying someone else's?*

- ***Organize your writing.*** Before you begin writing, outline what you have to say. Put your ideas in logical order, such as chronological order or order of importance. Use headings and subheadings to label different parts of your writing.
- ***Check your spelling and grammar.*** Use a spell checker on a computer. Keep a dictionary close by to check the spelling of words you don't know. Consult a style book for grammar rules.
- ***Watch your tone.*** Keep your audience in mind. Direct your words to the people who will be reading what you write. Be respectful and polite.
- ***Edit your work.*** When you think you are finished, go back and read through your work one more time. Make changes to what you have written until your message is clear.
- ***Proofread your work.*** Carefully check all of your work for any errors it may still contain.

Forms of Business Writing

You have many uses for writing right now. You may write journal entries, school reports, and e-mails. You'll discover many other uses for writing when you begin working. The basics of writing apply to business writing too. Some of the common forms of business writing are shown in **Figure 10.3** on pages 206–207.

Figure 10.3

COMMON FORMS OF BUSINESS WRITING

At some point in your job, you may need to write a memo, a letter, or a report. *What are the similarities and differences between these forms of writing and writing you do now?*

Businesspeople often use memos to communicate with others in the office. They also send memos to people outside the office who work closely with them. Memos are usually brief and focus on a limited topic. They are often fairly informal in tone.

Northeast Associates

Memo

To: Erica Sutton
From: Valerie Mendoza
CC: Scott Dennis
Date: September 16, 2002
Subject: Business Conference

I'll be attending the TBC Conference Monday, September 23 through Friday, September 27. I will return to work the following Monday, September 30.

While I'm away, Scott will be handling my projects. If anything urgent should come up, you can reach me at (924) 555-0191.

Northeast Associates

20 Winter Street, Wrightville, Vermont 05602 (921) 555-0160

September 20, 2002

Megabyte Computers, Inc.
252 Willoughby Street
Providence, RI 02012

Dear Sir or Madam:

I am writing to request your most recent catalog of computer hardware. I would also like any information you have on business discounts.

We are planning to update our computer system at Northeast Associates, and I am preparing a proposal that will outline our options and their cost.

Also, if you have a sales representative in this region, I would appreciate it if he or she would call me.

Sincerely yours,

Cristina Alvarez

Cristina Alvarez
Technology Specialist

In general, letters are more formal than memos. They are used to communicate with people outside the office who are customers or who work in other businesses.

The purpose of a report is to address a topic at length. The topic may be a possible new project or the progress of an ongoing project. Reports also often describe the results of research. People both within and outside an office may read reports.

The Mentor Project

An Evaluation

By Elizabeth Wang and Alexander Bain

September 2002

Overview

The Mentor Project appears to be one of the most successful of the many projects launched by Northeast Associates. With the help of business leaders in the community, we placed students in a variety of summer jobs in local businesses. We also paired each student with a mentor, an experienced coworker. It is the mentor's responsibility to teach the student about his or her job responsibilities.

Summer Results

More than 35 students worked under the direction of mentors over the summer. Most had little or no experience in the job they took. By the end of the summer, however, thanks to the direction of their mentors, all the students reported that they felt comfortable in the workplace and had no difficulty doing their jobs. Many observed that what they learned from their mentor was invaluable.

From: Rebecca Seidel <rseidel@megabyte.org>
To: Cristina Alvarez <c.alvarez@northeast.edu>
Date: Tuesday, September 24, 2002, 3:11 P.M.
Subject: Your Request

Dear Ms. Alvarez,

We received your e-mail request for our most recent catalog of computer hardware. We sent the catalog out today, as well as information regarding business discounts.

Our central sales region sales director, Mr. Rick Louvar, will be in touch with you this week to discuss your company's computer hardware needs.

Thank you for thinking of Megabyte Computers for your computer hardware needs. We look forward to doing business with you in the future.

Rebecca Seidel
Senior Manager
Megabyte Computers
rseidel@megabyte.org
Phone: (924) 555-0155
Fax: (924) 555-0154

Today, most written business communication is sent by e-mail. E-mail has become the method of choice because it enables fast communication. Although it has a reputation for informality, e-mail should be written carefully and formally. It should also be considered a public and permanent record.

Ideas and Images
There are many different ways to use images to express ideas. *Give an example of how an image can be used to present information.*

Using Images to Express Ideas

There's an old saying that says a picture is worth a thousand words. Look at magazine ads, TV commercials, posters, and billboards. Look at your favorite sites on the Internet. All use **images,** or pictures, as well as words to get their message across. Images include photographs, illustrations, videos, maps, and graphs.

Images are everywhere you look. They are used to communicate all kinds of information. They grab your attention and interest you in a subject.

Think of the different kinds of images you've used in work at school. You've probably drawn charts, maps, and graphs for social studies, science, and math projects. Maybe you've illustrated a report, book review, or science project.

More Than Words
People today are very visually oriented. They relate to images. *Why might you use images instead of words to communicate something?*

The Global Workplace

Do You Speak Metric?

Becoming fluent in the metric system is a great way to sharpen your math skills. More importantly, though, it will also help you survive on your trips abroad. That's because nearly every country in the world except the United States uses the metric system.

So, if you want to buy a snack in Egypt, you'll have to tell the fruit vendor how many kilograms of grapes you want. Or if you want to be sure you have enough time to drive to your next appointment while doing business in the Dominican Republic, you will need to know how far the distance is in kilometers.

Internet Activity

Using the Internet or library resources, do research on some of the problems American businesses have had because the United States does not use the metric system. Go to the *Exploring Careers* Web site at exploring.glencoe.com for a list of Web sites to help you complete this activity.

The posters, collages, dioramas, and bulletin board displays you've created have also included images. In each case, images were probably the best or most interesting way to present certain information.

Working with images takes practice. When you are thinking about using an image to convey a message, ask the following questions:

- Can this image say something that can't be said with words?
- Is the image accurate? Up-to-date? In good taste?
- Is the message of the image clear?
- Is the image interesting? Will it catch people's attention?

Images have a huge impact. Be sure to make using images one of your communication skills.

Lesson 10.1 Review and Activities

Key Terms Review

1. Imagine you're working in your first full-time job. You've volunteered to speak to middle schoolers about how communication skills helped you get your job. Give a talk on the subject to the class. Include the terms below in your talk.

- **communication**
- **purpose**
- **audience**
- **subject**
- **active listening**
- **previewing**
- **skimming**
- **context clues**
- **images**

Check Your Understanding

Choose the correct answer for each item. Write your answers on a separate sheet of paper.

2. Communication skills include ______.
   a. listening, reading, and math
   b. speaking, listening, reading, and writing
   c. reading, speaking, and math
3. Three common forms of writing in business are ______.
   a. memos, letters, and reports
   b. notes, letters, and deeds
   c. documents, reports, and trusts

Critical Thinking

Use complete sentences to answer the following questions. Write your answers on a separate sheet of paper.

4. Why should you know your purpose before speaking?
5. What kind of image especially grabs your attention? Why?
6. Why should business e-mail be written formally?

Connecting to the Workplace

7. **Taking Phone Messages** Imagine that you are working as a receptionist and you receive the following voicemail sent at 2:10 P.M. on September 24: "Hi, Andrea. Josh Liu here. I need to know if you want me to book that flight to Los Angeles for next week. If you let me know by the end of the day, I can still get the special rate. I'll be here until six o'clock. You can reach me at 555-0182. Thanks. Talk to you later." Write a message that summarizes this call.

Teamwork

8. **Create an Ad** Together with a group of classmates, choose a career in human services. Research the career to find out how communication skills are used in it. Use the information you find to create a poster that advertises the career. The ad should stress the importance of communication skills in the career.

Lesson 10.2

Applying Other Skills

What kinds of tools do you imagine yourself using in the different careers that interest you? None? Don't be fooled. Tools are not just objects like a hammer or a saw. A tool is anything that helps you accomplish something.

Many of the things you are studying now at school are tools for your future. Speaking, listening, reading, and writing are tools that will come in handy in the workplace. Math, science, and computer technology skills will also follow you out of the classroom. These skills are among the most important tools people use in careers today.

Discover

- How to strengthen your math and science skills
- How to build your computer technology skills

Why It's Important

Most careers today call for math, science, and computer technology skills.

KEY TERMS

- **mathematics**
- **science**
- **spreadsheet**
- **netiquette**

Math and Science

Mathematics is the study of numbers and their relationships. **Science** is the systematic use of observations and experiments to gain knowledge about the world. To you, either or both may just be interesting or challenging school subjects. What you are about to read, then, may surprise you.

Use Your Skills
The math, science, and computer skills you learn in school have many uses outside the classroom. *How do you think you might use these basic skills in a job someday?*

How Skilled Is Your Calculator?

Q: I don't really get why I should spend time sharpening my math skills. After all, I can always use a calculator.

A: Although a calculator might help you do a calculation quickly, you still need to have good math skills to know how to first set up the problem. For example, you need to know that you multiply 28.50 by .05 in order to calculate your local sales tax on a $28.50 purchase. So, you can see that a calculator is only as good at solving math problems as you are. The sharper your math skills, the more useful your calculator will be.

Everyday Skills

The truth is that people—and that includes you—use math and science every day in very ordinary activities. Math helps people understand their paychecks, pay bills, and buy goods and services. People use math and science to weigh, measure, cook, sew, make, and build things. Math and science skills help people play sports, garden, and operate vehicles and machines.

Learning to Think

Is math or science your favorite subject? If so, you may be thinking about careers that require special skills in those areas. Perhaps you see yourself becoming a zoologist, an engineer, or a laboratory technician.

Even if math or science is not a strong interest of yours, you still have something to learn from both. Math and science help you develop good thinking habits. Math teaches you to put things in order and take one step at a time. It also helps you to think logically and methodically. Science teaches you how to observe things and processes. Both math and science teach you how to solve problems.

Sharpening Your Skills

No matter what your interests or plans for the future, work on your math and science skills. You can't go wrong. Basic skills in math and science will help you in daily activities and in all kinds of careers. Do you need some suggestions for sharpening these skills? Take a look at **Figure 10.4**.

Computer Technology

Can you imagine a world not linked by computer technology? Computer technology has become a part of our everyday life.

Computer technology is used in nearly every kind of business. People use computers to get money from automated teller machines (ATMs). At stores, computers are used to scan bar codes on purchases. At school, you may use computers to do research on the Internet and to write and revise papers. You may also use computers to play games or communicate with others by e-mail.

Figure 10.4

TIPS FOR BUILDING MATH AND SCIENCE SKILLS

Strengthen or Expand What You Already Know	Look for library books about improving your math or science skills. Check TV listings for public television programs on math skills or science topics.
Use a Calculator Only to Check Your Work	Do math problems by yourself first. The more you work with numbers, the easier it gets.
Play Math Games	While you are waiting for the bus, for example, practice your multiplication tables. Think of other ways of testing your math knowledge.
Use Another Interest to Help Build an Interest in Math	If you like horses, for example, make up math problems for yourself based on that. Horses are measured in hands. How long is a hand? If a horse measures 16 hands, how tall is the horse in feet and inches?
Organize Information in Different Ways	Classify things and events. Classify your school supplies, for instance. Make a time line of highlights of your vacation or events in the school year. Present research you've done in the form of a table or graph.
Develop Your Observation Skills	Use your senses to observe your surroundings. Note entire objects or situations, and then details. Also practice using thermometers, scales, and other instruments to make observations.
Compare and Contrast	Identify likenesses and differences between things to learn more about what you observe.
Look for Causes and Effects	After something happens, think about why it happened. The answer to the question *why* is the event's cause. Also think about *what* happened as a result of an event. Effects of the event will answer the question *what*.
Go Metric	Become familiar and handy with the worldwide metric system, known as the International System (SI). Learn to convert other measurement units to metric. Practice converting to metric when you cook, sew, and build things.
Ask Your Math or Science Teacher for Special Help	There may be times when you miss a lesson that provides important information or helps you with a particular skill. Get help as soon as you need it so you can keep up and continue to learn.
Work With a Buddy	Improve your skills with a friend. Work together. If you are good in English and your friend is good in math or science, trade your knowledge. If you can't find a close friend who is interested, ask someone else to tutor you.

Learn a New Way Don't let fear of math or science stand between you and your career goals. Try these suggestions for improving your math and science skills. *What other methods work for you?*

Right now, you may not know exactly what you will be doing in the future. There's one thing you can count on, though. No matter where you work, you will use some type of computer technology in your job. Computer technology skills are as basic to work today as speaking, listening, reading, writing, math, and science.

Building Technology Skills

If you haven't spent much time using a computer, it's not too late to start. Begin building your technology skills now.

Learning to use different kinds of software is one basic computer skill. Software is a computer program or set of instructions for doing a particular kind of work on the computer. Most computer software is "user-friendly." That means it is designed to help you make computers work for you even if you know little about them.

Creative Documents
With desktop publishing software, you can create professional looking documents. *How could you use this kind of software in school? How could you use it in the workplace?*

There are different kinds of software you'll want to learn. You can use word-processing software to write letters, reports, and other documents. Word-processing software also allows you to edit what you have written quickly and easily. You can add, move, and delete letters, sentences, paragraphs, even a series of pages. Database software can be especially useful in school and later on the job. As you recall from Chapter 6, a database is a way of organizing and storing information on a computer. Databases are easy to search. Database software has many uses in business. A store owner might use a database program to track sales, items in stock, or customers.

Make a Database

Try This Activity

Try making your own database—of your CDs or books or your favorite sports figures or movies. Ask a teacher or other adult who enjoys working with computers to help you. When you've got your database up and running, share it with a friend. Ask your friend to ask you questions about your collection. Search your database to find the answers.

You can also use spreadsheets to view and work with information. A **spreadsheet** is a software program that arranges information, usually numbers, in rows and columns. Spreadsheet software can also display information in graphs and other formats. Many people and businesses use spreadsheets to keep track of schedules and of money coming in and going out. Perhaps you have a summer job. You want to know how much money you might be able to save over the summer. You could insert information in a spreadsheet about what you will earn and spend each month. Then you could use the spreadsheet program to predict how much money you'll have available for savings.

Microsoft Excel

Monthly Home Budget 1 [Read-Only]

Monthly Home Budget 1			
Expenses			
Withholdings	**Actual**	**Budgeted**	**Over/Under**
Federal income tax	175.00	175.00	at budget
State income tax	33.00	30.00	3.00 over
FICA	288.88	288.88	at budget
Medical	100.00	100.00	at budget
Dental	125.00	50.00	75.00 over
Total withholdings	**719.88**	**641.88**	**78.00 over**
Finance Payments	**Actual**	**Budgeted**	**Over/Under**
Credit card	77.50	50.00	27.50 over
Student loan	125.00	125.00	at budget
Auto loan	275.00	275.00	at budget
Home mortgage	1,240.00	1,240.00	at budget
Total finance payments	**1,717.50**	**1,690.00**	**27.50 over**
Fixed Expenses	**Actual**	**Budgeted**	**Over/Under**
Property taxes	65.00	65.00	at budget
Charitable donations			at budget
Auto insurance	125.00	125.00	at budget
Home insurance	125.00	100.00	25.00 over
Medical insurance			at budget
Cable TV	50.00	25.00	25.00 over
Telephone	66.98	50.00	16.98 over
Utilities	125.10	150.00	24.90 under
Total fixed expenses	**557.08**	**515.00**	**42.08 over**

Monthly Home Budget 1 / Sheet2 / Sheet3

Facts and Figures

Each box on a spreadsheet is called a cell. Changing a number in one cell automatically causes adjustments in other cells. *How might this be useful for making up or changing a project schedule?*

Being a Good Cyberspace Citizen

Like most people your age, you probably use the Internet. You may do research, visit favorite sites, e-mail friends, and buy products online. You're a citizen of cyberspace—the huge online world.

Like you, businesses use the Internet to buy and sell goods, find information, and communicate by e-mail. Businesses also use the Internet to save time and money. They e-mail documents and images, advertise and sell products, and provide information for customers. They post job openings and locate job applicants. Some companies even conduct job interviews on the Internet.

Whatever their reasons for going online, serious Internet users practice netiquette. **Netiquette** is a term for the accepted rules of conduct used on the Internet. Here are some basic rules of netiquette:

- Always complete the subject line on an e-mail so the receiver can identify the subject quickly.
- When responding, state to what you are responding, or copy the original message into your e-mail. Never just say yes or no.

Career Opportunities

Human Services

If you enjoy helping people, a career in human services may be for you. Jobs in this cluster range from child care workers to psychologists to massage therapists. What they have in common is making people's lives better.

Critical Thinking

What skills do you think would be most important for a family counselor? Why?

FAMILY COUNSELOR

Social services agency seeks counselor to help families resolve conflicts. Experience preferred, but will consider recent graduate with psychology or related degree. Master's degree a plus. Candidate must be caring and know how to lead discussions.

- Don't type in all capital letters. All capitals means you are screaming.
- Don't ramble. Internet users appreciate specific, focused messages.
- Use a definite close for your message.
- Avoid personal or sensitive issues. Never use obscene language. Do not make insulting remarks about people.

It's also important to pay close attention to security issues when using the Internet. **Figure 10.5** explains one security system that businesses use to protect their computer systems. There are some simple things you can do too. Be aware that e-mails with attachments can contain viruses, or programs that destroy computer files. You should never open or forward an e-mail file attachment from someone you don't know. It's also good practice to keep your Internet passwords private. If passwords fall into the wrong hands, computer information can be stolen.

Observing netiquette and security rules is an important part of being a good citizen—in cyberspace or anywhere else.

Figure 10.5

COMPUTER FIREWALLS

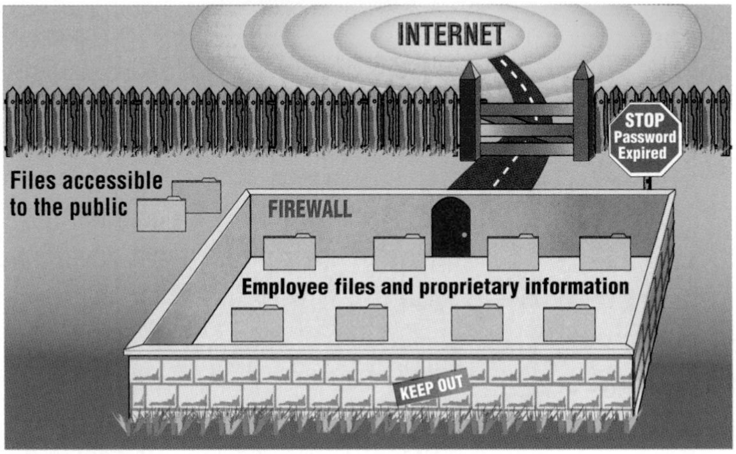

Firewalls Protect A firewall is hardware or software that restricts access to a business's internal network via the Internet. *Why would a company want to have a digital checkpoint at which incoming and outgoing data is checked to make sure that it is acceptable?*

Lesson 10.2 Review and Activities

Key Terms Review

1. Imagine that you are the teacher. Create a test to determine whether students have learned the key terms in the chapter. Write a series of questions—true/false, multiple choice, or fill-in-the-blank—to test students' knowledge of the key terms. Trade tests with another student and see if you can answer his or her questions.
   - **mathematics**
   - **science**
   - **spreadsheet**
   - **netiquette**

Check Your Understanding

Tell whether each statement is true or false. Rewrite any false statement to make it true. Write your answers on a separate sheet of paper.

2. Most careers today call for math, science, and computer technology skills.
3. E-mail messages should be typed in all capital letters.
4. Spreadsheets allow you to manipulate numbers and do calculations quickly and easily.

Critical Thinking

Use complete sentences to answer the following questions. Write your answers on a separate sheet of paper.

5. How does science teach people to think?
6. Why are computer skills considered basic skills?

Character Building

7. **E-mailing at Work** Evan just opened a chain joke e-mail on his home computer. It is about a sensitive topic. The e-mail says to forward the joke to five friends. Evan thinks his coworkers would get a good laugh from it and wouldn't be offended. Evan decides to forward the message to his friends at work. Write Evan a message explaining the problems that could result from forwarding the e-mail.

Community Involvement

8. **Participate in an Online Community** Many people connect online with others in their professional community by participating in e-mail discussion groups, chat rooms, or news groups. Think of a career that interests you. Use the Internet to find an online community for professionals in this field. E-mail or send a message to this group asking about jobs in the field. Follow the rules of netiquette.

Investigating Career Clusters

HUMAN SERVICES

Human Services • Services that improve people's quality of life and promote safe, healthy communities

Job Title	Work Description
Adoption Coordinator	Helps people adopt children
Child Care Worker	Takes care of children, either in a day care center, after school program, or in a home
Consumer Advocate	Protects consumers' rights by ensuring safe goods and services at fair prices
Cosmetologist	Shampoos, cuts, colors, chemically treats, and styles hair; gives manicures, pedicures, and facials; applies makeup
Counselor	Helps people handle personal problems
Health Care Social Worker	Helps patients by arranging aftercare, advocating patient rights, and providing counseling
Psychologist	Diagnoses and treats mental and emotional disorders
Substance Abuse Counselor	Helps patients and families deal with substance abuse and the problems it causes
Wedding Consultant	Helps couples plan weddings

Exploration Activity

Human Services Use library and Internet resources to research a career in the Human Services career cluster. Write a report on your findings. Include information about the kinds of work, the skills required, the working conditions, the training and education required, and the career outlook.

Cooperative Learning Interview a classmate about the career he or she researched. Find out as much information about that career as you can during the interview. Then have your classmate interview you about the career you researched. Afterward, share what you learned with the class.

Chapter 10 Review and Activities

Chapter Highlights

Lesson 10.1 Communication skills—speaking, listening, reading, writing, and using images—help you get information and share ideas.

Lesson 10.2 Math, science, and computer technology skills are basic skills for today's workplace.

Key Concept Review

Use complete sentences to answer the following questions. Write your answers on a separate sheet of paper.

1. How does it help to know your purpose, audience, and subject when speaking?
2. What two reading skills would you use if you needed to read a lot of material?
3. What thinking skills do math and science teach you?
4. Why is netiquette important?

Critical Thinking

Use complete sentences to answer the following questions. Write your answers on a separate sheet of paper.

5. Why are speaking, listening, reading, and writing called basic skills?
6. How can you practice active listening on the telephone?
7. What can you learn by practicing math without a calculator?
8. What do you think is one of the most important business uses of the Internet? Explain your answer.

Skill Building

9. **Information—Interprets and Communicates Information**
   Team up with a partner. Choose an article from today's newspaper and summarize the main point of the article in two or more sentences. Read the sentences to your partner. Then ask your partner to repeat back what he or she heard. Evaluate whether your partner understood your main point. Then discuss how you can improve your communication skills.
10. **Technology—Selects Technology**
    Create a chart that compares two brands of word-processing, database, or spreadsheet software. Research the software at the library and online. On a chart, list the

strengths and weaknesses of each brand.

Academic Applications

11. Social Studies

Ron is a truck driver for a moving company in your state. As his supervisor, you need to give him written directions for his next assignment. Using a state map, plan a route that begins at one point in the state and ends at another point. Write the directions on a sheet of paper. Map Ron's route on a road map of your state.

12. Computer Science

Create content for a Web page on a science topic of interest to you. Research the topic and collect images that illustrate it. Write text for the Web page. Compile a list of links to other Web sites that tell more about your topic.

Personal Career Portfolio

Interview Questions and Answers

- **List** 20 questions that you might be asked in an interview.
- **Decide** in advance what information and skills are pertinent to the career you are interested in so that you can reveal your strengths through your answers.
- **Compose** answers to each question. The answers should relate your experiences to the job, clearly articulate why you are the best person for the job, convey maturity, and avoid being too familiar.
- **Title** the document *Interview Questions and Answers* and file it in your Personal Career Portfolio.
- **Practice** speaking your answers with poise and assurance.
- **Revise** your *Interview Questions and Answers* as you gain new interests, aptitudes, skills, and experiences or as you choose new career pursuits.
- **List** your portfolio entry on your Personal Career Portfolio contents page.

Chapter 11

Staying Healthy and Safe

Lesson 11.1

It's Your Health

Lesson 11.2

Make Safety Your Business

CAREER CLUSTER

You will explore careers in the Information Technology career cluster.

What You'll Learn

- You will learn how to make healthful choices.
- You will discover how to handle stress.
- You will find out how to stay safe and deal with emergencies.

Get Ready!

Set Healthy Goals

Take an inventory of a friend's or family member's healthy habits. Ask this person to list the things he or she does in each of these areas to stay healthy: diet, exercise, and rest. Then take the inventory yourself.

Apply Review the inventory with a family member or friend. In which area could you both have more healthy habits? Together practice one new healthy habit for one week. Then discuss how you feel.

Lesson 11.1

It's Your Health

Discover

- What it takes to be healthy
- What stress is and how you can deal with it

Why It's Important

When you are healthy, you are able to do what you need and want to do. Good health is a solid foundation for success in all areas of your life, including a future career.

KEY TERMS

- health
- nutrients
- Food Guide Pyramid
- sedentary
- hygiene
- eating disorder
- addiction
- stress

Think about those you love most. That might include your brothers and sisters, your parents, other family members, your dog or cat, your best friend. Think about how much they mean to you. Imagine what you would do to keep them healthy and safe.

Now imagine having that same deep feeling of caring for yourself. Think of yourself as your own best friend.

Making Healthful Choices

When you care *about* yourself, you take care *of* yourself. Adult family members do their best to keep you healthy and safe while you are growing up. As you get older, however, you're expected to take responsibility for yourself. Making healthful choices is part of taking care of yourself. **Health** is the condition of both your body and your mind.

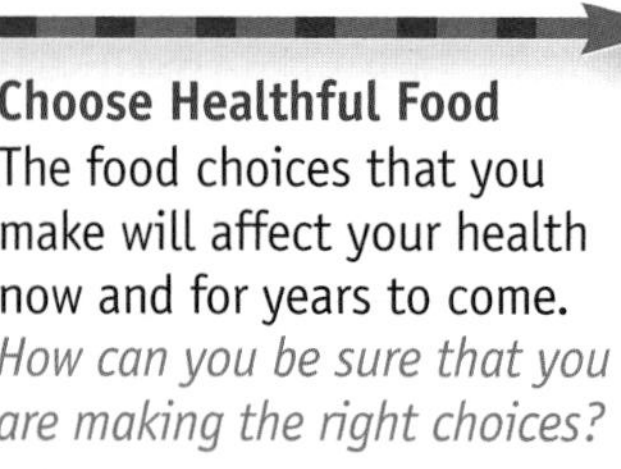

Choose Healthful Food The food choices that you make will affect your health now and for years to come. *How can you be sure that you are making the right choices?*

When you're healthy, you have the physical and mental energy you need to do things. This energy comes from eating wisely, getting exercise and rest, and guarding against sickness and harmful habits or behaviors.

Healthful Eating

Do you forget to eat because you're busy? When you're thirsty or hungry, do you reach for a soft drink or french fries?

If you answered yes to any of these questions, you may not be eating enough. In addition, what you are eating may not contain enough nutrients. **Nutrients** are the substances in food that the body needs to produce energy and stay healthy. The U.S. Department of Agriculture created the **Food Guide Pyramid** as a guideline for the nutrients you need each day. **Figure 11.1** shows how foods are grouped on the pyramid according to the nutrients they provide.

Figure 11.1

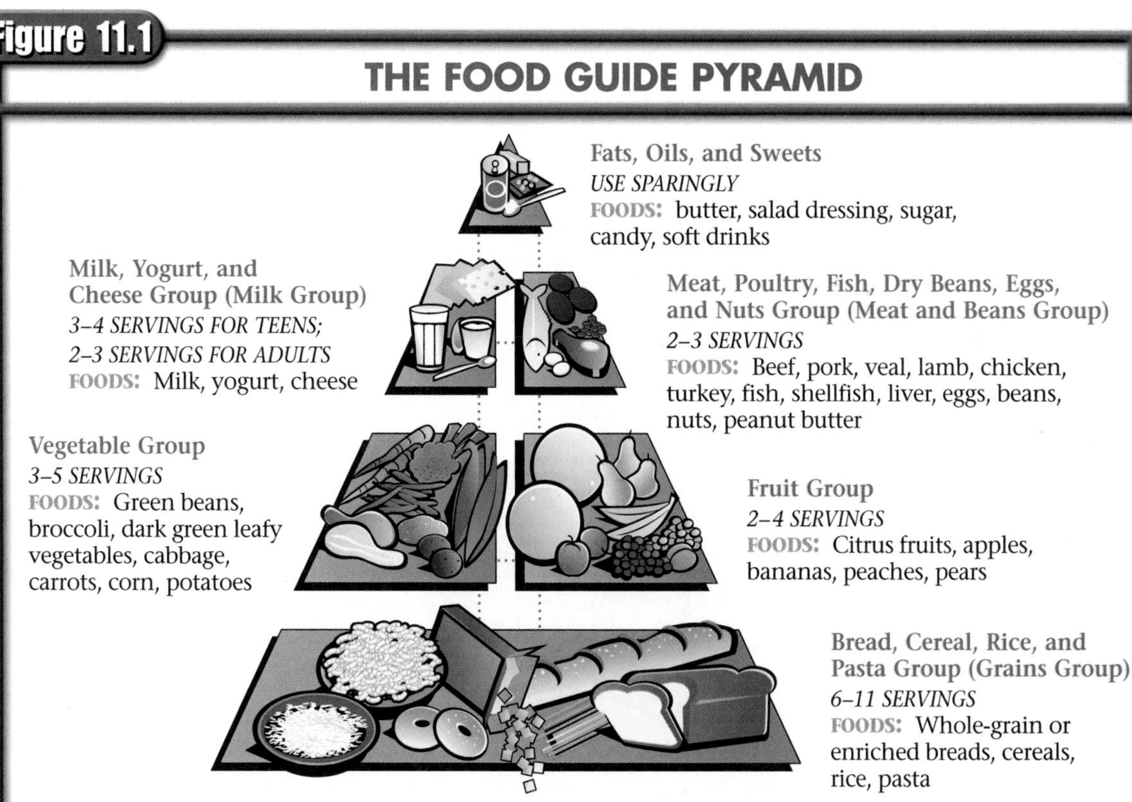

Important Nutrients Foods are grouped according to the nutrients they provide. This pyramid shows you how many daily servings you need from each food group. *Why does the Food Guide Pyramid recommend few or no servings of fats, oils, and sweets?*

Building good eating habits now will help you throughout your life. You can start to eat wisely by getting the number of servings of each food group suggested in the Food Guide Pyramid.

Here are some healthful eating suggestions from people your age:

- "Make a breakfast smoothie with milk or yogurt, your favorite fruit, and honey." (Daniel, age 13)
- "Buy veggies like tiny carrots for snacks." (Josie, age 15)
- "Have milk at mealtimes. Between meals, drink as much water as you can." (Mila, age 12)
- "Volunteer to make dinner once a week. Try new recipes. Have fun putting a meal together." (Patrick, age 14)

Exercise for Life

How do you feel when you exercise or play your favorite sport? Your heart races. You breathe harder. When the routine, run, or game is over, you're still raring to go. You're pumped.

Exercise takes energy, but it also gives it back. It helps you feel better physically, mentally, and emotionally. How? Exercise builds strength and endurance. It makes you more alert. It also helps you feel less tense and anxious about things.

Employers find that employees who exercise regularly do better work. They don't get sick as often as other employees do. Exercise is especially important if you have a **sedentary** job—one in which you spend much of your time sitting.

Get Active, Have Fun
Exercise can be a way to have fun with your friends. *What activities do you and your friends enjoy?*

Warm Up
Exercising for 20 minutes three times a week can do wonders for your health. *Why would making exercise a daily part of your life now pay off in the future?*

People often complain that they don't have time to exercise. The truth is, you don't need that much time. Exercising for 20 minutes three times a week can do wonders for your health.

Finding the time to exercise may not be a problem for you right now. The hard part may be choosing what to do. What do you like? Aerobics? Dancing? Basketball? Running? Whatever form of exercise you choose, make sure it's something you enjoy. Exercise should be fun, not a chore.

One last tip. Make exercise a regular part of your life now. Then you'll always make time for it. Exercise will be a natural part of your day or week, no matter how busy you are.

Time for Sleep

Perhaps your life is already quite busy. Your daily schedule may be something like Olivia Hartwell's.

After school twice a week, Olivia plays soccer. On the other days, she might go to a friend's house or have a friend over. If not, she talks on the phone with friends. In the evening, Olivia feeds and walks her dog. She also helps clean up after dinner. Then there's homework—about two hours a night. If she has any time left over, Olivia reads or watches some television.

Attitude Counts

Accepting Criticism

Learning new skills sometimes means accepting constructive criticism. If a teacher or supervisor offers constructive criticism, she or he is trying to help you learn. Remember, it's about the work, not about you! Helpful tips can strengthen your skills and teach you how to do your job more effectively.

Cooperative Learning Activity

- In small groups, share examples of comments you've received about a school project or a performance in a sport or hobby.
- Discuss how these comments helped you improve.

Set Your Alarm
It's a good idea to get up around the same time each day. *How much sleep do you get each night on average?*

Olivia is usually asleep by eleven o'clock. She is supposed to be up by seven. Frequently, though, she sleeps later than seven. When she leaves for school, she still feels sleepy.

Sleep restores the body and recharges the brain. It is also an important part of the growing process. Most people need at least eight hours of sleep a night. While you're still growing, you may need even more. If you're feeling sleepy like Olivia, your body's telling you that you need more sleep.

Without enough sleep, it can be difficult to think and concentrate. You're more likely to make careless errors. When you don't get the sleep you need, your performance can suffer. You don't want that to happen in the classroom now. You won't want it to happen later on the job.

Give yourself the rest you need to do your best. Try to go to bed about the same time each night. Also avoid foods and drinks that contain caffeine, such as chocolate and some soft drinks. You'll be better rested for your busy day ahead.

Remember, one of your best resources is exploring.glencoe.com

Protecting Your Health

Eating a balanced diet and getting the right amounts of exercise and rest are important. There's more to staying healthy, though. You need to protect your health. One obvious way to protect your health is to get regular medical checkups. It is also important to practice good hygiene and guard against eating disorders and addictions.

Hygiene is all the things you do to be clean and healthy. It includes brushing and flossing your teeth and taking regular baths or showers. It also includes washing your hands throughout the day, washing and grooming your hair and nails, and wearing clean clothes.

An **eating disorder** is a pattern of extreme eating behavior over time. When you have an eating disorder, you may eat too much or too little. You may have unrealistic ideas about how your body should look. If you think you might have an eating problem, ask a family member, teacher, school nurse, or doctor for help. Eating disorders can lead to serious illness or death.

The Right Size for You
You can't compare your own best weight with that of your friends. There are differences among people of the same age. *How can you find out what weight is right for you?*

Guard against addiction. **Addiction** is a physical or psychological need for a substance. Substances that can lead to addiction include tobacco, alcohol, prescription drugs, and illegal substances such as marijuana, cocaine, and heroin. Addiction can cause depression, heart attacks, lung or liver disease, and even death. Addiction affects every part of your life, including your relationships and your work at school or on the job. If you think you may have a problem with an addictive substance, talk to someone about it. Ask for help. Addiction is a serious health risk, but recovery is possible. Support groups help many people who are recovering from addiction.

Handling Stress

It's test day. You didn't sleep well last night. You couldn't eat much this morning. Your heart's pounding. Your palms feel sweaty. You can't concentrate. What's going on? You are experiencing stress. **Stress** is the mental or physical tension that is the body's natural response to conflict.

Good Stress, Bad Stress

Stress isn't always a bad thing. Runners may feel stress before a big race. Many musicians feel stress before a concert. Actors often feel it before performances. You may feel stress the first day of high school or before a job interview.

The kind of stress you feel before or during a big event tells you that what you are doing is important to you. You are excited and focused on what's happening. You want to be and do your best. At such times, stress can actually help you do a good job or get through an event. When the challenge is over, your body returns to normal. The stress goes away.

Sometimes, though, stress stays with you. You may be generally worried or fearful. You may simply feel tired a lot of the time. You may be distracted. You may have headaches or stomachaches. You may not feel like eating, or you may eat a lot. You may not be able to sleep, or you may want to sleep all the time. This kind of stress can wear you out.

You can feel stress anywhere—at home, in the classroom, or on the soccer field. Once you enter the work world, you'll feel stress there too. To perform well—wherever you are—you must learn how to handle stress.

Ways to Cope

What can you do about stress, especially bad stress? Here's what health experts recommend. First, try to identify the cause of the stress. Then deal with the problem directly. **Figure 11.2** shows some situations or problems that can cause stress. It also offers ideas for dealing with the stress.

Normal Stress
Some positive situations can be stressful. *Would you feel stress in this situation? Why or why not?*

Figure 11.2

COPING WITH STRESS

<table>
<tr><th>Causes</th><th>Ways to Cope</th></tr>
<tr><td>Major changes, such as marriage, divorce, moving, going to a new school, starting a new job, losing a job, or the serious illness or death of a family member</td><td>• Be patient. Give yourself plenty of time to adapt to the change.
• Try to limit changes in other areas of your life.
• Especially in the case of illness or death in the family, let someone at school or work know. Ask for lighter responsibilities (less homework or less demanding assignments at work) for a time. Most people understand and honor such requests.
• Gather a support system. Talk about what you are going through with someone. Friends, family members, and other people who care about you can provide insight and encouragement. Seek professional help from a counselor if necessary.</td></tr>
<tr><td>Conflicts or disagreements at home, school, or work</td><td>• Talk the problem out with a trusted friend, coworker, or supervisor.
• Look for common ground with the other person. Use your conflict resolution skills.
• Consider getting someone to mediate—to listen to what both sides have to say.</td></tr>
<tr><td>Too many things to do, too little time to do them</td><td>• Keep track of how you use your time. What can you change to make your life less stressful?
• Set realistic goals. You don't have to be a superhero—someone who does everything.
• Review your workload with a teacher, coworker, or supervisor. Get help handling your work.
• Set priorities, and then take them one step at a time.
• Make a schedule. Don't forget to include time for eating, sleeping, exercise, and relaxing. These activities will give you energy to do what you need and want to do.</td></tr>
</table>

Pay Attention Stress is a good alarm system—if you're paying attention. It often tells you that you need to take action or make a change. *What do you need to do before you can deal with stress?*

Relaxation techniques, or ways of relaxing, are also helpful in stressful situations. Here are several that many people use:

- ***Breathe deeply.*** Slowly fill your lungs with air. Count to 10 as you fill your lungs. Hold your breath, then slowly release, again to a count of 10. Repeat as needed.
- ***Visualize.*** Close your eyes. Picture yourself in a peaceful place, away from the stressful situation. The place might be a forest, the beach, a park—wherever you feel calm. What do you feel, smell, and hear there?
- ***Take a time-out.*** Get away from the stressful situation for a while. Take a walk. Give yourself time to calm down. You may see solutions you didn't see before.
- ***Vent.*** Share your feelings with a friend, family member, or other person you trust. Ask the person just to listen. Then try brainstorming solutions together.

There's no getting around it. Stress is a natural part of life. Why wait to do something about it? Try out what you've learned about handling stress right now at home and at school. You can use the same techniques later to manage stress on the job and in other parts of your life. Knowing how to manage stress is a life skill. It will help you stay healthy.

Career Opportunities

Information Technology

If you're the one people turn to when they have a computer problem, you might consider a career in information technology. This career cluster offers exciting opportunities for detail-oriented people.

Critical Thinking

Why should a help desk technician have excellent communication skills?

HELP DESK TECHNICIAN

Computer software firm seeks technician to assist customers on our help line. Must be patient, able to follow directions, and have excellent communication skills. Bachelor's degree in computer science required. Programming experience a plus.

Lesson 11.1 Review and Activities

Key Terms Review

1. Imagine you write articles for your company newsletter. Write a short article on tips for healthful living. Include the terms below.
   - **health**
   - **nutrients**
   - **Food Guide Pyramid**
   - **sedentary**
   - **hygiene**
   - **eating disorder**
   - **addiction**
   - **stress**

Check Your Understanding

Choose the correct answer for each item. Write your answers on a separate sheet of paper.

2. To be healthy, you need to ______.
   - **a.** exercise two hours every day
   - **b.** eat wisely, get exercise, and rest
   - **c.** skip meals
3. One way to manage stress is to ______.
   - **a.** put in more hours at work
   - **b.** eat more often
   - **c.** use relaxation techniques
4. If you exercise regularly now, you ______.
   - **a.** won't have to exercise when you're older
   - **b.** will always make time for it
   - **c.** will not get enough rest

Critical Thinking

Use complete sentences to answer the following questions. Write your answers on a separate sheet of paper.

5. Which area or areas of your health do you need to improve? What will you do?
6. What methods do you use to deal with stress at school?

Connecting to the Workplace

7. **Wellness Programs** Employers know that healthy employees are more productive. Many employers offer wellness programs to help keep their employees healthy. Wellness programs might include exercise classes, stress management classes, and weight loss classes. Do some research online or at the library on exercise. Identify three forms of exercise employees might do as part of a wellness program at the workplace.

Teamwork

8. **Create Catchy Signs** Team up with a group of classmates. Make a list of several tips for staying healthy. Think of a short and catchy way you could word each of these tips. For example, "Get your rest to do your best!" Then make an attention-grabbing sign for each catchy tip, one tip per sign. Post the signs in your school where students will see them.

Lesson 11.2

Make Safety Your Business

Discover

- What you can do to stay safe and prevent accidents
- How the government, employers, and employees make the workplace safe
- How to respond to an emergency

Why It's Important

Following safety measures can prevent injuries. That means fewer accidents at home, school, and work, and more time and energy for other activities.

KEY TERMS

- **Occupational Safety and Health Administration (OSHA)**
- **workers' compensation**
- **emergency**
- **first aid**

Accidents happen. Everyone knows that. What you might not know is that most accidents can be prevented. Accidents don't have to have the serious consequences, or results, that they often do. There are many ways that everyone can help prevent accidents.

Taking and Sharing Responsibility

Play it safe. That's good advice at home, at school, in the workplace—wherever people are active. When you practice safety, you protect yourself and others from harm or danger.

Many people are concerned about your safety and are there when you need help. Family members, teachers, and police are just a few of the people who are looking out for you. That's comforting to know. Even so, you can't always rely on others. It's a good idea to learn to look out for yourself. You need to make safety *your* business.

Prevent Accidents
By following the rules and avoiding unnecessary risks, you can prevent most accidents from happening. *What is this boy doing to stay safe?*

The Global Workplace

Don't Whistle While You Work

Your team just scored the winning point! The stadium erupts in shouts, cheers, and . . . whistles? Maybe in the United States, but in other countries whistling would be rude.

While whistling is a sign of appreciation or approval at U.S. sporting events or concerts, it is a symbol of disrespect in other countries. In Europe, whistling is the same as booing or jeering. In fact, in Russia whistling is not only rude, it's also considered unlucky.

Before you head out on your next trip, learn which behaviors are appropriate and which are not in the country you'll visit. It'll help you fit in and make new friends.

Internet Activity

Use the Internet and library resources to research the traditions and superstitions of one other country. What gestures or things do people in this country consider lucky or unlucky? Go to the *Exploring Careers* Web site at exploring.glencoe.com for a list of Web sites to help you complete this activity.

Safety Rules

You probably already take many steps to be safe. Think about the rules of the road that you follow, for example. As a pedestrian, or person traveling on foot, you pay attention to what drivers and others on the road are doing. You walk on sidewalks and not in the street, and you always cross the street at crosswalks or intersections. When you cross the street, you look out for vehicles turning right on a red light. When riding in a car, you always wear a seat belt whether you're seated in the front or back.

Before you get a driver's license, you'll need to learn how to operate a car safely. To do that, you will study a manual and take a class. You will practice on the road with someone who knows how to drive. Then you will take a road test and a written test on basic road safety rules.

Try This Activity

Write the Rules

With a partner, make a chart of rules you follow daily. Write at least five rules in one column. In a second column, write what you believe is the reason for each rule.

Rules Promote Safety! Which rules listed help keep you safe? How do they keep you safe?

Reducing Risk

Following rules is one part of safety. Avoiding unnecessary risks is another. Many activities involve some chance of harm.

You may enjoy outdoor activities like swimming, boating, hiking, camping, skiing, snowboarding, or skateboarding. You may also enjoy at-home activities, such as cooking, sewing, working on cars, and making or building things.

These and other activities you may enjoy are supposed to be fun. You don't want to get hurt doing them. Here are three safety tips for any activity:

- ***Respect your limits.*** Know how much you are really capable of doing. Pushing yourself beyond your training and ability is taking an unnecessary risk.
- ***Think before you act.*** Ask yourself: Is this situation safe? What are the risks involved? How can I protect myself?
- ***Don't give in to pressure from others.*** Don't let others push you into doing what you know or sense is not safe.

Think First
Remember, to be safe, you need to look out for yourself. *What should you do if someone suggests you do something that you know is not safe?*

Working With Others for Safety

It is said that there is safety in numbers. In other words, it is often safer to be with others than it is to be alone. That doesn't mean you shouldn't learn how to look out for yourself. It means that when people get together, they can be even safer than they would be individually.

Protect Yourself People in different jobs take different kinds of safety precautions. *How is this worker protected on the job?*

Just think of your own community. You probably already take steps there to protect yourself. For instance, you don't talk to strangers. You always let someone know where you'll be. You keep alert on the streets—especially at night. You also stay away from dangerous and poorly lit areas.

You can also take steps to make your community safe by working with others. You can work with your family and neighbors. Set up a Neighborhood Watch group. Neighborhood Watch members look after one another and one another's homes. They are trained by the police to identify and report suspicious activities. As members of a Neighborhood Watch group, neighbors and families share responsibility for community safety.

Safety on the Job

It's no different in the workplace than it is in your community. In the workplace, the government, employers, and employees team up for safety. They cooperate to create a safe working environment.

The Government's Role

The U.S. government protects workers by setting safety standards, or guidelines. It also makes sure injured workers receive care. A special branch of the U.S. Department of Labor, the **Occupational Safety and Health Administration (OSHA)**, is in charge of setting safety standards. It also inspects workplaces to make sure that the standards are being followed.

Be Calm and Prepared

Q: I panic in emergencies. I can't help it! How can I stay calm and provide help?

A: If you're prepared for emergencies, chances are you'll stay calm and know how to help. There are many ways to prepare for all kinds of emergencies before they happen. Participate in safety training programs at your school or work. Learn the correct way to use a fire extinguisher. Take a first aid class at your local American Red Cross chapter. Prepare a disaster supply kit for your family. Put one together for your pets, too.

Workers' compensation laws passed by the government protect workers who are hurt on the job. Under **workers' compensation,** injured workers receive financial help to cover both lost wages and medical expenses.

Employers and Employees: Partners for Safety

Of course, employers and employees must do their part for safety. It's up to employers to provide a workplace that is free of health and accident hazards, or dangers. The equipment and materials workers use must be safe. If work conditions are unsafe, employers must tell their employees.

Employers must also take the time to teach workers how to use equipment and materials. Training prevents all kinds of accidents. Workplace accidents are very costly. American businesses spend billions of dollars a year on lost wages, medical expenses, and insurance claims.

When you enter the work world, you will take on new responsibilities. One of those responsibilities will be your own safety on the job. You may operate a piece of heavy equipment or work at a keyboard. Whatever you do, you will have health and safety concerns to consider. You will need to follow safety rules. When you notice unsafe conditions or practices, you will need to report them right away. Safety will continue to be your business, as it is now.

In Case of Emergency

No matter how careful people are, accidents happen. Would you know what to do in case of an emergency?

Is It an Emergency?

An **emergency** is something serious that happens without warning and calls for quick action. Some emergencies are more obvious than others.

Unusual noises, sights, odors, or behavior can be signs of an emergency. You might hear crying, moaning, or a call for help, for instance. Alarming sounds such as breaking glass, screeching brakes, or crushing metal can also signal an emergency. You may see sparks, smoke, or fire or find someone lying on the ground. The smell of gasoline, smoke, or some other strong odor can also alert you to an emergency. A person who does not look well or who is breathing or speaking with difficulty may need immediate help.

Once you've identified an emergency, you need to evaluate the scene. Before doing anything, figure out what has already happened. Think about what may happen next. Consider your own safety. It won't do much good to jump in the water to save someone if you can't swim. Other hazards may prevent you from offering to help someone.

Be Prepared
Be prepared to handle emergency situations. *What should you do even if you aren't sure whether someone is seriously injured?*

What to Do

If someone is injured or sick and you are nearby, stay calm. Then follow these easy-to-remember American Red Cross emergency action steps—Check-Call-Care.

- ***Check the scene and the victim.*** First check the scene to make sure it's safe for you to approach. Then check the victim for consciousness and life-threatening conditions.
- ***Call for help.*** Dial 911 or another local emergency number. Remain calm as you explain the situation to the dispatcher. If possible, stay with the victim and ask a passerby to call for help.
- ***Care for the victim.*** Stay with the person until help arrives. Do not move the victim unless the scene becomes unsafe. Help the victim rest comfortably and provide reassurance while you wait.

Knowing first aid can often save someone's life. **First aid** is the emergency care given to an injured or sick person before help arrives. First aid might be needed anywhere, at any time, and without warning. Any time first aid is needed, it's important to stay calm.

While you are caring for a victim, it helps to know your ABCs. As **Figure 11.3** below shows, the ABCs are an easy way to remember what to check and care for in an emergency.

To reduce the risk of disease transmission while checking and caring for a victim, keep these guidelines in mind: Be careful not to touch blood or other body fluids. Wear disposable gloves. Use protective breathing barriers when giving rescue breathing. Wash your hands and any area of your skin that comes in contact with the victim with soap and warm water immediately after giving care.

Figure 11.3

KNOW YOUR ABCs IN AN EMERGENCY

The ABC guidelines help you remember priorities, or what to do first, while caring for a victim in an emergency. *Where might you learn more about these first aid methods?*

A

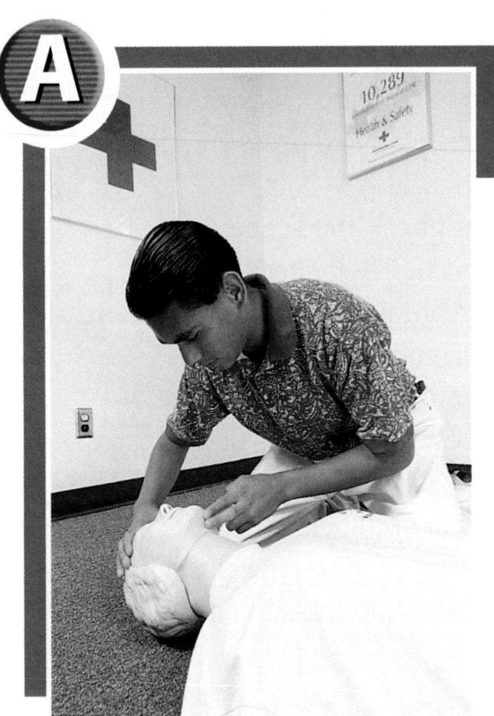

Airway

If necessary, clear the victim's airway (the passage that allows the person to breathe). Do this by placing one hand on the person's forehead. At the same time, place two fingers of the other hand under the person's chin. Tilt the head back by pushing on the forehead and lifting the chin.

You never know when you might need to know first aid. Take it from Robby and Carlos. They were just standing at the mall talking when an older man sitting nearby began to have trouble breathing. While Carlos went for help, Robby sat with the man and helped him stay calm. "The emergency team said our quick thinking saved that man's life," Robby explains. "I'm glad we were there and knew what to do."

You may be glad you know what to do someday too. Safety is everybody's business.

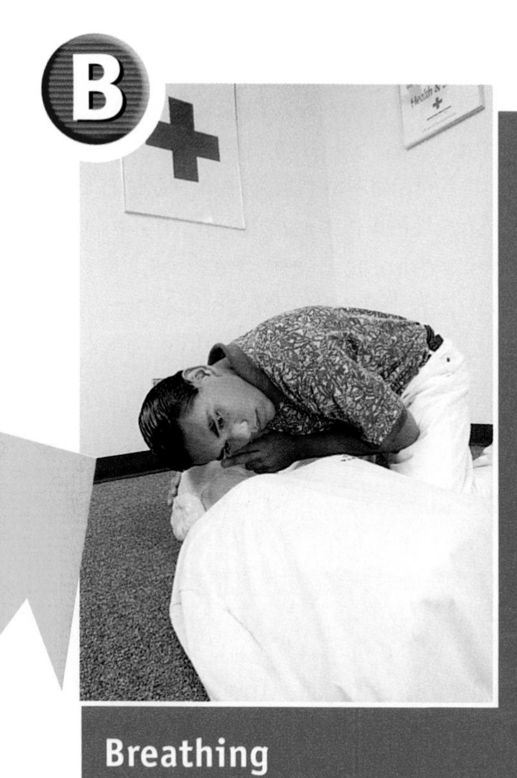

Breathing

Check to see if the victim is breathing. Watch for rising or falling of the chest. Also listen and feel for air moving out of the mouth and nose. If the person is not breathing, administer rescue breathing if you know how.

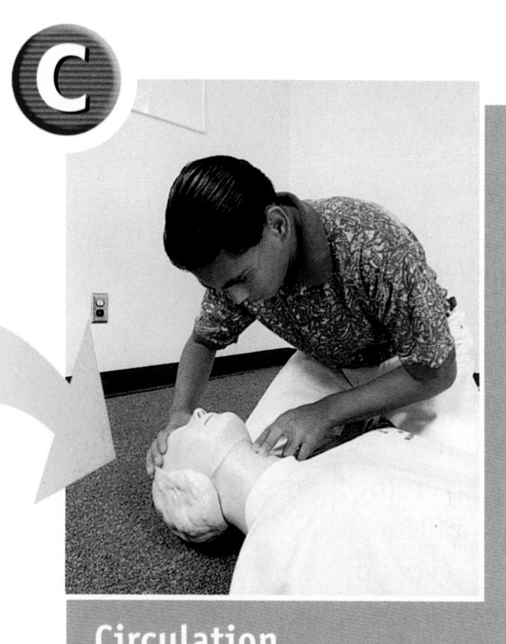

Circulation

Check the victim for signs of circulation (such as breathing, coughing, and movement) and a pulse if you know how. If there is no circulation, begin CPR if you know how. Also check to see whether the victim is bleeding severely. If so, press a clean cloth on the wound. Then hold firmly with your palm.

Lesson 11.2 Review and Activities

Key Terms Review

1. Your next assignment for the company newsletter is an article about safety on the job. In your article, tell how the government, employers, and employees cooperate to make the workplace safe. Use the terms below.
   - **Occupational Safety and Health Administration (OSHA)**
   - **workers' compensation**
   - **emergency**
   - **first aid**

Check Your Understanding

Tell whether each statement is true or false. Rewrite any false statement to make it true. Write your answers on a separate sheet of paper.

2. It is only the responsibility of the employer to create a safe work environment.
3. In the event of an emergency, first check the scene and victim, then call for help and care for the victim.

Critical Thinking

Use complete sentences to answer the following questions. Write your answers on a separate sheet of paper.

4. What precautions do you take to stay safe at home?
5. Why do you think the government sets workplace safety standards?
6. Why is it important to check the scene of an accident before acting?

Character Building

7. **Being Responsible** Jessica just started a part-time job at a fast food restaurant. Every month the restaurant offers a safety and first aid training class to all new employees. Jessica missed the class. She doesn't think it's important to take the class next month either. She feels her employers have made her workplace safe. Besides, if anything does happen, she thinks her coworkers will know how to handle the emergency. Explain to Jessica why it's important for her to take the class.

Community Involvement

8. **Create a Bulletin Board** Invite a member of your local American Red Cross chapter to talk to your class about the organization's services. Ask questions about the work the Red Cross does. Find out what kinds of classes and programs the Red Cross sponsors in your community. Ask how young people can get involved in the Red Cross. Then with others in your class, create a bulletin board display about the Red Cross.

INFORMATION TECHNOLOGY

Information Technology • The technology used to design, develop, set up, operate, and support computer systems

Job Title	Work Description
Computer Hardware Engineer	Designs and develops computer hardware
Computer Operator	Oversees the operation of large mainframe computers or groups of microcomputers
Computer Programmer	Writes, tests, and maintains computer software
Computer Scientist	Conducts research in information technology
Help Desk Technician	Assists computer users who encounter problems
Network Administrator	Installs, maintains, repairs, and upgrades computer network hardware and software
Systems Analyst	Studies how institutions process information and designs better ways of processing it
Technical Writer	Creates user guides and online help guides that tell people how to use software, hardware, and other high-technology products
Webmaster	Designs and maintains sites on the World Wide Web

Exploration Activity

Information Technology Use library and Internet resources to research a career in the Information Technology career cluster. Write a report on your findings. Include information about the kinds of work, skills required, working conditions, training and education required, and career outlook.

Cooperative Learning Interview a classmate about the career he or she researched. Find out as much information about that career as you can during the interview. Then have your classmate interview you about the career you researched. Afterward, share what you learned with the class.

Chapter 11 Review and Activities

Chapter Highlights

Lesson 11.1 To be healthy, you need to eat wisely, get exercise and rest, and guard against sickness and harmful habits or behaviors.

Lesson 11.2 Government, employers, and employees share the responsibility for creating a safe workplace.

Key Concept Review

Use complete sentences to answer the following questions. Write your answers on a separate sheet of paper.

1. What are the six groups of food in the Food Guide Pyramid?
2. What are four ways you can protect your health?
3. What is stress?
4. What is OSHA, and how does it help workers?
5. What are the Check-Call-Care emergency action steps?

Critical Thinking

Use complete sentences to answer the following questions. Write your answers on a separate sheet of paper.

6. What foods would you include in a healthful breakfast?
7. What are two ways you could get more sleep on school nights?
8. What techniques do you use to deal with stress? Why?
9. How can knowing your limits help reduce your risk?
10. How can clear thinking skills help you in an emergency situation?

Skill Building

11. **Information—Organizes and Maintains Information**
    For one week, write down what you eat each day. Then categorize your daily food choices according to the groups in the Food Guide Pyramid. From which groups do you need to eat more servings? Fewer servings? Change your daily eating habits to reflect the Pyramid's recommendations.
12. **Personal Qualities—Self-Management**
    Take a personal safety inventory. First, list safety precautions you already take. Then, make a list of ways in which you could act more safely.

Academic Applications

13. Science

Repeating the same motions throughout the workday can cause repetitive stress injuries, or RSIs. Engineers in the field of science called ergonomics are working on the problem of RSIs. Visit OSHA's Web site and use library resources to learn about ergonomics. Present your findings in an oral report.

14. Health and Physical Education

With your classmates, design a wellness program for your school. Include choices of exercise, healthful snacks, and stress-beating activities. Work with teachers, school cafeteria staff, the school nurse, and interested parents to make your wellness program a reality.

Personal Career Portfolio

Pertinent Documents

- **Gather** together the documents you will need in order to fill out a job application. These include a work permit, a photo identification card, and your Social Security number.
- **Make** copies of these documents. Don't forget to copy the back side of a document if it also contains information you will need for an application.
- **File** the copies of your documents in your portfolio.
- **Label** this section of your portfolio *Pertinent Documents.*
- **Add** new documents to this section as you receive them. For example, add a copy of your driver's license when you get it.
- **Replace** copies of documents that expire with copies of the updated documents. For example, replace the copy of last year's photo ID with a copy of this year's ID as soon as you receive the updated one.
- **List** your portfolio entry on your Personal Career Portfolio contents page.

Chapter 12

Moving Toward Your Goals

Lesson 12.1
School-to-Work Transition

Lesson 12.2
Reevaluating Your Goals

CAREER CLUSTER

You will explore careers in the Law, Public Safety, and Security career cluster.

What You'll Learn

- You will discover ways to learn and grow in everything you do, including a job.
- You will find out why it is important to reevaluate your goals.
- You will learn about changes you might make in a career plan.

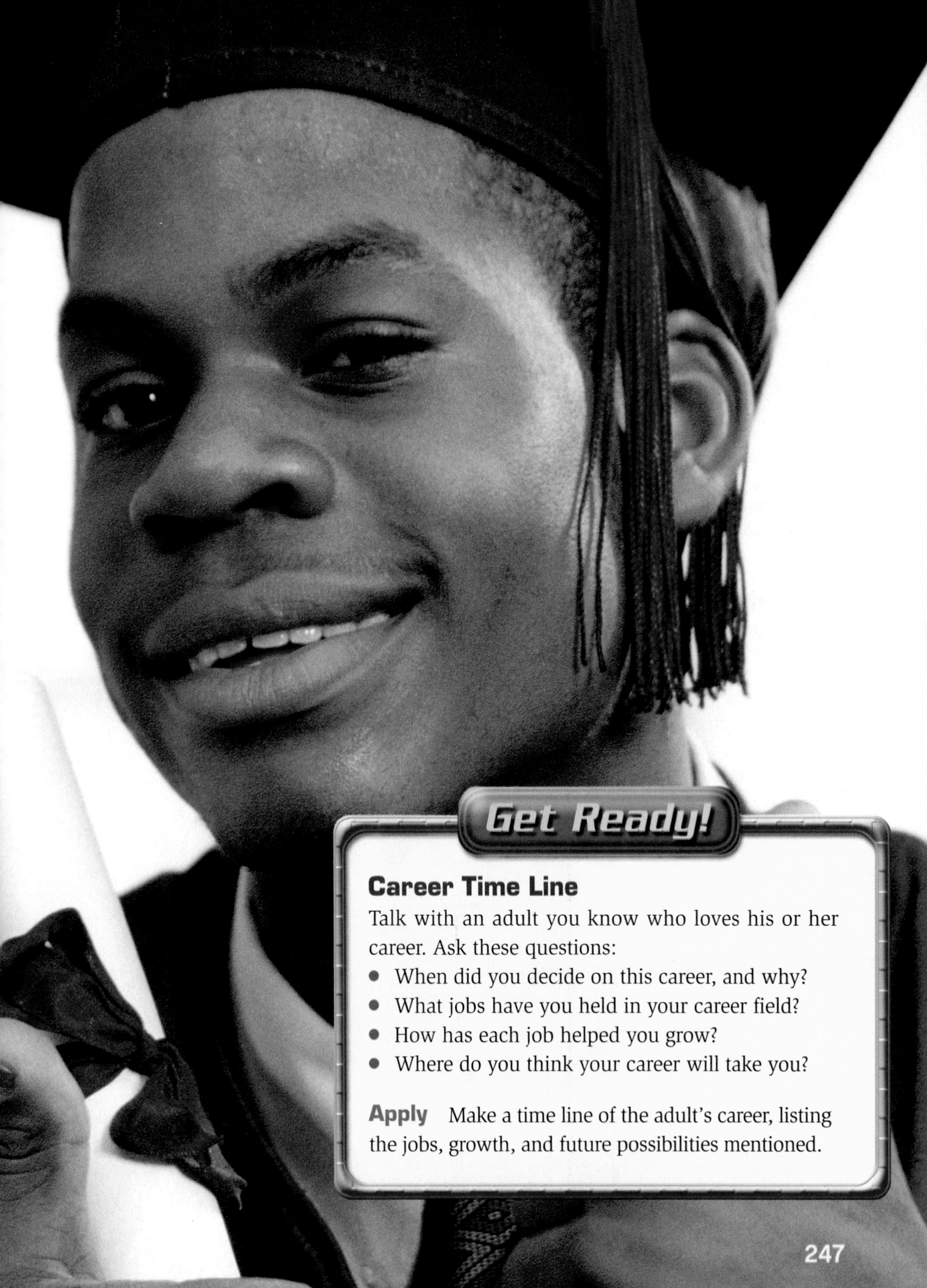

Get Ready!

Career Time Line

Talk with an adult you know who loves his or her career. Ask these questions:

- When did you decide on this career, and why?
- What jobs have you held in your career field?
- How has each job helped you grow?
- Where do you think your career will take you?

Apply Make a time line of the adult's career, listing the jobs, growth, and future possibilities mentioned.

Lesson 12.1

School-to-Work Transition

Discover

- How to get the most out of everything you do, including a job
- How to get and handle more responsibility on the job

Why It's Important

Making the most of everything you do is like making an investment in your future and your happiness.

KEY TERMS

- **promotion**
- **raise**

To make a successful transition from school to work, you need to understand and plan for your future. You have to set goals and achieve them. You're in charge of your future, and you've got a good idea of where you're going.

Getting the Most Out of All You Do

You're working hard in school and looking ahead to high school. You may have some ideas about interesting careers. Maybe you volunteer or have a part-time job. You're probably working toward a variety of goals. Are you getting the most from everything you do?

Live and Learn
There is something to learn from everything you do. What activities are you involved in right now? *What have you learned by participating in them?*

The Right Attitude

"I'm bored." "I wish I were somewhere else." Sound familiar? Everyone has thoughts like these from time to time. Many people have these thoughts at work each day. Thoughts like these can have a negative effect on what you're doing.

Usually it's not your situation—where you are, what you're doing—that triggers this kind of thinking. It's your attitude, or basic outlook on things. A change of attitude can make a huge difference in everything you do.

Try This Activity

Develop a Positive Attitude

The next time you feel bored or wish you were somewhere else, try this. Challenge yourself to find something worthwhile in what you are doing.

Open Your Mind Take your least favorite class, for instance. Go into the class with an open mind. Focus on the subject. Practice active listening. Think about what your teacher is saying. Pay attention to what your classmates have to say. Contribute to discussions.

Keep a Journal For one week, keep a journal to reflect on your new attitude. Record what happens in the class. Also record what you discover about the subject of the class, yourself, and your classmates. You may be amazed at what you learn, thanks to your new attitude.

Learn and Grow With a positive attitude, you are always ready to learn and grow. You'll find every situation inviting and interesting. Everything you do will have value. Every experience will be a step on the way toward your goals.

Always Giving Your Best

Success in school and work requires effort and a good attitude. You hear that from everyone—teachers, parents, coaches.

Giving your best is not about being the best. It is giving your best effort to something. It means sticking with it and not giving up. What you do may be something you like or don't like. You may succeed or fail. In the end, though, you have the satisfaction of knowing you gave it your all.

Giving Criticism

The way you give constructive criticism makes all the difference. When critiquing someone's work, use a calm voice. Begin by praising something about the work that is positive. Then suggest improvements. Focus on the problem and not on the person. Do not make any hurtful remarks. At its best, criticism is a helpful way for people to learn new things.

Cooperative Learning Activity
With a small group, take turns giving and receiving criticism using the following role-play situations.

- A friend asks you to review a story she wrote.
- You are asked to critique a painting in art class.
- You need to give your teammates some tips for winning a game.

Like having a positive attitude, giving your best can bring unexpected rewards. Jules Veanor knows that from experience. He did well in math, but it was not his easiest or favorite subject. Jules's math teacher suggested he take honors math in eighth grade, based on his work in seventh grade. Jules wasn't sure. He was afraid the class would be too hard.

In the end, Jules took his teacher's advice and signed up for the class. "It definitely was a challenge," Jules admits.

> "I gave it everything I had, but I got something back. I learned a lot. I improved my math skills. More than that, though, I feel more confident now about what I am able to do. I won't be afraid of a challenge next time around."

Growing on the Job

You can learn on a job just as you do in school and in other activities. Learning allows you to grow. You continue to grow in different ways throughout your life.

In the workplace, there are opportunities to learn and grow at every level. It will be up to you to look for them and take advantage of them. How will you do that? Again, it's a matter of attitude and effort.

Attitude is Susan James's secret to getting the most out of her volunteer job at a local nursing home. "I look at my job as the most important position at the nursing home," explains Susan. "Of course, there are many other people who have more responsibility than I do. I fill a real need of the residents, though. I offer them companionship and friendship. To me, that's the most important job of all, and I take it seriously."

Showing Initiative

Extra effort will also help you get the most from a job. Imagine two employees in the same job. One always does only what he is told to do. The other does what she is asked and more. She shares new ideas. She volunteers to help out when needed. She is open to suggestions. She is willing to try something new. In other words, she shows initiative. As you recall from Chapter 8, when you show initiative, you do what needs to be done without being told to do it. Which employee do you think learns and grows more on the job?

Making the Most of Any Job

Here are some suggestions for making the most of any job.

- ***Do your job as well as you can.*** That is, do your assigned work to the best of your ability.
- ***Volunteer to do more.*** When you've finished your regular duties, ask your supervisor if there is something else you can do.
- ***Look for opportunities to learn on the job.*** Learn to do new tasks that will help you move ahead in your career plan. You never know how you might use what you've learned.
- ***Get more education or training.*** Take advantage of every opportunity to further your education. The more education and training you have, the more career choices you will have. Remind yourself of the many options available for education and training by reviewing the chart on page 86 in Chapter 5. When you interview for a job, find out what kind of training the employer offers. Ask if the employer will help pay for continuing education. Once you have a job, take courses you need to get a promotion.
- ***Be willing to try new things.*** You may have a favorite way of doing something. You feel comfortable with it and see no reason to change. That doesn't mean you shouldn't try new ways to see how they work. You never know—they may work better. They may give you new ideas. If you want to grow, you need to be open to new things.

Learning Is Everywhere
You learn in many other places besides school or on a job. *What skills have you learned at home?*

Getting More Responsibility

Growth often leads to more responsibility. Think of the responsibilities and privileges you've begun to enjoy at home now that you're older. At school, you may be a leader in class, on a team, or in a club. You probably became a leader because of your attitude and the skills, knowledge, or experience you have. In high school and beyond, you will have even greater responsibility and independence.

As you grow on a job, you may be given more responsibility. You may even get a promotion. A **promotion** is a job advancement to a position of greater responsibility and authority. A volunteer, for example, might advance to a paid position. A salesperson might be promoted to supervisor of sales. Promotions offer new challenges. They also usually include a **raise,** or increase in pay.

Learn From a Mentor In some businesses, a new employee is paired with a coworker who acts as a mentor. A mentor is an informal teacher. *What do you suppose a new employee might learn from a mentor?*

How to Get a Promotion

At the end of each school year, your teachers decide whether to promote you—to the next grade. To make their decision, they review your work and grades. They think about whether you can handle work at the next grade level.

Employers take similar steps. They want to make sure that employees they promote can handle additional responsibility and authority. How do they determine this? They review their employees' performances on the job. They also look for certain qualities in employees. Some of these qualities are shown in **Figure 12.1**.

Carlos Cordona has many of these desirable qualities. They helped him get more job responsibilities and promotions.

Figure 12.1

CHECKLIST OF DESIRABLE EMPLOYEE QUALITIES AND SKILLS

- Seniority, or length of time on the job
- Knowledge and ability to perform basic skills
- Willingness to learn
- Initiative
- Perseverance, or ability to finish what you start
- Cooperativeness
- Thinking skills
- Listening skills
- Communication skills
- Teamwork skills
- Social skills
- Problem-solving skills
- Decision-making skills
- Planning and organizing skills
- Technology skills
- Adaptability and flexibility
- Education and training

Important Skills and Qualities These are just some of the qualities and skills employers prize in employees. You can begin to develop many of these skills and qualities right now in school and in other activities. *Which are already strong qualities of yours? When do you use or show your skills?*

Carlos was promoted several times by Shady Grove Day Camp. When he was 13, he was a volunteer camp counselor for a month. He worked with a high school student named Ed who was a full counselor. Together, they were in charge of 12 first- and second-grade campers.

The first week on the job, Carlos carefully observed Ed. He paid attention to how Ed interacted with the campers. By the end of the month, Carlos felt comfortable in his position. He even suggested some new activities. He volunteered to lead a nature walk, for example—and it was a big success.

Ed recommended Carlos for a paid position as an assistant counselor the following summer. In his new job, Carlos was responsible for leading the afternoon activities. He tried out many new ideas.

The next summer, Carlos returned to Shady Grove as a full counselor. In this position, he earned twice as much as he had the summer before. That's because he was experienced and had twice as much responsibility. He even supervised an assistant counselor.

Deciding Whether to Accept More Responsibility

Each time Shady Grove Day Camp offered him new responsibilities, Carlos thought carefully before accepting. He had to decide whether he wanted more responsibility.

These were easy decisions for Carlos. He liked working at the camp. He was also ready for new challenges. Trying new tasks in familiar surroundings appealed to him.

Deciding Whether More Responsibility Can Be Handled

Of course, Carlos also had to ask himself if he could handle the added work. Carlos's first promotion involved more time on the job. Accepting the assistant counselor's job meant that Carlos would spend eight weeks as a camp counselor. This would cut into his summer activities. He would also have less time to spend with family and friends.

Carlos worked out a schedule that allowed time for everything he needed and wanted to do. The schedule took into account his work at Shady Grove during the day.

Career Opportunities

Law, Public Safety, and Security

Do you insist that everyone play games by the rules? Perhaps a career in law, public safety, and security is for you. This career cluster includes lawyers, police officers, prison guards, prosecutors, judges, and other professionals who uphold the law.

ASSISTANT DISTRICT ATTORNEY

Experienced prosecutor needed in busy district attorney's office. Must have proven track record of convicting criminals in court. Law degree and three years experience required. Must be hard-working, self-confident, and knowledgeable about all aspects of criminal law.

Critical Thinking

Why must an assistant district attorney be hard-working and self-confident?

Other Things to Consider

There can be other things to consider when you are offered more responsibility. When Carlos was promoted to full counselor, for instance, he became a supervisor. He was responsible not only for his own work, but also for the work of an assistant counselor.

When you become a supervisor, your relationships with your coworkers will change. You will be the boss. You will oversee their work and give them direction. You will review their performance. It may be difficult to have close friendships with people you supervise. You will need to ask yourself whether you'll be able to adjust to these changes.

A promotion sometimes requires you to move to a new place. You may have to travel more in your new position. That may mean that you have to live far from family and friends or be away from them for periods of time. Will you be willing to move or travel? Handling more responsibility often involves making personal sacrifices such as these.

Talk Face to Face
When you decline a promotion, talk to your supervisor face to face. *Why do you think meeting in person is important?*

Deciding Whether to Accept a Promotion

When you're offered a promotion, you must take an honest look at yourself and at your goals. Being offered a promotion is always a good thing. It shows you've earned your employer's trust and appreciation. Not every promotion, however, will be right for you. You may have good reasons for not wanting more responsibility. You may know that you cannot handle what's involved. It's okay to decline, or say no, to a promotion. Just because you are not ready for more responsibility now doesn't mean you won't be ready later. If one promotion is not right, the next one might be.

The important thing is to be honest with yourself and your employer. Leave a door open for the future. Look at all you do in a positive way and keep at it. A positive attitude and your best effort will help you move toward your goals.

Lesson 12.1 Review and Activities

Key Terms Review

1. Imagine that you are an employer. Tomorrow you will discuss a promotion and raise with an employee. Write what you plan to say. In your remarks, explain the following key terms.
   - **promotion**
   - **raise**

Check Your Understanding

Choose the correct answer for each item. Write your answers on a separate sheet of paper.

2. A positive ______ and your best effort will help you get the most out of everything you do.
   a. source
   b. company
   c. attitude
3. When you receive a ______, you receive a position of greater responsibility and authority.
   a. diploma
   b. promotion
   c. raise

Critical Thinking

Use complete sentences to answer the following questions. Write your answers on a separate sheet of paper.

4. What experience might you benefit more from if you have a positive attitude? Explain your answer.
5. How can a willingness to try new things help you grow?
6. What would you do if you were offered more responsibility in your job?

Connecting to the Workplace

7. **Working Toward a Promotion** Linda has worked as a clerk at a movie rental store for two years. The position of assistant manager has become available. Linda thinks she is qualified for the promotion. The manager, however, has not offered her the position. Linda feels overlooked. Role-play a meeting between Linda and the store manager. Then discuss Linda's handling of the situation. How else could she handle the situation? Role-play these other options.

Teamwork

8. **Conduct a Debate** Some companies give promotions based on the amount of time a worker has been with the company. Other companies give promotions based solely on the worker's ability and performance on the job. Which promotion policy do you think is more fair? Why? Team up with others in your class who feel as you do. As a team, prepare for a debate on the issue. Debate with a team with the opposite point of view.

Lesson 12.2

Reevaluating Your Goals

Do you ever wish that you could see the future? Just imagine knowing what the future was going to be like. You might do certain things differently in the present.

No one can really know the future, though. There's no way to be sure of exactly what you will be doing 10, 20, or 50 years from now. You can be certain of one thing, however. Some of your goals will change. As your life unfolds, you will need to make adjustments in your plans.

Discover

- Why it is important to check your progress toward your goals
- Why you might make changes in a career plan

Why It's Important

As you grow and change, your goals will change. You'll need to be prepared to adjust your plans.

Key Terms

- **notice**
- **letter of resignation**

Review Your Progress You should review your career plan on a regular basis. Check to see how well you are moving toward your goals. *Which goals would you expect to meet first—long-term goals or short-term goals?*

Reviewing Your Career Plan

Do you get a progress report between report cards at school? A progress report tells you how you're doing in your classes. It may include suggestions for improving your work or raising your grades.

Your progress in school is your focus right now. Although you're exploring careers, you probably haven't launched a real career plan yet. More likely, your main goals are to finish this part of your education and go on to high school. Doing well in school, graduating, and continuing your education are important goals. These are the most important things you can do right now to prepare for any future career.

When you reach high school, you may begin to follow an actual career plan. You may choose classes, activities, and maybe even a part-time job that are related to a particular career. As you work on goals included in your plan, you'll need to review your progress occasionally.

The earlier you develop the habit of reviewing your career plan, the better. That way, your plan will keep pace with your growth. Remember, a career plan isn't set in stone. It should grow and change as you do.

At different points in a career, you'll want to see if you're moving toward the goals you set. You'll also want to make adjustments in your plan to fit the person you have become. You will update your plan throughout your career.

Explore Different Opportunities Continue to explore who you are in high school and beyond. *What activities or classes do you look forward to in high school?*

Making Changes

Many things can change your career plan. Just think back over your years in school. How have you changed? In the years ahead, changes will continue to occur.

Changing Direction

In high school and the years beyond, you will just be starting to move toward a career. You will still be learning a great deal about who you are. You will continue to develop your values. Your interests and skills will keep expanding in new directions.

At this early stage in your career plan, you will still be gathering a lot of information. You'll talk to people. You'll do research. You'll work part-time or volunteer your time.

A world of possibilities will be open to you. New careers and new choices will emerge. Don't be surprised if you decide to go in an entirely different direction than you had planned. That's what happened to Jocelyn Sanders. Jocelyn had a career plan and knew exactly where she was headed. At least she thought she did.

A Career Change
You may have several careers in your lifetime. *How might you identify a new career direction for yourself?*

Q&A

Job-Hopping

Q: I've heard that the only way to get ahead is by job-hopping. Is this true?

A: Many people do advance in their careers and move closer to their long-term goals when they change jobs, but changing jobs too often can be a disadvantage. Employers value workers who are loyal and can commit to them for at least a year. They won't risk hiring a person with a track record of quitting too soon and too often. Take job opportunities that bring you closer to your long-term career goals, but also recognize when it's best not to job hop.

New Opportunities
Changing your career plan may seem frightening at first. In the end however, such a change may open up many new opportunities. *What might these opportunities be?*

"I grew up by the ocean, and my dream was to be a marine biologist. When it was time, I chose a college known for its marine biology program. My first years in college, I had to take a broad range of courses to meet various requirements. One way to meet the language requirement was to study abroad for a semester.

"I had studied French and chose to go to France. The experience completely changed my mind about a career. I found living in another culture fascinating. I began to think about careers in the global marketplace. Today, I have a career in international banking. I travel frequently and work out of a major U.S. bank's office in Hong Kong."

You can learn from Jocelyn's experience. Don't be afraid to change your career plan. At this early stage, you'll still be discovering what fits you best. When you find it, go with it. It's okay to change direction.

Changing Jobs

Remember the difference between a job and a career? A job is any work you do for pay. A career is one or more jobs in the same area of interest. During a career, you will hold a series of jobs.

The Global Workplace

Handy Advice

Keeping track of your hands during your travels is tough work. In Hindu and Muslim countries the left hand is considered unclean; avoid using it in public. In these countries use only your right hand to eat, accept gifts, or hold money.

In Australia, Poland, and Nigeria giving the thumbs up sign to signal a job well done might get you in trouble. In these countries this hand gesture is offensive. If you think it's safest to just hide your hands in your pockets, guess again. The Thai, Scottish, and Japanese cultures consider this bad manners.

The best advice for handling your hands is to watch how locals use their hands and then follow their lead.

Internet Activity

Use the Internet and library resources to research one other country. What are some common gestures used in this country? What do they indicate? Go to the *Exploring Careers* Web site at exploring.glencoe.com for a list of Web sites to help you complete this activity.

Some of these jobs may be part of your original career plan. Doors to other jobs will open as your career goes forward. Look at **Figure 12.2** on pages 262–263 to see the job changes one person made in the course of a career in education.

As **Figure 12.2** shows, people change jobs during the course of a career for a variety of reasons. You may feel another job would better fit your skills or personality. You may want new responsibilities or challenges. Maybe the idea of working for a different employer appeals to you.

Changing jobs is never a snap decision. Whatever your reason, you should always make sure you think the change through carefully. Think about how the change fits your career plan and your long-term goals. Use the steps of the decision-making process discussed in Chapter 4 to carefully consider your options and make your decision.

Figure 12.2

ONE CAREER, MANY JOBS

Gina Cacciotti has held many jobs in her career. She may change jobs several more times. *What kinds of jobs might be part of a career that interests you?*

1

Gina had always wanted a career in education. As a high school student, she prepared for college by taking a variety of classes. In college, she majored in biology, her favorite subject. She took courses that would help her earn a teaching certificate. She also worked as a student teacher in a middle school.

2

After college graduation, Gina got a job as a middle-school science teacher. She taught seventh-grade science five periods a day. She quickly became a popular teacher. Students loved her science activities and projects.

3

The school principal recommended Gina to a textbook publisher looking for teachers to write science activities. Gina put together activities for a seventh-grade workbook. She later agreed to write a science textbook for seventh graders for the same publisher.

4

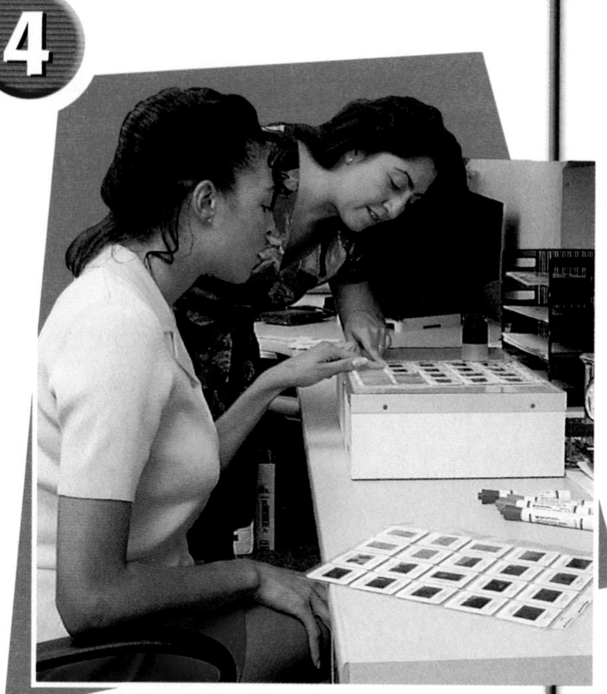

Gina continued to teach and do other writing projects for the textbook publisher. When a position as science editor opened up, the publisher offered it to Gina. Gina decided she was ready for a change from classroom teaching. She took the job.

5

After several years as a science editor, Gina was looking for a new challenge. She spotted a job opening for an editor in a different department at her company. The department specialized in educational multimedia products, such as software, videos, and Web sites. Gina applied for and got the job. In her latest project, she is helping create interactive science Web sites for middle school students.

When to Leave a Job

It is better not to leave your job until you have a new one. This ensures a steady source of income, and prospective employers generally prefer interviewing candidates who are currently employed. This is because employed people tend to be more current with their skills and active in their profession.

Leaving a Job

You may decide to leave a job to take a different job in the same company or organization. You may also find a new job with a new employer. Once you've accepted a job with a new

Figure 12.3

LETTER OF RESIGNATION

Ved Madanda
2827 Suncrest Drive
Mason, Illinois 66140

August 1, 2002

Mr. Albert Ziegler
Mason Times
1732 Hedgeview Lane
Mason, Illinois 66138

Dear Mr. Ziegler:

Thank you for giving me the opportunity to work with you at the *Mason Times*. I thoroughly enjoyed working on the paper's staff.

On August 26, I will be returning to Edison High School to begin my senior year. My schedule and responsibilities as a student will not allow me to continue my job as an editorial assistant.

I appreciate all you did to teach me about newspaper editing. I know my experience at the *Mason Times* will be useful in the career I hope to have someday.

Sincerely,

Ved Madanda

Ved Madanda

Proper Notice Even if you are leaving a job you don't like, you still must give notice. It's the right thing to do. *What does a letter of resignation show your employer?*

employer, be sure to give proper notice to your current employer. **Notice** is an official written statement that you are leaving your job. It is customary to give notice at least two weeks before you are going to leave. Then your current employer has time to find a replacement.

In some places of business, you may need to submit a formal letter of resignation. In a **letter of resignation,** you explain why and when you are leaving. **Figure 12.3** shows a letter of resignation.

It doesn't matter what kind of job you have. It is professional—and courteous—to give notice. Giving notice helps you leave your employer on good terms. As **Figure 12.3** shows, Ved Madanda found out how valuable that can be.

"I worked part-time at a newspaper last summer," explains Ved. "I was going back to school soon, so I knew I couldn't continue working there. I wrote a letter to my boss. I told him that I would be leaving in two weeks to start school. I mentioned how much I had liked my job. I also told him what I had learned. I thanked my boss for hiring me. When I gave the letter to him, he thanked me for writing it. Before I left, he gave me a letter of recommendation. Writing that letter of resignation took just a few minutes of my time. Now, I have a recommendation for that next job in my career plan."

Changing Careers

People today change jobs frequently. As a matter of fact, the average American holds at least seven jobs before he or she reaches age 30. What may be more surprising, though, is that many people have several careers in their lifetime.

People have many reasons for making career changes. Some reach the end of their career plan. Others find their career plan is no longer right for them. Many people change careers to pursue personal interests. Many people choose to run their own businesses, as you'll learn in Chapter 13.

Discovering who you are and what you want to do is a lifelong process. You can learn and grow every step of the way—in new experiences, new jobs, and new careers. Stop now and then to check your progress. It's an important part of your journey.

Lesson 12.2 Review and Activities

Key Terms Review

1. In a short paragraph for an employee handbook, explain the rules for giving notice. Use and explain the terms below.
   - **notice**
   - **letter of resignation**

Check Your Understanding

Tell whether each statement is true or false. Rewrite any false statement to make it true. Write your answers on a separate sheet of paper.

2. Your goals will change as you get older. You will need to make changes in your plans.
3. Once you determine a career plan, you shouldn't change it.
4. It is usual to give notice two days before you are going to leave your job.

Critical Thinking

Use complete sentences to answer the following questions. Write your answers on a separate sheet of paper.

5. Why should you make a habit of reviewing your career plan from time to time?
6. Why is periodically checking your career progress an important part of your lifelong journey?

Character Building

7. **Changing Jobs** Hoshi plans to be a paramedic. For the past two years, he has worked as a lifeguard at the local swimming pool. He loves this job because it gives him the opportunity to learn and practice first aid. Hoshi had planned to work as a lifeguard again this summer. However, a Web site design firm also offered him a summer job. He isn't interested in Web site design, but the job pays double what he makes as a lifeguard. Should Hoshi switch his summer job? What should he consider while making his decision?

Community Involvement

8. **Organize a Speaking Event** Network with adult friends and family members to identify someone in your neighborhood or community who has changed careers. Invite the person to talk to your class about his or her career change. With your classmates, prepare a list of questions for your guest before he or she visits. Have the person share the things he or she considered while making the decision to change careers. Follow up by sending a thank-you note to your guest.

LAW, PUBLIC SAFETY, AND SECURITY

Law • The rules by which a society governs itself

Public Safety • Efforts to keep the public safe

Security • Privately funded protection of persons and property

Job Title	Work Description
Arbitrator	Decides disputes between people or groups who do not agree
Correctional Officer	Guards inmates in prisons or jails
Emergency Medical Technician (EMT)	Gives immediate care to injured persons and transports them to medical facilities
Firefighter	Responds to fires and other emergency situations
Judge	Hears and decides legal cases in court
Lawyer	Conducts criminal and civil lawsuits, prepares legal documents, advises clients on their legal rights, argues cases in court
Parole Officer	Supervises people who have been released from prison
Police Officer	Keeps order, protects lives and property, and investigates crime
Sheriff's Deputy	Keeps public order, protects lives and property, and investigates crime in a county or other large region

Exploration Activity

Law, Public Safety, and Security Use library and Internet resources to research a career in the Law, Public Safety, and Security career cluster. Write a report that includes information about the kinds of work, the skills required, the working conditions, the training and education required, and the career outlook.

Cooperative Learning Interview a classmate about the career he or she researched. Find out as much information about that career as you can during the interview. Then have your classmate interview you about the career you researched. Afterward, take turns sharing what you learned from each other with the class.

Chapter 12 Review and Activities

Chapter Highlights

Lesson 12.1 A positive attitude and your best effort will help you move toward your goals. In the workplace, there will be opportunities to learn and grow at every level.

Lesson 12.2 It is important to reevaluate your goals now and then. As you grow and change, your goals will change. You will need to make changes in your plans.

Key Concept Review

Use complete sentences to answer the following questions. Write your answers on a separate sheet of paper.

1. Why does giving your best make you feel good about yourself?
2. What can you do to increase your career options?
3. What personal sacrifices might be involved in a promotion?
4. Why do people change careers?

Critical Thinking

Use complete sentences to answer the following questions. Write your answers on a separate sheet of paper.

5. What is your attitude toward school? How does it affect your performance at school?
6. How can you tell if you're ready for a promotion?
7. Why do you think employers consider seniority when considering promotions? Explain.
8. When do you think you should review your career plan?
9. Name an advantage and a drawback of changing careers.

Skill Building

10. **Thinking—Reasoning**
    Think about what you could do to earn a raise. Make a list of at least three ways you can show that you are ready for more responsibility.
11. **Interpersonal—Exercises Leadership**
    Adam received a promotion and now supervises Paul, a coworker who is also a good friend. Paul has begun coming in to work late and leaving early. When Adam talks with Paul, Paul says, "I thought you were my friend. You sure have changed since you became boss." What would you say to Paul if you were Adam?

Personal Career Portfolio

Academic Applications

12. Mathematics

You have worked as a guide at the aquarium for two summers. This summer you have been offered the job again, but with a 4 percent raise. Last summer you worked two and a half months and earned a total of $1,875. How much more will you earn per month this summer than you did the last two summers? What will your earnings be for the entire summer?

13. Language Arts

Pretend you are president of the student council. You've been asked to give a speech to the incoming students on the theme "Giving Your Best." Write a three-minute speech on giving your best at home, at school, on the job, and throughout your life. Practice your speech before an audience of your classmates.

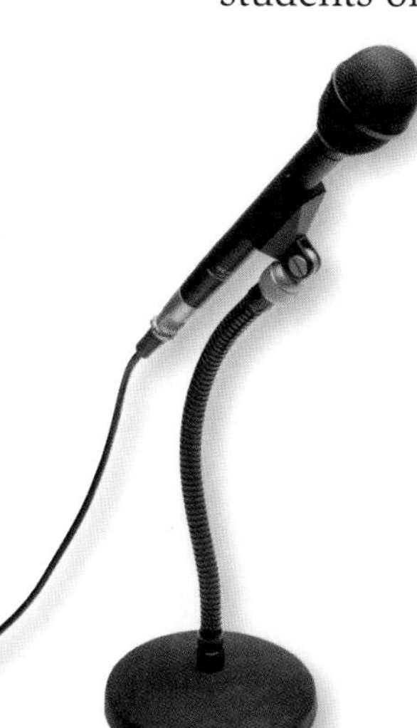

Performance Records

- **Acquire** copies of your school transcripts.
- **Gather** copies of successful performance evaluations.
- **Make** copies of any thank-you letters or notes of praise you may have received from teachers, supervisors from jobs, internships, or volunteer positions, teammates, and coworkers.
- **File** these documents in your Personal Career Portfolio.
- **Label** this section of your portfolio *Performance Records*.
- **Add** new documents to this section as you receive them. For example, include your final middle school and high school transcripts when you have them. Also include copies of job performance evaluations as you get them.
- **List** your portfolio entry on your Personal Career Portfolio contents page.

Chapter 13

Our Economic System

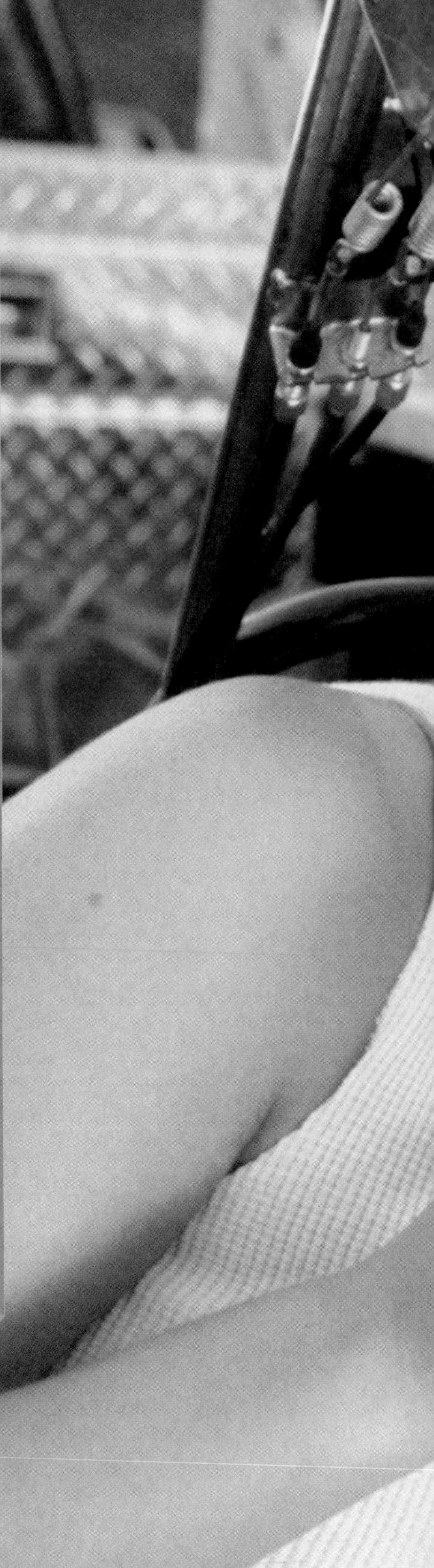

Lesson 13.1

The Free Enterprise System

Lesson 13.2

Being Your Own Boss

CAREER CLUSTER

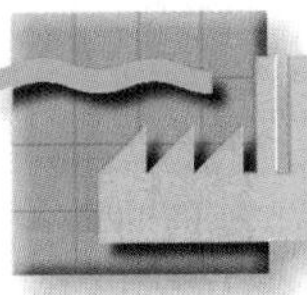

You will explore careers in the Manufacturing career cluster.

What You'll Learn

- You will discover your place in the economy now and in the future.
- You will learn about the U.S. free enterprise economic system.
- You will find out what is involved in starting your own business.

Get Ready!

Conduct Interviews

Interview three family members or friends you know who work. Ask these questions:

- What items or services does your company sell?
- Who is your company's competition?
- What does your company do to make sure people buy its products?

Apply Write down the information you collect. What does it tell you about our economic system?

Lesson 13.1

The Free Enterprise System

Discover

- The meaning of free enterprise
- How the free enterprise system works
- How you fit into our economic system

Why It's Important

The more you understand about our economy, the better your chances of reaching your career goals.

KEY TERMS

- economics
- economic system
- capitalism
- free enterprise
- regulate
- command economy
- socialist economy
- consumers
- producers
- profit
- supply
- demand

As a teen, you are a member of a group with a great deal of spending power. You and others your age buy all kinds of goods and services. Goods, as you recall from Chapter 2, are *items* that you buy, such as sports equipment, jeans, and computer games. Services are *activities* people might do for you for a fee, such as tutoring, bike repair, and teeth cleaning.

Many companies that provide goods and services take the interests of young people very seriously. These companies make it their business to know what young people want.

What do *you* know about these companies? What do you know about how the prices for goods and services are set? Do you understand why prices rise or fall?

Economic Systems

You can find the answers to these questions by studying economics. **Economics** is the study of how people produce, distribute, and use goods and services. *Producing* means creating goods or services. *Distributing* means making goods and services available to the people who want or need them.

Purchasing Power Young people are an important part of the economy. *What kinds of goods and services have you purchased in the last month?*

The Global Workplace

Mind Your Meal Manners

Minding your manners during a dinner abroad is usually a matter of common sense. For example, you should always try all foods your hosts offer.

Sometimes, good table manners aren't what you'd expect. Go ahead, slurp your noodles and belch during a dinner in China, where such behavior is a sign that you're enjoying your meal. In the Philippines and Russia, don't clean your plate. A clean plate is a sign that you didn't get enough to eat—a terrible insult. Finally, forget about saying "thank you" to your dinner hosts in India. That's considered payment for the meal and very rude.

Internet Activity

Use the Internet and library resources to research one other country. What are the traditions and customs observed during meals in this country? Go to the *Exploring Careers* Web site at exploring.glencoe.com for a list of Web sites to help you complete this activity.

Delivering and selling are two ways of distributing goods and services. *Using* is what people do with goods and services.

How do people produce, distribute, and use goods and services? That depends on their country's economic system. An **economic system** is a country's way of making choices about how to use its resources to produce and distribute goods and services.

The Free Enterprise System

The economic system of the United States is known as **capitalism.** Capitalism is also known as a market economy or a free enterprise system. **Free enterprise** means that individuals or businesses may buy and sell goods and services and set prices with little governmental control.

Assert Yourself

Assertive people confidently present themselves and their abilities to those around them. The first step in practicing assertiveness is to be friendly and outgoing. Use positive body language and speak with confidence. Share your ideas and opinions. Keep in mind though that nobody likes people who are bossy or arrogant. Be assertive, but always respect other people and their abilities.

Cooperative Learning Activity

- Team up with a group of classmates.
- Brainstorm a list of things you can do in school to show that you are confident and assertive.
- Share your list with the class.

In a free enterprise system, individuals and businesses have a good deal of free choice. The government does not plan what or how many goods or services will be available. It does not tell people where to work. It also usually does not tell individuals or businesses what prices to charge.

That doesn't mean, however, that the government has nothing to do with business in a free enterprise system. In fact, the government plays a very important role. As you learned in Chapter 11, it passes laws that set workplace safety standards. It also passes laws to **regulate,** or set rules for, some prices and wages. Laws passed by the government protect workers and consumers.

Other Economic Systems

There are other types of economic systems in other countries. In a **command economy,** the government makes all of the key economic decisions. In such a system, there is little economic freedom. There is also little incentive for people to increase their productivity. The main advantage of a command economy is that every citizen has an equal standard of living. The government provides each citizen with a job, a place to live, and health care.

In a **socialist economy,** there is private enterprise, but the government controls key industries and makes many economic decisions. Socialist countries tend to provide the public with more social services, such as health care and education, than capitalist countries do. They also tend to ensure a certain standard of living for everyone.

How the U.S. Economy Works

People like you who buy and use goods and services are **consumers.** Consumers are an important part of the free enterprise system. In the United States, consumers decide which products will be produced and which companies will stay in business. They do this by shopping. Every time they make a purchase, they are "voting" with their dollars. The more votes (or sales) a product gets, the more likely the product and the company that produces it will succeed. Consumers decide how much demand there is for a product.

Producers and Consumers

Where do the goods and services that consumers buy and use come from? Individuals or companies known as **producers** make or provide them. Producers are another important part of the free enterprise system.

Remember, one of your best resources is exploring.glencoe.com

Many young people are producers. If you design T-shirts, for example, you are a producer of goods. If you baby-sit, you are a producer of a service. Have you ever been a producer? What goods or services did you make or provide?

Once goods and services are produced, people or other businesses consume, or buy and use, them. The people who buy your T-shirts are consumers. The people for whom you baby-sit are also consumers. You become a consumer when you buy lunch, ride the subway, or get your hair cut.

Producers and consumers can't exist without each other. People and business and industry need each other. **Figure 13.1** on page 276 shows how business flows between these groups.

The Producer's Goal: Making a Profit

Although they can't exist without each other, producers and consumers have very different goals. Producers try to make goods or provide services that consumers will buy. Consumers try to get what they need and want within the limits of how much money they have.

New Enterprises New businesses are always opening in a free enterprise system. An enterprise is something a person or group of people plans or tries to do. *Why do you think our economic system is called the free enterprise system?*

There are tens of thousands of producers in our economic system. Some are large companies owned by groups of people. Others are individuals who own and operate small businesses. Bike repair shops, hair salons, bakeries, and restaurants are just a few examples of small businesses. Your pet-grooming service and your friend's business selling handmade crafts are two more.

All businesses, both large and small, must earn a profit to keep operating. A **profit** is the amount of money left after the business pays its expenses. The main goal of a producer is to make a profit.

Q&A

Not-for-Profit Organizations

Q: I don't want to work for a business whose main goal is making a profit. Am I a misfit?

A: Perhaps a job in a not-for-profit, or *nonprofit*, organization would be a perfect fit for you. Most businesses want to make a profit, but not all. Some nonprofit organizations exist to serve charitable causes, not to make a profit. Churches, homeless shelters, and the YMCA are examples of nonprofit organizations. Public organizations, such as schools, libraries, and museums don't make a profit either.

Figure 13.1 THE PATTERN OF THE ECONOMY

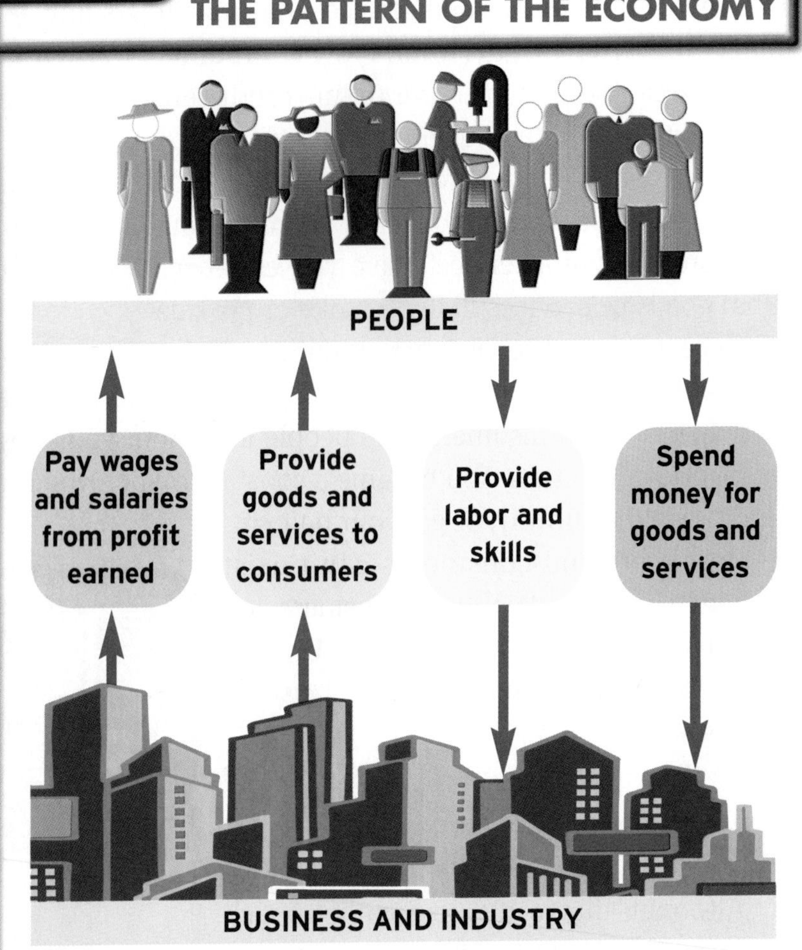

Everyone Plays a Part You play a part in the free enterprise system. This diagram shows how the money that you spend goes into businesses and comes back to you as a worker. It also shows how your skills help produce goods and services that consumers like you need and want. *How does the freedom of choice of a free enterprise system affect these processes?*

One Producer's Experience

Take a look at Tom Hanshaw's business. Tom grows and sells flowers and vegetables in Peoria, Illinois. His first year in business he had no expenses and made a 100 percent profit.

Tom's parents bought him vegetable seeds and the other supplies he needed. He sold the vegetables he grew to his neighbors. His total sales at the end of the summer were $50. Because Tom had not spent any money to do business, the money he earned was total profit. Tom's profit the first summer was $50, or 100 percent of his sales.

The first summer, Tom's customers kept asking for flowers. The second year, Tom used part of his profit from the year before to buy both flower and vegetable seeds. It was an easy decision to grow flowers in addition to vegetables.

Tom spent a total of $40 on seeds. He had no other expenses. The garden space was ready to be planted, and he had all the tools he needed. By the end of the summer, Tom had made $253 selling his produce. He made a profit of $213 the second summer.

The Business of Profit Making a profit is important to both large and small businesses. *What kinds of expenses do businesses have?*

The third summer, Tom decided to expand his garden. He planned to sell what he grew at a booth at the local farmers' market on Saturdays. What additional expenses do you think Tom faced when he made his garden bigger? Tom is looking forward to his fourth summer selling what he grows. He expects his profit to continue to grow. What are the secrets to Tom's success as a vegetable and flower producer? First, he has few expenses. Like other producers, Tom also tries to provide goods or services that consumers will buy. In addition, he listens to what his customers want. That also helps him make a profit.

Factors That Affect Prices

Like any producer, Tom wants to make a profit. Like other consumers, Tom's customers want to get what they need and want for the money they have to spend. You might say a consumer's main goal is to get the most for his or her money.

With that goal in mind, consumers pay a lot of attention to prices. They note changes in prices. They compare prices. Don't you? (You'll learn more about how to be a smart consumer in Chapter 14.)

Think about the last time you had your hair cut. Did it cost more or less than the haircut you had six months before? What kinds of prices have you paid for CDs? Do you always pay the same price for jeans?

There's nothing unusual about changing prices. In a free enterprise system, it's normal for prices to go up and down. Three main factors cause prices to change: supply and demand, production costs, and competition.

- ***Supply and demand.*** **Supply** is the amount of goods and services available for sale. **Demand** is the amount of goods and services that consumers want to buy. When supply is greater than demand, producers lower their prices. When demand is greater than supply, producers raise their prices.
- ***Production costs.*** The more it costs to make a good or provide a service, the higher its price. Remember, producers want to make a profit. To do so, they must sell their goods or services for more than it cost to produce them.
- ***Competition.*** When producers offer similar goods or services for sale, they are in competition. Sometimes competition is great—many producers are offering the same or similar goods or services. When competition is great, prices tend to be lower. When there is little or no competition, prices tend to be higher.

See the Big Picture
During your lifetime, you will fill many different roles in the economy. *How might keeping up with news about the economy help you fill these roles?*

The Big Picture

Consumers, producers, profits, prices, supply, demand, competition—each is an important part of our free enterprise economic system.

You already have a role in the economy. You are already a consumer because you buy goods and services. If you're not already a producer, you will be one day. In your work life, you will provide goods or services for other consumers. You will also be a voter helping decide what economic policies the government should follow.

To prepare to play these different roles in our economic system, stay informed. Pay attention to what is going on around the world. The global economy links the free enterprise system of the United States to all the other economic systems in the world. As you learned in Chapter 2, what is happening in our economy can affect other countries' economies. What is happening in other countries' economies can affect our own economy.

As part of the free enterprise system, you already have a role in the global economy.

Evaluate International Career Opportunities

Try This Activity

Knowing the similarities and differences among different types of economies will help you make wise career choices. It will help you compare employment opportunities in our free enterprise system to those available in the international job market. It will also help you set your career goals.

Study Economic Systems Research the market economy of the United States and the command or the socialist economy of another country. Create a chart with a column for each economic system. Enter into the chart your answers to these questions about these two economies:

- Why are jobs created?
- Who creates the jobs?
- How are wages determined?
- What are incomes based on?
- Who makes the production decisions?
- What determines the demand for labor?
- Is there a demand for technical skills?
- Is there equal employment opportunity under the law?
- Who is responsible for protecting workers' health and safety?
- Who sponsors retirement systems?

Create a Venn Diagram Prepare a Venn diagram comparing and contrasting the employment opportunities in the U.S. free enterprise system to those in the economic system of the other economy you researched. A Venn diagram is a visual way of showing how two ideas are similar and how they are different. It uses two overlapping circles to show the two ideas. The overlapping portion of the two circles shows the similarities among the two ideas. The remaining portions of the two circles show the contrasts, or differences, between the two ideas.

Fill in Your Diagram Label the left circle "Market Economy" and label the right circle either "Socialist Economy" or "Command Economy," depending on which type of economy you researched. In the overlapping portion of the two circles, write down any similarities of the two economic systems. In the non-overlapping portions of the circles, write down the contrasts between the two economic systems.

Lesson 13.1 Review and Activities

Key Terms Review

1. Write a series of questions and answers that use the terms below.

- **economics**
- **economic system**
- **capitalism**
- **free enterprise**
- **regulate**
- **command economy**
- **socialist economy**
- **consumers**
- **producers**
- **profit**
- **supply**
- **demand**

Check Your Understanding

Choose the correct answer for each item. Write your answers on a separate sheet of paper.

2. In a free enterprise system, individuals and businesses buy and sell ______.

a. goods and services
b. government control
c. enterprises

3. Someone who buys and uses goods and services is a ______.

a. producer
b. regulator
c. consumer

Critical Thinking

Use complete sentences to answer the following questions. Write your answers on a separate sheet of paper.

4. Why does the government regulate prices and wages?

5. Is it ethical for companies to make a profit by selling people things they can't really afford? Explain.

6. What happens to prices when supply is greater than demand? When demand is greater than supply? Explain why this happens.

Connecting to the Workplace

7. **Making a Profit** Jordan makes jewelry. He wants to sell his pieces at a craft show. He knows that there are already two other jewelers signed up to sell at the show. Most of their jewelry is in the \$15 to \$30 range. What could Jordan do to compete with the other jewelers and still make a profit?

Teamwork

8. **Create a Skit** Work with a group to create a skit about the free enterprise system. Dramatize the way the system works. Include the roles of producers, consumers, and competitors. Use and explain the terms *profit*, *supply*, and *demand* in your dialogue. Make the skit simple enough for younger students to understand the basics of free enterprise. Perform your skit at an elementary school.

Lesson 13.2

Being Your Own Boss

Dreamer, doer, inventor, organizer—do any of these words describe you? Are you someone who likes to take risks, take action, take responsibility? If so, you may have a future as an entrepreneur. An **entrepreneur** is someone who organizes and runs a business.

If the idea of being your own boss appeals to you, you're not alone. The idea appeals to many people in the free enterprise system. Businesses owned and operated by individuals are an important part of our economy. They employ many people. More than 95 percent of U.S. workers work for small businesses.

The Rewards and Challenges of Entrepreneurship

Being an entrepreneur offers many rewards and many challenges. Ask any entrepreneur how he or she likes running a

Discover

- The rewards and challenges of working for yourself
- How to start your own business

Why It's Important

In the free enterprise system, many people own and operate their own businesses. One day, you may be one of them.

KEY TERMS

- **entrepreneur**
- **business plan**
- **marketing**

Work for Yourself
You can gain experience as an entrepreneur by starting a business at home. *Why do you think many entrepreneurs like to work at home?*

business. You're likely to hear the same list of advantages and disadvantages.

Victor Klepack has been in business for himself since he was 17. He creates logos, or symbols that identify companies. Victor doesn't hesitate when asked about the rewards of being an entrepreneur.

"I'm in charge. That's the big thing. I'm the one who decides how to operate the business. When I work, how hard I work—it's all up to me. I like having that control over my life."

"Every project gives me satisfaction. I make a good income, too. In fact, there's no limit to what I can earn. It's just a matter of deciding how many customers I want to handle."

Victor is just as open about some of the challenges he faces as an entrepreneur. "I've never had an eight-hour workday," he notes. "When I've got several jobs going, I may be up until midnight or later working. I have to put in long hours because there's a lot of competition out there. I need to deliver quality work. I also need to deliver it on time. If I don't, my customers will find someone else to do the job."

Career Opportunities

Manufacturing

If you love to build things or make things, a career in the Manufacturing career cluster may be for you. Workers in this career cluster make everything from bathing suits to computer chips.

Critical Thinking

What people do you think a quality assurance manager would need to communicate with? Why?

QUALITY ASSURANCE MANAGER

Experienced manager needed to supervise quality assurance team and maintain quality of products manufactured in large factory. Requirements: bachelor's degree in science or engineering, teamwork skills, management skills, math and analytical skills.

Long hours and stiff competition are concerns that every entrepreneur shares. That's not all that's on the minds of most entrepreneurs. Running your own business involves financial risk. You can lose the money you've invested, or put into, your business. You may even lose more than you invested. In addition, there are no guarantees of success. Almost two out of three new businesses fail within their first four years.

Would you enjoy the rewards of being an entrepreneur? Would you be able to meet the challenges of running your own business? **Figure 13.2** on pages 284–285 shows qualities most entrepreneurs share. What kind of entrepreneur do you think you'd make?

Market Yourself
Marketing is important no matter what the size of your business. *How would you advertise a business you might like to start?*

Launching Your Own Business

Is being an entrepreneur for you? You may picture yourself running your own business someday. Maybe you have an idea for a business right now. Whether you launch your business this weekend, next summer, or in the future, you will need a plan.

The Importance of Planning

You already know why planning is important. As you learned in Chapter 5, a plan of action helps you reach your goals. To run a successful business, you need a business plan.

A **business plan** is a written proposal that describes your new business. It is often shown to people who can lend you money to start your business. It identifies the goods or services you will offer. It tells where your business will be located. It outlines your goals and gives a timetable for meeting them. It also describes who your customers will be and your marketing plan. **Marketing** is the process of developing, promoting, and distributing goods and services to consumers. Marketing includes market research, finance, pricing, promotion, service, distribution, and selling.

Whatever type of business you launch, you'll probably need some money to get it going. As part of your business plan, you'll figure out how much it will cost to start and run your business. You will decide how many employees you need, if any, and what you will pay them. You will also predict what your profits will be.

To start a business, you may just use money you have saved or you might borrow some from a family member. Many entrepreneurs borrow money from a commercial lender, such as a bank.

Figure 13.2 QUALITIES OF ENTREPRENEURS

Entrepreneurs have many qualities in common. *Which qualities do you see in yourself? Which might you have to develop?*

A

Motivation

Successful entrepreneurs know what they want to achieve. They believe in their ability to achieve it. They keep themselves motivated by setting short-, medium-, and long-term goals. Then they make and follow a plan for reaching those goals.

B

Sight and Foresight

Entrepreneurs recognize opportunities. They see problems that exist now. They also foresee, or look ahead to, problems that may occur later. They find ways to build success on the problems they identify. They brainstorm solutions and put their ideas into action.

Sometime in the future, you may apply for a loan for a business you want to start. When you do, you'll need to have a detailed business plan ready for the lender.

Putting an Idea on Paper

Now use your imagination. Make a plan for a business you would like to start and run right now. You don't actually have to start the business. Just dream a little. Then make a business plan detailing how your business can make money out of your dream.

C

Decision Making

Entrepreneurs make business decisions every day. Their decisions must be good ones. The operation and success of their business depends on them.

D

Human Relations

To operate a successful business, entrepreneurs must be able to interact with other people. Entrepreneurs need to build and keep good relations with both employees and customers. They do this by listening to employees and customers and responding to their needs.

Try This Activity

Develop a School-Based Business

Use all of the information you have gathered about careers, industries, and entrepreneurship to develop a small school-based business. Work with a group of students. Brainstorm a list of businesses that would be successful at your school. Conduct market research in your school to find out if students would patronize your business. Then work as a team to prepare a written business plan.

Develop Your Business Plan Now develop the business plan. The plan should answer the following questions.

- What goods or services will the business provide?
- Where in the school will the business be located?
- What are the goals of the business?
- What is the timetable for meeting the business's goals?
- Who do you expect your customers to be?
- What kind of marketing will you do?
- How much will it cost to start the business? Where will the money to start the business come from?
- How much will it cost to run the business?
- How many students will work for the business? How much will they be paid?
- How much profit do you expect the business to earn?

Conduct Research, Then Carry Out Your Plan To answer these questions, your group will need to do some research. Talk to students at other schools who run businesses similar to the one you have in mind. Ask businesspeople for advice. Make sure your plan includes all the information listed. Then carry out your plan by starting the school-based business.

Making a business plan is hard work, but it's also exciting. A business plan is a dream on paper. See **Figure 13.3** for a list of business ideas for young entrepreneurs. The list of business possibilities is endless!

Running your own business, being your own boss, is an adventure. It's not for everybody, but you never know—it could be for you.

Figure 13.3

BUSINESS IDEAS FOR YOUNG ENTREPRENEURS

- Baby-sitting
- Tutoring
- Party planning
- House-sitting
- Obedience training
- Videotaping events
- Raising animals for sale
- Catering
- Car washing and cleaning
- Plant-sitting
- Lawn or garden care
- Pet bathing and grooming
- Grocery shopping
- Housekeeping
- Repairing bikes
- Making and selling crafts
- Designing T-shirts
- Pet-sitting
- Delivery or messenger service
- Garage cleaning
- Snow shoveling
- Washing and ironing
- Clothing repair
- Typing service
- Computer tutoring
- Wake-up service
- Growing and selling flowers or vegetables
- Baking services

Endless Possibilities The list of business possibilities is endless. *Have you ever done any of the jobs listed? Which ones? Which ideas would you like to pursue as a business of your own?*

Lesson 13.2 Review and Activities

Key Terms Review

1. Write a one-paragraph description of a business you would like to start someday. Use the following key terms in your description.
   - **entrepreneur**
   - **business plan**
   - **marketing**

Check Your Understanding

Tell whether each statement is true or false. Rewrite any false statement to make it true. Write your answers on a separate sheet of paper.

2. One of every three new businesses fails within its first four years.
3. You need to make a business plan before starting a business.

Critical Thinking

Use complete sentences to answer the following questions. Write your answers on a separate sheet of paper.

4. Imagine that you are an entrepreneur. What would you like most? Least?
5. Which of the qualities listed in **Figure 13.2** on pages 284–285 do you think an entrepreneur needs most? Why?
6. What should you consider in choosing a location for a business?

Character Building

7. **Starting a Business** Lori is starting a garden care business in her neighborhood. From her research she learned that overusing pesticides to rid gardens of pests and weeds is bad for the environment. Pesticides make garden care easier and quicker, though. This means more customers and profits. So, if Lori wants to have a pesticide-free business, she will need to charge more for her services. Which type of garden care service do you think Lori's business should provide? Why?

Community Involvement

8. **Survey Marketing Methods** Together with a small group of classmates identify three successful small businesses in your community. Survey these businesses about the different kinds of marketing they do to target their customers. For example, do they give away free samples to advertise? Do they charge lower prices than their competitors? Share the results of your group's survey with the class. As a class discuss the marketing methods that were mentioned most. Why do you think they are successful?

Investigating Career Clusters

MANUFACTURING

Manufacturing • The process of making products by hand or by machine

Job Title	Work Description
Boilermaker	Creates and maintains steam boilers used to heat large buildings
Electrical/Electronics Engineer	Designs, develops, tests, and supervises the manufacture of electrical and electronic equipment
Industrial Designer	Develops and designs products such as cars, home appliances, and computer and medical equipment
Machinist	Uses machines such as lathes and drill presses to make metal parts
Mechanical Engineer	Designs tools, engines, and machines
Plastics Machine Operator	Sets up and operates machines that produce items from plastic, such as toys and car parts
Production Manager	Coordinates the activities of a production department
Textile Designer	Designs fabrics for clothes, upholstery, rugs, and other products
Tool and Die Maker	Produces tools, dies, and other devices that help machines mass-produce parts

Exploration Activity

Manufacturing Use library and Internet resources to research a career in the Manufacturing career cluster. Write a report on your findings. Include information about the kinds of work, the skills required, the working conditions, the training and education required, and the career outlook.

Cooperative Learning Interview a classmate about the career he or she researched. Find out as much information about that career as you can during the interview. Then have your classmate interview you about the career you researched. Afterward, take turns sharing what you learned from each other with the class.

Chapter 13 Review and Activities

Chapter Highlights

Lesson 13.1 In a free enterprise system, individuals and businesses buy and sell goods and services and set prices with little government control.

Lesson 13.2 Owning your own business offers both rewards and challenges. A business plan is a proposal that describes a business.

Key Concept Review

Use complete sentences to answer the following questions. Write your answers on a separate sheet of paper.

1. What are two names for the economic system of the United States?
2. What roles will you play in our economic system?
3. What is an entrepreneur?
4. What kind of information needs to be included in a business plan?

Critical Thinking

Use complete sentences to answer the following questions. Write your answers on a separate sheet of paper.

5. Why do workers in a command economy have less incentive to be productive than workers in a free enterprise system?
6. Which qualities of entrepreneurs are also important to have when you work for someone else? Why?

Skill Building

7. **Thinking—Creative Thinking**
   Do you, like most entrepreneurs, see problems as opportunities? Think of a need in your school or community that you could fill by starting a business. Write a summary of the need and how your business would fill it. Share your summary with the rest of the class. As a class, vote on the most creative business solution.
8. **Systems—Understands Systems**
   List the advantages and disadvantages of each economic system you have read about in this chapter. Use this list to help you write an essay about the positives and negatives of a capitalist economy, a command economy, and a socialist economy. In your essay state your opinion on which economic system offers the most opportunities for workers and why.

Academic Applications

9. Mathematics

Gema sells sodas and ice cream at outdoor sports events. She buys sodas for 50 cents each and ice cream bars for $75 per hundred. She marks up all the items by 100 percent, selling the sodas for $1.00 and the ice cream bars for $1.50. One day, she sold 100 sodas and 90 ice cream bars. Her expenses totaled $31.50. What was her profit?

10. Social Studies

With a partner, research a country that had a command economy or a socialist economy in the past, but has now changed to a free enterprise system. What effect has this change had on the country? Use the Internet and library resources to get the information you need. Then write a report about the changes that have happened in this country.

Personal Career Portfolio

Awards and Honors

- **List** the academic, work, and extracurricular honors and awards you have received.
- **Write** a sentence or two that describes each honor or award and explains why you achieved it.
- **Include** on your list any special recognition you have earned for service and leadership.
- **Note** which recognitions were earned while working on teams with others. Write a sentence or two about the teamwork skills you used while working on the teams.
- **Title** the document *Awards and Honors* and file it in your Personal Career Portfolio.
- **Update** the document when you receive new awards, honors, or special recognitions.
- **List** your portfolio entry on your Personal Career Portfolio contents page.

Chapter 14

Managing Your Money

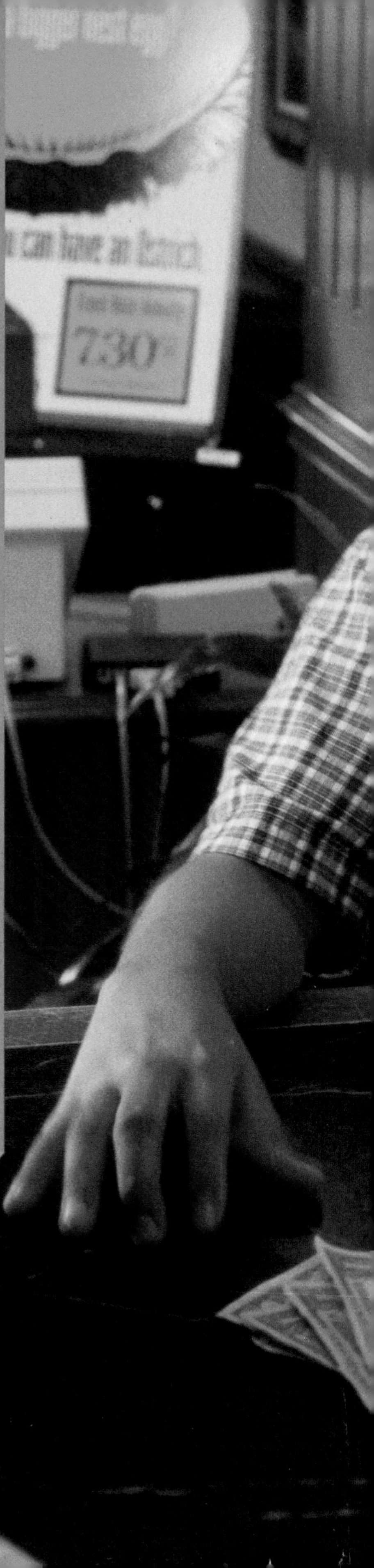

Lesson 14.1

The Money You Earn

Lesson 14.2

You, the Consumer

CAREER CLUSTER

You will explore careers in the Marketing, Sales, and Service career cluster.

What You'll Learn

- You will discover why it is important to manage your money.
- You will learn how to make a plan for spending and saving money.
- You will learn how to finance your education.
- You will find out how you can become a smart shopper.

Get Ready!

Manage Your Money

In what ways do you try to make the most of your money? Make a list of three things you do. Now ask three friends or family members to list three things they do to manage their money so it will last longer. Compare their lists with yours.

Apply Choose one of the money management methods friends or family members listed that's new to you. Try it with your money.

Lesson 14.1

The Money You Earn

Discover

- What your sources of income are
- How to make a plan for spending and saving money
- How to finance your education

Why It's Important

Having a spending and savings plan will help you make the most of your money.

KEY TERMS

- income
- gross pay
- net pay
- withhold
- income tax
- Social Security
- Medicare
- F.I.C.A.
- budget
- fixed expenses
- flexible expenses
- interest
- scholarship
- loan
- work-study program
- grant

Money—most people want more of it. At the same time, many people don't pay much attention to how they spend the money they have. That just doesn't make sense.

You will be earning, spending, and saving money all of your life. You may have only a small amount of money to spend. You may have a large amount. The important thing is to make your money work for you. *What* you have to spend is less important than *how* you spend what you have. That's the key to managing your money.

Your Income

The first step in managing your money is to know your income. Your **income** is the amount of money you receive or earn regularly.

What Are Your Sources of Income?

Where does your money come from? How frequently do you receive money? Maybe you get a set amount of money as an allowance once a week or once a month.

Sources of Income One day, a job will be your main source of income. *What are your sources of income right now?*

From time to time, you may receive gifts of money from family members. You may earn money in a part-time job. An allowance, gifts, and earnings from part-time jobs are the main sources of income for most young people.

Making Sense of a Paycheck

You're probably used to being paid immediately for any part-time work you may do. At the end of an evening of babysitting, you receive money for your work. At a part-time or full-time job sometime in the future, however, you probably won't be paid as quickly. If you work by the hour, you may receive your pay once a week. If you are on salary, your pay may come every two weeks or once a month.

You will also probably receive your pay in the form of a paycheck. Most paychecks have two parts. One part is the check itself. The other part of a paycheck is the stub. The paycheck stub shows how much you were paid. It also shows the different amounts taken out of your check and why. **Figure 14.1** shows an example of a paycheck stub.

Figure 14.1

PAYCHECK STUB

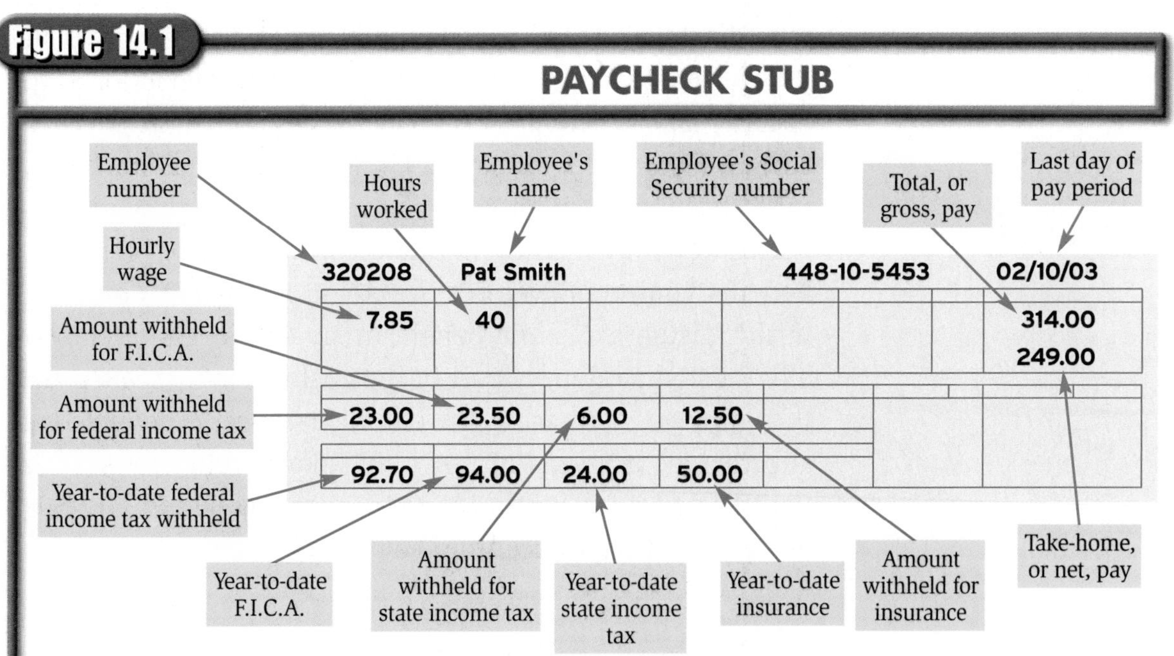

Important Information Pat Smith's Social Security number is on her paycheck stub. A Social Security number is a permanent identification number issued by the government to track contributions and work history. *How else is Pat Smith identified on her paycheck stub?*

Understanding Withholding

Take a close look at Pat Smith's paycheck stub shown in **Figure 14.1** on page 295. Compare the payment amounts. Pat's **gross pay,** or total pay, each week is $314.00. However, Pat doesn't take home all the money she earns. Her **net pay**—the amount she actually takes home—is $249.00. Like other employers, Pat's employer must **withhold,** or take out, money from her paycheck.

As Pat's paycheck stub shows, her employer withholds money for both federal and state income taxes. As you might guess, **income tax** is tax you pay to the government based on your income, or the money you make. Income tax money pays for government services, such as police and fire protection and public education.

Employers also withhold money from employees' paychecks for Social Security and Medicare taxes. **Social Security** is a federal government program that provides benefits for people of all ages. Workers pay Social Security taxes so they can receive benefits when they retire or are disabled. **Medicare** is a health care program provided by the federal government primarily for retired persons. Most workers rely upon Social Security benefits at some time in their lives. The money withheld for Social Security and Medicare taxes is labeled F.I.C.A. on the paycheck stub in **Figure 14.1** on page 295. **F.I.C.A.** stands for Federal Insurance Contribution Act.

Money may also be deducted from your paycheck for benefits your employer offers. As you learned in Chapter 8, health insurance is one benefit many employers offer. Usually the company pays part of the cost of the insurance, and the employees pay part. The employee's part is deducted, or subtracted, from his or her pay. Take another look at Pat Smith's paycheck. As you can see, each pay period, $12.50 is deducted for insurance from Pat's pay.

Making a Budget

Right now, you may not have much money, so you may not have a plan for managing your money. When you are working regularly and earning more money, you'll need a budget.

Career Opportunities

Marketing, Sales, and Service

Do you love shopping for the latest fashion styles or the newest gadgets? Do you look forward to school fund-raisers because you know you'll win an award for selling the most items? If so, you might consider a career in marketing, sales, and service.

BUYER
Local department store seeks buyer for men's clothing department. Responsible for purchasing merchandise from wholesalers and manufacturers. Requires knowledge of fashion trends and pricing strategy. Bachelor's degree required.

Critical Thinking

Why do you think a buyer would need a college degree?

A **budget** is a plan for saving and spending money. It is based on your income—the money you expect to have coming in. A budget is also based on your expenses—the money you will pay out for goods and services. Try to make and use a budget now. That way, you'll get started on the right foot. Just follow these steps.

Decide on Your Goals

To make a budget, first list the things you need or want. Do you need money for a new pair of shoes? Do you want to pay for singing lessons so you can try out for a part in a school musical? Are you saving money to buy a birthday present for a friend? Maybe you'd also like to put away money for college.

Divide your goals into short-term and long-term goals. Short-term goals are what you need or want to spend money on now or within the next 12 months. Long-term goals are spending or savings goals that take a year or more to reach.

Write down the amount of money each goal will cost. You may have to look in stores, at newspaper ads, or on the Internet to get an idea of what things cost. You can also get this information by calling businesses and talking to people.

The Global Workplace

Hurry Up and Wait

Your meeting is set for 10:00 A.M., but the exact time it'll actually begin depends on the country in which your meeting is being held. In Switzerland, punctuality is admired and your meeting will start on time. You will even impress your Swiss associates by arriving early. In Colombia, expect to be kept waiting. Meetings there usually start 15 to 30 minutes later than scheduled. If your meeting is in Russia, bring a book to read while you wait. There it's not unusual to be kept waiting one or two hours. No matter where you are, *always* arrive on time and have a good attitude if you have to wait.

Internet Activity

Use the Internet and library resources to research work schedules in one other country. What are the typical work day hours? What days make up this country's work week? Go to the *Exploring Careers* Web site at exploring.glencoe.com for a list of Web sites to help you complete this activity.

Prioritize Your Goals

Now look at your lists. You'll probably have more items listed than you have money for. That's why prioritizing is the next step in making a budget. As you know, when you prioritize, you put items in order from most to least important.

Think about which goals are most important to you. These will be at the top of your list. Your most important goal will be number 1 on your list. The next most important goal will be number 2, and so on.

Prioritizing will help you see clearly which goals are wants and which are needs. It will help you make choices. You may have to give up or put off reaching some of your goals in order to meet others. You may need a bike to get to your summer job, for example. To get the bike, you may have to give up the new clothes or CD player you want.

Figure Out Your Income and Expenses

The next step in making a budget is to figure out your income and expenses for each month. First, write down how much money you expect to have coming in. Include all your sources of income: allowance, gifts, earnings, and possibly tips from a job.

Pay Your Way Paying for part of your education is an excellent goal. *Why is it important to set and work toward such a goal now?*

Then write down your expenses for each month. You'll have two kinds of expenses: fixed expenses and flexible expenses. **Fixed expenses** are expenses you have already agreed to pay and that must be paid by a particular date. They are usually the same each month. To have your own telephone line, for example, you may pay your parents a set amount each month. You may pay bus or subway fare to get to school each day. Someday you may have a car payment due each month. Rent is another fixed expense.

Flexible expenses are expenses that come irregularly or that you can adjust more easily. These expenses may be different each month. Entertainment costs, such as concert tickets, are flexible expenses. Clothing and medical costs are others.

Set Up Your Budget

Now you're ready for the next step, setting up your budget. A written plan for spending and saving is best. The form shown in **Figure 14.2** on page 300 is a good place to start.

Fill in the information about your income and expenses first. Your income should be equal to or more than your total expenses. If it isn't, you may have to make some changes.

If you need to make changes, take a look at your flexible expenses. They are usually easier to change than fixed expenses. You may pack your lunch every day instead of buying it, for example. You may decide to buy new clothes next month instead of this month. Another way to approach the problem is to increase your income. You may decide to get a part-time job or work more hours, for instance. You may consider getting a job that pays more.

Figure 14.2

A BUDGET FORM

Categories	Budgeted Monthly Expenses	Actual Monthly Expenses
Savings		
Fixed Expenses		
Flexible Expenses		
Total Spent		
Total Income		

Keep Track of Your Money Many people use a form like this for their budget. *How would you use the column at the far right?*

Set Savings Aside

Don't forget savings. It's a key step to making a budget. Remember, a budget is a spending and savings plan. A savings plan helps you put aside money for long-term goals and unexpected needs. You may begin saving for your college education.

All you have to do is set aside part of your income each month. You may save 10 percent of your monthly income, for example. Jesse Reeves knows how quickly savings can add up. Jesse's monthly allowance is $40. He also makes $90 a week repairing bikes and skateboards at a shop in town. Jesse saves 10 percent of his monthly income. In one year he will save $516 of his income.

Jesse keeps his savings in a savings account at a local bank. You can make more money by keeping your money in a bank. The bank will pay you money known as **interest** to use the money in your savings account. The interest is added to the money that is already in your savings account. It's another source of income for you!

Stay Within Your Budget

You prepare a budget and begin to follow it. Your job isn't over, though. There's one last step. Like any other plan, your budget should be adjusted to fit your needs and wants. Check your budget at the end of every month. Does your income cover your expenses? Do you have money for savings? Do you need to adjust some of your flexible expenses?

You'll find other tips for staying within your budget in **Figure 14.3** on page 302. These spending rules will also help you be a smart and responsible consumer. You'll learn more about that in the next lesson.

Ways to Save the Most

Q: I want to put my savings in a bank. Do all banks pay the same amount of interest?

A: You need to be a smart shopper when choosing a bank. You'll find that some banks pay more interest than others. You'll also discover that banks offer other ways to save money in addition to savings accounts. Savings bonds, money market accounts, and certificate of deposit (CD) accounts are some other types of saving plans. These can pay more interest than a regular savings account, but they have more rules about the amount of money you deposit or how long the money has to stay in the account. So, compare banks and savings plans to find what's best for you.

Financing Your Education

Going to school is no small expense. The sooner you start planning how you will finance your education, the more likely you will achieve your educational goals. You may be saving money for your education right now. You may have already included savings for education in your budget.

There are many ways to pay for education, you just have to know where to look. Most schools have financial aid departments to help you find the financing that is best for you. When you apply for financial aid, you will have to fill out a Free Application for Financial Student Aid (FAFSA). The FAFSA uses information from the income tax returns of you and your parents to determine your financial need. The results of your FAFSA need analysis is listed in a Student Aid Report (SAR).

The following are some of the ways you can finance your education:

- A **scholarship** is money for education awarded to students because of their need, or academic or athletic achievement. Scholarships do not have to be repaid.

Figure 14.3

STAYING WITHIN YOUR BUDGET

Keep Track of Your Spending	• Carry a small notebook. • Note every penny you spend so you know where your money goes.
Don't Carry Around a Large Amount of Cash	• Take only as much cash as you think you'll need when you go out and you'll avoid impulse buying.
Shop Smart	• Think before you spend. • Compare prices. • Shop at discount stores.
Pay With Cash Whenever Possible	• Credit cards can make overspending too easy.

Simple Guidelines You can stick to your budget if you follow a few simple spending rules. *Which suggestion do you find most helpful? Why? Which suggestions do you already practice?*

- A **loan** is money borrowed from the government or a lender that must be repaid.
- A **work-study program** allows students to earn their education by working full- or part-time jobs in a related field throughout the student's academic career.
- A **grant** is money for education provided by the government, schools, or private donors. Grants do not have to be repaid.

No matter how much your educational goals will cost, one of these finance options can make it possible for you to reach your goals. All you need to do is plan ahead.

Lesson 14.1 Review and Activities

Key Terms Review

1. Write a report on managing your money. Include the terms below in your report.

- **income**
- **gross pay**
- **net pay**
- **withhold**
- **income tax**
- **Social Security**
- **Medicare**
- **F.I.C.A.**
- **budget**
- **fixed expenses**
- **flexible expenses**
- **interest**
- **scholarship**
- **loan**
- **work-study program**
- **grant**

Check Your Understanding

Choose the correct answer for each item. Write your answers on a separate sheet of paper.

2. Money that you earn regularly is your ______.
   a. flexible expenses
   b. F.I.C.A.
   c. income
3. Employers ______, or take out, money from employees' pay for various taxes.
   a. itemize
   b. withhold
   c. budget

Critical Thinking

Use complete sentences to answer the following questions. Write your answers on a separate sheet of paper.

4. What do you think is the main source of income for young people?
5. What problems might arise if you are too flexible about your budget?
6. What would you do if you needed to increase your income right now?

Character Building

7. **Making Choices** Ella's grandparents put money into her savings account for Ella to buy a car. Ella agreed to add $40 each month to her savings account so she'll have enough money to buy a car when she starts driving. Ella has recently taken up tennis, and she has been paying for tennis lessons instead of saving for a car. Should Ella use her money for tennis or save for a car? Why or why not?

Teamwork

8. **Create a Budget** Working in a group, create a fictitious teen. Make up facts about the teen's finances, including goals, income, and expenses. Then create a budget and work out money-management solutions for the teen you invented. Explain your budget and money-management recommendations in a group presentation.

Lesson 14.2

You, the Consumer

Discover

- How you can get the most for your money
- Ways that people pay for purchases

Why It's Important

Thinking before you spend pays off. When you do research and comparison shop, you get more for your money.

KEY TERMS

- **impulse buying**
- **warranty**
- **exchange**
- **refund**

You save for months to buy something you want. Maybe you have your eye on a new pair of athletic shoes or a computer. Finally you have enough money set aside to make your purchase. You go to the store, hand the salesperson your money, and the item is yours.

A few days later, you pass a different store. In the window, you see a similar item for less money. In fact, it not only costs less but it also has more features or is of higher quality. How could that be?

You took the time to save, and you reached your goal. Between saving for your purchase and actually making it, however, you forgot something. You skipped several important steps. Smart shoppers can tell you what those steps are.

Shop Carefully
Price, selection, and services may vary widely among different types of stores. *What factors are most important to you? What types of stores provide these for you?*

Becoming a Smart Shopper

Smart shoppers get the best value for their money. They get great satisfaction from the purchases they make. They also save a lot of money over time. What can you do to become a smart shopper? It's simple, really. You need to gather information, compare quality and price, and read the fine print.

Knowledge Is Power

Smart shoppers gather information before making a purchase. They find out as much as they can about the item they want or need. This kind of research helps them make an informed choice when they decide to buy something.

When you get in the habit of gathering information about products, you also can avoid impulse buying. **Impulse buying** is making a sudden, unplanned decision to buy. Everybody is prone to it from time to time. Just think of the last time you decided to buy candy or a magazine while waiting in a checkout line. The problem with impulse buying is that you often purchase things you don't need. You may also purchase items that are not worth the money you spend. More often than not, these items are not part of your budget.

Those are good reasons to get information about products in advance. How do you get information? Believe it or not, it's possible to find out quite a bit without even walking into a store.

Make Smart Shopping Decisions
Consumer magazines can help you decide which brand of product to purchase. You can also ask friends and family members for recommendations. *What questions might you ask them about product brands?*

Sources of Information

Newspapers are one source of information. Check out newspaper ads for products you wish to purchase. Use the ads to find out which stores in your area carry the products you want. You may also find product prices in newspaper ads. You can use this information to comparison shop without leaving home.

Smart shoppers often do research on products in magazines. *Consumer Reports* is just one magazine that helps consumers make choices. It compares prices, quality, and features of several brands of the same product. It also reports on how easy different brands are to use and how often they need to be repaired.

The Internet is another source of information. Online you can find product prices, as well as information on product features. Many Web sites compare products side-by-side. There are also sites where consumers report on their satisfaction with products they have purchased.

No Returns
Items you want to buy for a reduced price may be marked "As Is" or "All Sales Final." Be sure to check them carefully for defects. Try them on if appropriate. *Why is it important to do this before purchasing such items?*

Many smart shoppers also depend on word of mouth. They get information about products by talking with friends and family members. Are they satisfied with a product? What do they like or dislike about it? Would they buy the product again? Think of people whose opinions and judgment you trust.

Compare Quality and Price

You've got some information. Now you're ready to do some comparison shopping. Always compare both the quality and the price of an item you want to buy. You may be surprised. A more expensive product isn't always the better product, for example. Jerome Ticknor found that out the hard way.

"If one item was more expensive than another, I just assumed it was higher quality. That's not always true. I bought a high-priced jacket with a designer label. The first time I washed it, it fell apart. I saved for three months for that jacket. I didn't even think of checking how well it was made."

Items on sale can also fool you. They may be less expensive than regular-priced items. At the same time, they may not be of the same quality. Remember quality when you shop at a sale. Before making a purchase, make sure the goods on sale are real bargains. A good-quality item at a low price is a bargain.

There may be times, on the other hand, when you are willing to pay a high price. A higher-priced item may very well be good quality. Stop and think about whether it is right for you, though. Higher-priced items may have more features than you need. For instance, having 10 speeds on your bike may not be a feature you want or need. If so, this feature won't be worth the extra money to you.

Read the Fine Print

Smart shoppers don't stop there. To get further information about a product, they always read the labels on the item. Labels tell about the features of a product. Labels describe use and care. They also give information required by law on products such as clothing and food.

Clothing labels must contain the name of manufacturer, or maker, the country of origin, the fiber content, and instructions for care. Food labels provide the name of product, the name and address of manufacturer, the weight of contents, the ingredients (with the greatest quantity first), and the nutrients contained.

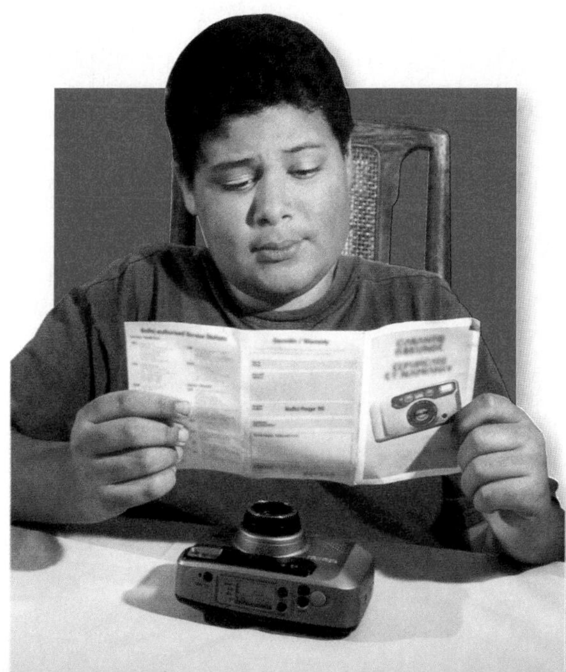

Check the Warranty
If an item you purchased breaks or does not work as it should, check the warranty. *What have you purchased that included a warranty?*

In addition to labels, many items come with a warranty. A **warranty** is a guarantee that a product meets certain standards of quality. Sometimes a product does not work as claimed in the warranty. When that happens, the manufacturer must either repair or replace it.

A warranty protects you after your purchase. If you're a smart shopper, though, you'll find out what the warranty covers before you purchase the item. Then you'll know what the manufacturer promises. Some warranties apply only to certain parts of the product or to specific conditions. Some expire, or end, after a certain period of time. Be aware of what you're getting into. Read the fine print in both labels and warranties.

Making a Purchase

You've done your homework as a shopper. You've gathered information. You've compared quality and prices. You've read labels and checked the warranty. What's next? You're ready to make a purchase. How are you going to pay?

Comparison Shop
Comparing quality and price helps you get the best value for your money. *Have you ever done any comparison shopping? Describe your experience.*

Ways to Pay

Most teens just use cash when they make a purchase. That's not the only way to pay, however. **Figure 14.4** on pages 310–311 shows some of the different methods people use to pay for their purchases. These methods include cash, checks, debit cards, layaway, and credit.

Be responsible about your purchases. Think carefully before you make your selection. Choose a way of paying that is both convenient and practical for you. All your purchases should fit your budget.

Refunds and Exchanges

Have you ever been unhappy with a product you purchased? Your new video game system may not have worked properly. Maybe the zipper on the jeans you bought turned out to be faulty. What did you do?

When purchases don't work out for one reason or another, you usually have two options. You can ask for either an exchange or a refund. An **exchange** is a trade of one item for another. You might ask to trade the pair of jeans for another pair, for example. A **refund** is the return of your money in exchange for the item you purchased. If you decide you just don't want the jeans because you question their quality, you might ask for your money back.

When you're unhappy with something you purchased, follow these rules. If you do, you'll be more likely to get an exchange or refund.

- ***Know the store's policy.*** Every store sets its own rules for exchanges and returns. These are usually posted where you pay. Read the rules. If you don't understand them, ask the salesperson before paying for your purchase. Never assume you can return an item.
- ***Keep proof of your purchase.*** The sales receipt is proof of the price, date of purchase, and store where you bought the item. At most stores, you will have to show your receipt to make an exchange or receive a refund.
- ***Make sure an exchange or refund is possible.*** Damaged or sale items may be marked "As Is" or "All Sales Final." In these cases, you cannot return the item.

Relax

Ready-set-relax! Those are good starting instructions for a job interview, a major test, or any other potentially stressful situation. Take the time to prepare yourself in advance. Shortly before the interview or test, review carefully. Then relax! Feeling calm and confident will help you do your best.

Cooperative Learning Activity

- With a small team of classmates, research one relaxation technique.
- Practice the technique for one week.
- Discuss how well it worked with your teammates.
- Compare this relaxation technique with the techniques other teams researched.

- ***Be prompt and prepared.*** If you have a problem with a purchase, don't waste time. Take the item, the sales receipt, and warranty (if any) to the store. Be ready to describe the problem. You may have to fill out a form that includes your reason for returning the item.

Alma Perez of Buena Park, California, found out about these rules too late. "My favorite store was having an incredible clearance sale. Some things were marked down 75 percent!

Figure 14.4 **WAYS TO PAY FOR PURCHASES**

Cash is not the only way to pay for a purchase. Compare and contrast the different methods of payment consumers can choose. *When might you use each?*

A

Check

A check is a written document that permits the transfer of money from a bank account to a person or business. To pay by check, you must open a checking account with a bank or credit union. You deposit, or put, money into the account. Then you can write checks up to the amount of money in your account.

B

Debit Card

Many people use debit cards to pay for purchases. When you use a debit card, money is withdrawn directly from your account. You might use a debit card to pay for groceries rather than carry a large amount of cash to the store.

I got a little carried away. I bought a huge bag of clothes, many of which I didn't even bother to try on. Two of the sweaters and one pair of jeans didn't fit me. When I tried to return them, the manager explained that these items fell under the 'All Sales Final' rule. I was out $60. I'll never make that mistake again!"

Becoming a smart shopper takes some time and some practice. It pays off, though. The next time you're thinking about buying something, put what you've learned to work. See for yourself how your money can work for you.

D

Credit

Credit allows you to receive a good or service now and pay for it later. Credit cards are the most common type of credit. You receive a monthly bill for your credit card purchases. If you cannot pay the bill in full, you must still pay a minimum amount. You also pay interest on the money you owe.

C

Layaway

When you do not have enough cash to buy something, you might use a layaway plan. A layaway plan is a scheduled payment plan for a purchase. You pay a small amount of money down on the item you want. Then you make regular payments until you have paid the full amount for the item. When you have paid in full, the item is yours to take home.

Lesson 14.2 Review and Activities

Key Terms Review

1. Use the following terms to write a dialogue between two friends about how to be a smart shopper. Then, with a friend, perform the dialogue for the class.
   - **impulse buying**
   - **exchange**
   - **warranty**
   - **refund**

Check Your Understanding

Tell whether each statement is true or false. Rewrite any false statement to make it true. Write your answers on a separate sheet of paper.

2. Smart shoppers compare quality and price before they purchase products.
3. A higher-priced item is always a better product than a lower-priced item.

Critical Thinking

Use complete sentences to answer the following questions. Write your answers on a separate sheet of paper.

4. Why might it be important for people to read about the use and care of a product before deciding to purchase it?
5. Do you think buying designer or brand-name products can be a good use of your money when comparable generic products are available? Explain.
6. What are some of the risks involved in using credit?

Connecting to the Workplace

7. **Developing a Purchase Plan** You've learned HTML in your computer class and are very good at creating Web pages. Online photo albums are your specialty. You would like to offer Web page creation services to family and friends. You have a computer, but will need a scanner in order to scan photos that your customers will want on their Web pages. You have savings you could use to purchase a scanner. Make a checklist of the steps you would take to get the best scanner for your money.

Community Involvement

8. **Create a Teen Consumer Guide** Work with your classmates to put together a consumer guide of the best businesses in your community for teens to shop for goods and services. List the name, address, and business hours of each store. Then write a short description of the kinds of goods or services each offers. Include some "insider" comments about bargains or special items or services at the places listed. Make copies of the guide to share with other students at your school. Also donate a copy to your school library.

Investigating Career Clusters

MARKETING, SALES, AND SERVICE

Marketing • Developing, promoting, and distributing goods and services to consumers

Sales • Providing goods and services to consumers

Service • Performing tasks for consumers

Job Title	Work Description
Advertising Copywriter	Writes advertisements
Buyer	Meets with manufacturers to buy merchandise to be sold in stores
Cashier	Totals bills, receives money, makes change, and gives receipts
Counter Clerk	Answers questions, takes orders, and receives payments and returns
Public Relations Manager	Develops, maintains, and evaluates a favorable public image for a business
Retail Salesperson	Assists customers in selection and purchase of goods and services
Sales Manager	Assigns sales territories and establishes training programs for sales representatives
Store Manager	Provides day-to-day supervision of the operation of a store

Exploration Activity

Marketing, Sales, and Service Use library and Internet resources to research a career in the Marketing, Sales, and Service career cluster. Write a report that includes information about the kinds of work, the skills required, the working conditions, the training and education required, and the career outlook.

Cooperative Learning Interview a classmate about the career he or she researched. Find out as much information about that career as you can during the interview. Then have your classmate interview you about the career you researched. Afterward, take turns sharing what you learned from each other with the class.

Chapter 14 Review and Activities

Chapter Highlights

Lesson 14.1 The money you receive or earn regularly is your income. Income sources include allowance, gifts, and earnings from a job. Making a budget is a smart way to manage your money and save for future expenses, such as education.

Lesson 14.2 Thinking about how you spend will help you get more for your money. Smart shoppers gather information about a product before purchasing it. They compare quality and price. They also pay close attention to labels and warranties.

Key Concept Review

Use complete sentences to answer the following questions. Write your answers on a separate sheet of paper.

1. What is income?
2. What must you do before you can set up a budget for yourself?
3. What should every budget include?
4. Name some ways that you can help finance your education.

Critical Thinking

Use complete sentences to answer the following questions. Write your answers on a separate sheet of paper.

5. Why is it important to be honest with yourself about income and expenses when making a budget?
6. Why do you need to be careful when you gather information about products from newspaper ads?
7. What advice would you give someone who has just started to use a credit card?

Skill Building

8. **Information—Organizes and Maintains Information**
   Develop a filing system that organizes sales receipts, warranties, and product instructions. Write a paragraph describing your filing system.
9. **Systems—Monitors and Corrects Performance**
   Use the budget form on page 300 to make a one-month budget. At the end of each week, check to see how well you are staying within your budget. Make changes as needed. At the end of the month, make a new budget that will span six months.

Personal Career Portfolio

Academic Applications

10. Social Studies

Most people are used to paying money for goods and services. Another way to get the items you need is by bartering. When you barter, you trade goods and services without the use of money. If you've ever swapped comic books or baseball cards, you've done some bartering. Arrange to barter services with a friend or family member. Write a paragraph about your experience.

11. Mathematics

Imagine that you bought $250 worth of clothes and charged it to your credit card. The credit card charges 18 percent interest annually (1.5 percent per month). If you pay the minimum payment of $20 each month, what will you owe after three months? How much will you have paid in finance charges?

Samples of Work

- **Gather** together examples of outstanding work from school, work, and extracurricular activities.
- **Select** examples of work that show you in your best light.
- **Include** a variety of different types of work you have completed, including reports and essays, computer programs, blueprints, photos, tapes of oral presentations, copies of assessments showing academic growth, and summaries of projects showing artistic or other abilities.
- **Include** work that shows your problem-solving skills, communication skills, and critical-thinking skills.
- **Label** this section of your portfolio *Work Samples*.
- **File** these work samples in your Personal Career Portfolio.
- **List** your portfolio entry on your Personal Career Portfolio contents page.

Chapter 15

Living a Balanced Life

Lesson 15.1

Work Isn't Everything!

Lesson 15.2

Giving Something Back

CAREER CLUSTER

You will explore careers in the Science, Technology, Engineering, and Mathematics career cluster.

What You'll Learn

- You will discover how to balance work responsibilities and personal responsibilities.
- You will learn how to manage your time and how to make your time count.
- You will find out what is involved in being a good citizen.

Get Ready!

Make a Mobile

Ask adult friends or family members for tips on how they juggle the responsibilities they have at home, at work, and in the community.

Apply On separate small strips of construction paper, write down the different responsibilities and corresponding tips. Attach string to each strip. Use them to create a mobile in which the "responsibilities" hang in balance with the corresponding "tips."

Lesson 15.1

Work Isn't Everything!

Discover

- Why it is important to balance the different parts of your life
- How to make time for school, work, family, and friends

Why It's Important

Life is more than work. Friends, family members, and activities other than work bring meaning to life. They may also give meaning to the work you do.

KEY TERMS

- **balance**
- **leisure**
- **time management**

You do work at school and at home. You may also volunteer your time or have a part-time job. Your life, however, most likely includes other kinds of activities. In other words, your life probably has balance. There is **balance** when the parts of something have the same weight, amount, or force. You probably spend time and energy on all the parts of your life. You pay attention to your responsibilities at school, at home, and on the job if you have one. You also have **leisure,** or time to do what you like.

In the future, work is likely to take up a great deal more of your time and energy than it does now. You may begin to feel a pull between work and other parts of your life. Finding a balance and keeping it may become a challenge.

Balancing Work and Family Life

Julie Myers is a flight attendant. She has been a flight attendant for 15 years. Here's Julie's advice:

"Just keep this in mind. No matter what happens at work, don't forget what you're working for."

Play Time
To be mentally and physically healthy, people must have time to play. *What physical activities do you enjoy in your free time?*

The Global Workplace

What Time Is It?

You might be puzzled when the alarm clock in your Austrian hotel says 20:00. No, the clock isn't broken. It's just telling the time using the 24-hour clock system. This system, known as "military time" in the United States, is used in many countries. In this system 8:00 A.M. is 08:00 hours; 3:00 P.M. is 15:00 hours. The trick? Add 12 to the hours after 12 noon.

You may notice that Europeans drop the "hours," calling the time just by the number. In casual conversation some people might not use the 24-hour system, but don't be surprised if your international travel agent reminds you that your flight leaves at 22:00!

Internet Activity

Use the Internet and library resources to research one country. What is the format for writing the date in this country? Is it the same as in the United States? Go to the *Exploring Careers* Web site at exploring.glencoe.com for a list of Web sites to help you complete this activity.

"Take it from me," Julie goes on. "When I first started out, my work was my life. I spent a huge amount of time on the job. I love my profession, and I couldn't get enough of it. I was always ready to fill in when others wanted extra time off.

"My schedule caught up with me, though. I'll never forget the morning seven years ago when I woke up in a hotel in Los Angeles. I was on the crew for the early flight east. I felt tired and empty. I was working all the time. I sat up in bed and thought, 'Is this what life is all about?' "

These days, Julie is in the air only three days most weeks. She usually spends just two nights each week away from home. Then she has a block of time off, which she spends with her husband and two sons at their home in Pittsburgh. Julie's new work schedule allows her to keep the job she loves and spend more quality time with her family.

Family Time
Sharing activities with family members can bring you closer together. *What kinds of things does your family do together?*

"After that 'wake-up call' in Los Angeles," explains Julie, "I took a close look at what is important to me. My family is at the top of my list. Then there's running, gardening—well, the list goes on. My life is more balanced now. I feel much happier."

What's Your Life About?

As Julie realized, life is about much more than work. Work is an important part of life and has many rewards. However, your personal goals and interests, and the activities you spend time on outside of work are also valuable. The people you care about and who care about you bring meaning to your life, too.

Whatever your career someday, remember that you have a responsibility to yourself as well as to your job. Try to balance the different parts of your life—your work and your commitments to yourself and others. The right balance will make you happier and healthier. It will make you more satisfied with everything you do.

Try This Activity

What's Important to You?

Take some time to think about what your life is about. Who is important to you? What is important to you? Make a list of people and activities that make your life meaningful.

Reflect Do you think that your list will change as time goes on? How? Why?

Making Your Time Count

Identifying what is important to you is the first step in the balancing act of life. The next step is to figure out how to manage your time so that you can balance the different parts of your life.

Managing Your Time

How well do you manage your time? Do you usually stay up late to finish your homework? Do you run out of time when you're working on a big project? Do you allow interruptions to disrupt your work? Are you often late for school? Does your family complain that they never see you? If you have any of these problems, you need to learn and practice time management. **Time management** involves choosing how to spend your time and creating a schedule for your choices. You can budget your time just as you do your money.

Time management skills will help you in all areas of your life. Time management is an important part of reaching goals. You will have more time for special activities, such as sports and hobbies. You won't constantly be late or forget to do important tasks. You will have more time for yourself and others, and your stress level will be reduced.

You can begin to develop time management skills now. Soon time management will become a habit. It will serve you your entire life. Effective time management skills will help you be recognized as someone who may be able to assume more job responsibilities.

Try some of the tools and techniques shown in **Figure 15.1** on pages 322–323. They'll help you make time for everything that's important to you.

Being Present

Time management skills help you make time for all kinds of things. If you manage your time well, you may even feel as though hours have been added to your day.

Having time for everything that is important to you isn't all there is to it, though. You want the time you spend to count. Making your time count is all about being present. When you are present, you are fully alive and alert to whatever you're doing.

Make Your Time Count

Q: I'm bored! I never have interesting things to do with my free time. Am I just a slug?

A: Having a balanced life not only means having free time, but it also means making the most of this free time by spending it on activities that you enjoy. If you've got too much time on your hands, you're out of balance. Think of ways to challenge yourself. Make a list of things you would like to learn or do. Then, just do it! Filling your free time with satisfying activities will help you grow as a person and bring balance to your life.

You may be working on a homework assignment, a task around the house, or a project on the job, for example. How can you be present? How can you pay close attention to what you are doing? Here are a few suggestions.

- ***Avoid interruptions.*** If a friend calls while you are doing your homework, for instance, tell him or her that you will call back when you are finished.

Figure 15.1

TIME MANAGEMENT TOOLS AND TECHNIQUES

Think of time management as making choices. If you have just a few choices, finding the time may be easy. If you have lots of choices, you may need help organizing your time. Many people find these tools and techniques helpful. *Which have you used before?*

A

Make a "To-Do List"

Some people use a list as a reminder of tasks to complete. Once a day or once a week, make a "To-Do List" for the next day or week. As you complete each task, cross it off the list. You'll get a feeling of accomplishment as you complete each task.

B

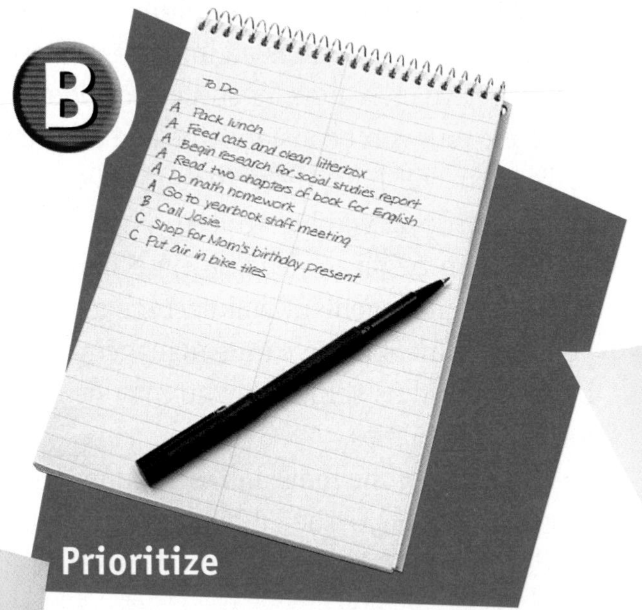

Prioritize

If you have a long list of tasks, you may not know where to begin. Try ranking the tasks in order of importance. Label top-priority activities with an A. Mark the activities you need to complete next with a B. Activities marked with a C are the least important.

- ***Stay on task.*** Stick with what you're doing until it is done. Don't stop to read that magazine you find while cleaning your room. Save it for later. Later will arrive sooner when you focus on what you are doing.
- ***Don't try to do too many things at once.*** Concentrate on one task or activity. Give it your best. You'll complete tasks more quickly, and you'll do a better job.

Break Big Projects Into Small Steps

Large or long-term projects can be difficult to manage because you may overlook things that need to be done later. Try breaking big projects into manageable steps. Then treat each step as a separate task.

Set Up a Schedule

Once you know what tasks you have to do, make a schedule showing when tasks must be completed. Many people use a calendar or day planner for scheduling. You can enter tasks on your schedule as soon as you know about them. Then you always know what's coming up.

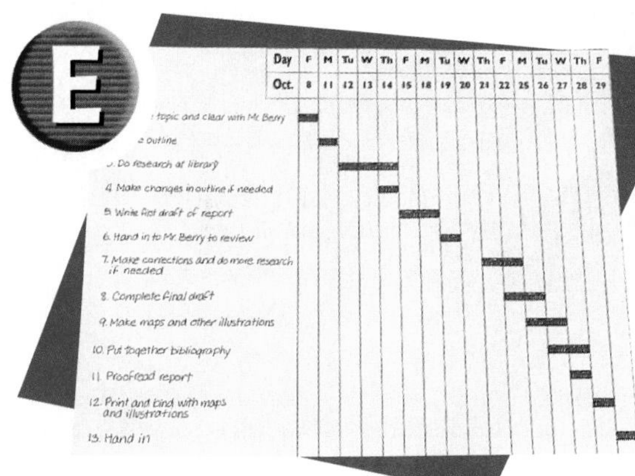

Make a Time Line

For big projects, you may want to create a time line. This kind of chart shows the order of events in time. A time line can help you see the stages in a complicated or long-term project. You will be able to see where you are in a project at a glance. You will also see what you need to do now.

Exercise

Exercise is great for your physical health, but its benefits go beyond fitness. Regular exercise can improve your attitude. So, when the stresses of school or work make you feel crabby and tired, be sure to take a half-hour exercise break. Not only will this do wonders for you physically, but it will also help you mentally.

Cooperative Learning Activity

- With a group, choose an exercise and do it for one week.
- Make a list of the benefits of exercise.

Staying Focused

Being present at work means using your time wisely and being focused on what you are doing. Being present in your activities with others also involves focus. When you focus on others, you show them love, care, and attention. Here are some ideas for making your time with others count.

- ***Communicate.*** Make talking and listening to friends and family members a priority. Share your thoughts and feelings. Listen to what others have to say, what problems they're facing, and what interests them. Practice active listening.
- ***Be considerate.*** Pay attention to the little things that make life more pleasant for everyone. Do things without being told. Surprise others with small favors.
- ***Offer praise and encouragement.*** Remember how good it feels to hear an encouraging word. Show your appreciation for the efforts of others. Give others support.
- ***Keep promises.*** If you say you'll be somewhere or do something, stick to your word. Be dependable.

Time at work is valuable. Time with others is precious. Be present wherever you are, whatever you are doing. That's the best way to make your time count.

Find Your Own Balance
Everyone's situation for balancing work and family responsibilities is different. *How do day-care centers help some parents fulfill their work responsibilities? What can working parents do to make the most of their family time?*

Lesson 15.1 Review and Activities

Key Terms Review

1. Create a diagram that shows the connections between balance, leisure, and time management. Include the terms below in your diagram.
- **balance**
- **time management**
- **leisure**

Check Your Understanding

Choose the correct answer for each item. Write your answers on a separate sheet of paper.

2. It is important to balance your work time and your ______ time.
a. business
b. life
c. personal

3. To help you make time for what is important to you, use ______.
a. time management
b. other people's time
c. free time

Critical Thinking

Use complete sentences to answer the following questions. Write your answers on a separate sheet of paper.

4. Why is it especially important to set aside personal time when you have a consuming job?

5. Which time management strategy would you use to set aside time for homework? Which would help you manage a long-term project?

6. What does it mean to be "present" on a task?

Character Building

7. **The Importance of Time Management** Sarah has a busy life. She wants to fit as many tasks and activities as she can into her day. So, she's created a new schedule that limits her to 30 minutes per task. Every half hour she moves on to the next task—even if she didn't finish the last task. Whenever possible she does two tasks at the same time. For example, she reads her e-mail while she helps a friend with homework over the phone. Does Sarah manage her time well? What time management suggestions would you give her?

Teamwork

8. **Create a Time Line** Team up with a group of classmates to plan an end-of-year celebration for your class. At the celebration you will serve refreshments and exhibit the projects your class completed during the year. Invite family members, teachers, counselors, and members of the school administration. Create a time line for planning the class celebration. Begin with today's date and end four weeks from now.

Lesson 15.2

Giving Something Back

Discover

- Your responsibilities to your community
- How you can contribute to the life of your community

Why It's Important

Taking an active part in your community is not only your responsibility, but also a way to enrich your life. When you get involved, you meet people, learn new skills, and make your community a better place to live.

KEY TERMS

- citizen
- register
- civic minded
- community service

What group are you a part of? You probably think first about your group of friends or your athletic team, club, or musical group. Beyond that, you are a part of your school, your family, your neighborhood, your state, your country, and the world.

Within each of these groups, you enjoy certain rights, and you hold certain responsibilities. In general, these responsibilities boil down to "good citizenship," which means being a productive and responsible member of your community.

What Is a Citizen?

People use the word "citizen" to mean different things. Legally, a **citizen** is someone who is recognized by the government as having the rights and protections of a country. Everyone born in the United States is automatically a legal citizen, but people from other countries can also become U.S. citizens through an official process called *naturalization*.

Everyone in the United States, whether he or she is a legal citizen or not, has certain rights, such as freedom of speech and religion. Everyone has a responsibility to be a "good citizen" to others.

Participate in Your Community When members of a community work together, they make life better for everyone. *In what kinds of community projects have you participated?*

When we talk about being a good citizen, we mean that you should be a responsible, contributing member of society. In this general sense, everyone is a citizen—of a school, a town, and a state.

Respecting Others

Remember the key to getting along with others? You learned it in Chapter 9. The key is respect, or consideration, for others.

When you show respect for others, you make a good member of any group. Showing respect for others is everyone's responsibility. Show respect for other community members by treating them as you—and they—would like to be treated. Wait your turn, for example, instead of trying to cut into the front of a line.

Speak respectfully to adults, such as older citizens, teachers, and police officers. Greeting adults and calling them "Mr.," "Ms.," or "Mrs." is another way to show your respect.

Remember to show respect to everyone, not just people you know or like or who are like you. If someone holds different values or beliefs from yours, be open and accepting. If you disagree with someone, give that person a fair chance to explain his or her opinion.

Help Raise Money Good citizens often help raise money for worthy causes. *What fund-raising events take place in your community?*

Caring for What You Share

You also have a responsibility to take good care of the property you share with others in your community. Be as careful with library books or playground equipment, for example, as you would be with your own possessions. Do the same with other community property, such as recreation areas, the school building, streets, and sidewalks. Take a moment to pick up litter and discard it in the proper place, for instance.

Career Opportunities

Science, Technology, Engineering, and Mathematics

If you love figuring out how things work, then a career in science, technology, engineering, and mathematics may be for you. Some jobs in this cluster are entry-level, but many require advanced education.

Critical Thinking

Why would a research assistant need communication and computer skills?

RESEARCH ASSISTANT

Oceanographer seeks research assistant to perform laboratory experiments, gather samples, and maintain a database of research results. Top candidate will have a degree in biology or related field, with extensive lab work.

Staying Informed

Knowing what goes on in your community is also your responsibility. You need to stay informed about issues and events.

Read your community newspaper and listen to local radio and television reports for news about community happenings. Talk to your family members and neighbors to learn what they think about issues.

Making Your Voice Heard

One of the main things that separates legal citizens from other members of the community is the right to vote. Voting is both a right and a responsibility. It is one of the most important responsibilities of citizens.

By voting, citizens express their points of view. They help to decide who the nation's leaders will be and under what laws everyone will live. To be eligible to vote, you must be a legal citizen and at least 18 years old, and you must **register,** or officially sign up as a qualified voter. When you choose not to vote, you let other people make these decisions for you. You disregard an important responsibility and an important right.

Try This Activity

Learn About Voting

Methods for registering to vote vary from place to place. Find out how registering is done in your area. Call the League of Women Voters or your county election commission. Ask how, when, and where citizens can register to vote. Also ask what documents they need to bring along to register.

Create a Voting Information Pamphlet Create a pamphlet about how to register to vote. Include in your pamphlet a sample voter registration form. Ask your teacher to make photocopies of the pamphlet. Distribute the pamphlet to your classmates.

Doing Your Part

Your responsibilities as a citizen will grow as you get older, move into the work world, and get your own place to live. One of the ways you can practice good citizenship and stay connected to your community as your life changes is by being civic minded. Being **civic minded** means being concerned about and active in community affairs. People who are civic minded remember that they are an important part of a community.

You may already be playing a very important role in the life of your community. You may be donating your time and energy to others by serving as a volunteer.

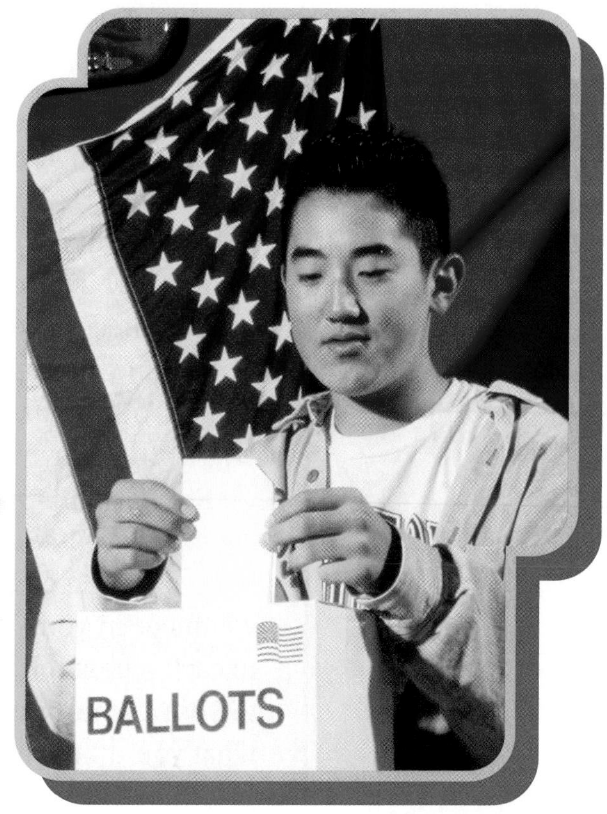

Get Out and Vote
Voting is one of your most important responsibilities as a citizen. Remember to register when you turn 18. *How important will your vote be? Will it matter in an election in which millions of people vote? Why?*

Ways to Lend a Hand

Aaron picks up groceries for his elderly neighbor once a week. Casey helps out at the local community recycling center on Saturdays. Davon reads to young children at the public library after school. Yoko helps paint houses with her Habitat for Humanity group. Don regularly takes part in events such as walk-a-thons to raise money for different causes.

All of these young people are performing **community service,** volunteer work that benefits the community. Young volunteers are active in every community. Do you and your friends volunteer your talents and skills to your community? What do you do? How can you make a difference?

A personal commitment to your community can also be helpful to you in your job search and in your career. Employers consider community involvement important because of the initiative and commitment it demonstrates. Community service is also evidence of your ability to manage your time and energy. Many companies prefer to hire employees who will represent them through community service work. If you have community service experience, be sure to include it on your résumé.

Try This Activity

Explore Service Learning

There are many ways you can help others in your community. There might be a service learning program in your community. Through a service learning program, your community service becomes part of your schoolwork. You might collect used clothing for the needy or hand out magazines and newspapers to people in a hospital or nursing home. You might volunteer at your local library. There are many other ways you can volunteer.

Reflect on Opportunities Find out about service learning programs in your community. If there aren't any, find out how you could create one. Then think of three ways you could volunteer in your community. Write a paragraph about each. In each paragraph, explain what you could contribute, or give, to your community as that kind of volunteer. Also describe what you think you would get out of the experience.

The Rewards of Good Citizenship

There are many rewards of being a volunteer. One of the most important is that you feel good about yourself. When you help someone else, you see how valuable your time and energy can be to others. That gives you a sense of self-worth. You have the sense of accomplishment that comes from a job well done. When you volunteer, you also gain valuable work experience.

Here's what Alberto Fuentes of Falls Church, Virginia, has to say about giving back to his community: "I've been tutoring English for the past six months. I'm from Peru, so we speak mostly Spanish at home. Last summer a boy from Puerto Rico moved in across the street. He's my age and ended up being in my class. I noticed that he was having trouble in English and science. I remembered what it was like when I first came to the United States. Sometimes I didn't even understand the instructions on a test. I asked him if he'd like some help. We meet twice a week for about an hour, and he's doing much better now. He called me last night to tell me he got a B+ on his last English paper. I can't tell you how good that made me feel. I think I was even happier than he was! When you help someone else, it's an awesome feeling, and the experience you get can help you, too. Maybe I'll be a teacher someday!"

Use Your Skills
There may be a volunteer opportunity for you as close as next door or just around the corner. *What skills or interests could you contribute to your community?*

There's no doubt about it. Being a good citizen helps you in many ways. It gives you a sense of belonging and a feeling of pride. You are able to share community spaces, such as libraries, parks, and museums, with others. You are also able to share your ideas, interests, and skills. Along the way, you develop skills that will be useful to you throughout your life. Some may even lead to a career one day. You get so much from your community. It's your responsibility to give something back.

Lesson 15.2 Review and Activities

Key Terms Review

1. Create a poster that encourages people to register to vote. Use words and images on your poster to illustrate and explain why voting is such an important responsibility. Use all of the following key terms on your poster.
   - **citizen**
   - **register**
   - **civic minded**
   - **community service**

Check Your Understanding

On a separate sheet of paper, tell whether each statement is true or false. Rewrite any false statement to make it true.

2. Only legal citizens need to stay informed about issues and events.
3. The key to getting along with others is showing responsibility.
4. It is the government's responsibility to care for community property.

Critical Thinking

Use complete sentences to answer the following questions. Write your answers on a separate sheet of paper.

5. Why do you need to be well-informed in order to fulfill your responsibility as a voter?
6. What contribution could you make to the community by participating in a volunteer activity?

Connecting to the Workplace

7. **Applying Citizenship Skills** Think of a job that interests you. How could you apply your citizenship skills to this job? Make a list of the citizenship skills described on pages 327–331. Next to each write an example of how you would use this skill on the job. Use this information to create a large chart to display for the class. Then describe the job you are interested in to the class and share your examples of applying citizenship skills on that job.

Community Involvement

8. **Extend Your Business** Many companies feel it's important to give something back to the communities in which they do business. They contribute to local charities and encourage their employees to do volunteer work. Suppose you have a lawn-and-garden or baby-sitting service. Your business is good, and you have many customers. You'd like to offer the same services in your community from time to time as a volunteer. How could you serve your community doing yardwork or baby-sitting as a volunteer? Name two ways.

Investigating Career Clusters

SCIENCE, TECHNOLOGY, ENGINEERING, AND MATHEMATICS

Science • The systematic use of observations and experiments to gain knowledge about the world

Technology • The practical use of scientific knowledge

Engineering • Solving practical problems by combining science and mathematics with technology

Mathematics • The study of numbers and their relationships

Job Title	Work Description
Anthropologist	Studies the development of humans and human society
Astronomer	Studies space, stars, and planets
Biological Technician	Assists scientists who study living things
Botanist	Studies plants
Chemical Engineer	Applies principles of chemistry and engineering to solve problems involving the production and use of chemicals
Entomologist	Studies insects and how they affect plants and animals
Oceanographer	Studies and explores the oceans

Exploration Activity

Science, Technology, Engineering, and Mathematics Use library and Internet resources to research a career in the Science, Technology, Engineering, and Mathematics career cluster. Write a report on the kinds of work, skills required, working conditions, training and education required, and career outlook.

Cooperative Learning Interview a classmate about the career he or she researched. Find out as much information about the career as you can during the interview. Then have your classmate interview you about the career you researched. Afterward share what you learned with the class.

Chapter 15 Review and Activities

Chapter Highlights

Lesson 15.1 Balancing your work time and your personal time will make you more satisfied with everything you do.

Lesson 15.2 Citizens have certain rights and responsibilities. Voting and volunteering are two important responsibilities of citizens.

Key Concept Review

Use complete sentences to answer the following questions. Write your answers on a separate sheet of paper.

1. Why should you try to balance the different parts of your life?
2. What does time management involve?
3. What are five tools or techniques of time management?
4. What are the requirements for voting?
5. How does volunteering help you feel good about yourself?

Critical Thinking

Use complete sentences to answer the following questions. Write your answers on a separate sheet of paper.

6. Does your life have balance? Explain your answer.
7. How do you practice being focused?
8. Which citizenship skills do you need to work on?
9. What are some ways you can make your voice heard until you are old enough to vote?

Skill Building

10. **Resources—Allocates Material and Facility Resources**
    Zach collects and trades comic books, giving the money he makes to a local homeless shelter. For $5, Zach could reserve a display table at the upcoming comic book fair. Zach could also rent a table for $3 or buy a used table for $10. What should Zach do? Why?
11. **Resources—Allocates Human Resources**
    Use the Internet and library resources to find out about a "family-friendly" benefit. In an oral report, explain how the benefit helps reduce employee stress and increase employee productivity.

Academic Applications

12. Social Studies

U.S. citizens have many rights and responsibilities. Some of these responsibilities, such as paying taxes, are required by law. Some, such as caring for shared property, are not. In a small group, identify a problem in your community. Find out what, if anything, is being done about it. If something's being done, join the effort. If not, plan a way to solve the problem and carry out your plan. Write an account of your group's effort for a local newspaper.

13. Language Arts

Write a self-evaluation of how you manage your time. Do you procrastinate? Do you meet deadlines? Are you always on time? Read your self-evaluation. What would you like to change? How would you go about changing?

Personal Career Portfolio

Evaluate and Refine Your Portfolio

- **Evaluate** the contents and organization of your Personal Career Portfolio.
- **Review** your portfolio from a prospective employer's point of view.
- **Consider** the logical organization of documents, appearance, creativity, neatness, content, and breadth of types of documents.
- **Consider** how these documents show what you have learned and how you have improved your skills.
- **Consider** your reasons for including each document.
- **Proofread** the entire portfolio.
- **Write** a list of improvements that can be made to your portfolio.
- **Make** the improvements to your portfolio.
- **Reevaluate** and refine your portfolio on a regular basis.

Chapter 16

Looking Beyond Today

Lesson 16.1

Dealing With Change

Lesson 16.2

Lifelong Learning

CAREER CLUSTER

You will explore careers in the Transportation, Distribution, and Logistics career cluster.

What You'll Learn

- You will learn about life changes you may experience.
- You will explore ways to handle challenging personal and job-related changes.
- You will discover how to think about, plan for, and move toward your future.

Get Ready!

Life Changes Word Web

Write the word "change" in the center of a piece of paper. Write two major life changes you have experienced on the paper and connect each to the word "change" with a line. Ask three adults how they handled similar changes. Write these down and connect them to the changes listed on the word web.

Apply Compare your web with classmates' webs. What changes and coping strategies were common?

Lesson 16.1

Dealing With Change

Discover

- How to deal with personal changes beyond your control
- Kinds of personal changes you might choose in the future
- How to handle job and career changes
- Ways of looking at and preparing for change

Why It's Important

Thinking about future changes gives you an idea of what to expect. You'll feel confident about dealing with the changes that come your way in life.

KEY TERMS

- **stepparent**
- **blended family**

One thing you can count on in life is change. You may know this already from your own experience.

Some changes are expected. Others are not. Even when we know to expect change, it can still take us by surprise. Change is also hard to predict. The idea of it makes many of us nervous or uneasy. In some situations, change is beyond our control. We have no choice but to accept it.

Personal Changes Beyond Your Control

You've probably already experienced many changes in your life—some pleasant, some not. You can be sure that more change will come your way. You may even look forward to some changes. You were probably eager to become a teenager. Maybe you can't wait to get a driver's license. You may be looking ahead to the day when you graduate from high school. Moving into your own place may be something else you see yourself doing one day. As you get older, you will continue to experience all kinds of personal changes.

Big Changes, Small Changes
Life is full of changes. *What big changes have you already experienced? What changes are you looking forward to?*

Many changes are predictable. You can plan for them. You know that you will soon be entering high school, for example. Other changes happen to you. Many are not changes you would choose. They can be difficult to handle.

Divorce, remarriage, moving, illness, and death are all unexpected changes. Like a sudden storm, changes such as these can catch you by surprise. They can even upset and uproot you.

Family Changes

Many families have to deal with the changes that divorce brings. Divorce can be very difficult for children of all ages. If your parents divorce, you may feel as though your world has been turned upside down. You may worry about who will take care of you or where you will live. You may wonder how or if you will continue to see both your parents.

Family Responsibilities Family changes often bring about new roles and responsibilities for family members. *What roles and responsibilities do you have in your family?*

The remarriage of a divorced parent is also a big change. It means there is a new adult in the house. This **stepparent** — the spouse of your mother or father—may also have children. They become your stepbrothers and stepsisters. Together you form a **blended family.** Blended families consist of a parent, a stepparent, and one or more children. As you might expect, it can take time for everyone in a blended family to feel like a family.

Everyone adjusts to the changes after divorce or remarriage in his or her own way. You need to be patient. It is also helpful to have some support. Cassidy Turner tells how she dealt with the changes in her family.

"I wasn't prepared at all when my parents divorced," Cassidy recalls. "I was 10 at the time. My mother and I moved in with my grandparents in a different town.

"I missed my school and my friends, and I really missed my dad. We only saw each other a few times a month. It was such a hard time. Almost everything in my life changed.

"I wasn't sure how to handle all the changes. I really needed help, but I didn't know where to turn. My mom and dad were going through a lot of changes themselves. My grandmother was around, though. I started talking to her. I told her what I was feeling. I talked about everything on my mind." Cassidy offers this advice to others:

> "I guess if I had one word of advice for others going through what I did, it would be this. Don't be afraid to ask for help. Find someone to talk to. Oh, and there's something else I can say from my own experience. Things do get better."

Changing Places

In addition to adjusting to the changes that divorce brought, Cassidy had to deal with moving to a new place. Families move to different places for many reasons. Most children and young adults don't choose to move. Adult family members usually make the decision. The rest of the family may not have much choice in the matter.

If you've ever moved to a new place, you know how hard it can be. You almost always have to change schools. You may leave friends, neighbors, and even family members behind. Feeling comfortable in your new environment takes time.

Change Happens
Families move to different places for a number of reasons. *Have you ever moved to a new place? How long did it take before you felt comfortable in your new environment?*

Illness and Death

The serious illness or death of a friend or family member is another change beyond your control. You may feel scared, worried, nervous, helpless, sad, or restless. Friends and family members may have their own feelings to deal with. They may not notice what you are going through.

People deal with illness and death differently. Remember, there is no "right" way to react or grieve. It does help to talk through your thoughts and feelings with someone, though. The support of others can help you adjust to the difficult changes that come with illness or death.

Dealing With Changes You Can't Control

Changes you can't control can affect your relationship with others, your work at school or on the job, and your health.

What can you do? Focus on the things you can control. Talk about your feelings. Ask a relative, neighbor, teacher, counselor, or religious adviser for advice. Listen to and respect the feelings of other family members. Be patient with yourself. You can't control everything that happens, but you can learn to be flexible.

Choosing Change

Think of changes you might choose—now or in the future. When you are older, you will move into your own place. You will choose where and how you will live. You may also choose to start your own family someday.

The changes you choose—and the timing of your choices—will affect other parts of your life. How will you choose wisely?

You may listen to the advice of people close to you. You may read books on the subject. You may make a list of the pros and cons of the change you have in mind. You may search your heart to discover what's right for you. You may think about how the change will fit or affect your personal and career goals.

You may find it helpful to review the seven basic steps of decision making in Chapter 4. If you are already practicing these steps, you'll be prepared when you need to make a major life decision. By then the process should feel natural.

Ask for Help
Changes beyond your control can be difficult to handle alone. *Who would you go to for help if you were going through a difficult change?*

Even when you choose to make a change, you won't know exactly what will happen. What you can be sure of is that it will affect every aspect of your life. You should also know that you will make mistakes. Don't panic. You can learn from your mistakes. You can get help if you need it.

Changing Jobs or Careers

Personal changes are one kind of change you will experience throughout your life. You will also face changes at work. In the years to come, you'll continue to discover more about yourself. You'll grow and change. Your experiences, interests, and previous jobs may lead to new jobs and career choices.

You may decide to change jobs or careers. Some work-related changes you experience, however, may be the result of decisions made by others. What are these unwanted changes, and how can you deal with them?

Losing a Job

Have you ever lost a school election? Been passed over by the swim team? Been replaced by someone else at a job such as baby-sitting, newspaper delivery, or yardwork? How did you feel? In general, no one of any age likes to lose.

People do lose jobs, though. **Figure 16.1** describes some of the reasons why.

There's a good chance that you'll lose a job at least once during your working career. If you do, you'll probably feel angry, afraid, depressed, or discouraged.

Figure 16.1

REASONS FOR LOSING A JOB

You are fired.	If you are fired, it's important to find out why. It usually means that your employer wasn't happy with you or your work. That information will be helpful in your job search and in future jobs.
Your company is downsizing.	When a company goes through downsizing, it gets rid of jobs. Jobs are cut to make the company more efficient or to cut costs.
You refuse a transfer.	Your employer may want to send you to work in another location. The job might be in another office, city, state, or even in another country. If you are unwilling to transfer, you may lose your job.
You are laid off.	Some companies lay off workers when business becomes slow. If you are laid off for a long time, you may have to look for other work.
The company is sold.	You may lose your job if your company is sold to another company. The new company is now in charge. It may decide that it doesn't need all the people in your company.

Time for a Change People lose jobs for many reasons. *Has anyone you know lost a job for one of these reasons? Which reasons are new to you?*

Don't be ashamed of feeling such strong emotions. It's only natural. Don't let these feelings take over, though. Keep your chin up. Remember that losses always present opportunities. You have a chance to make a fresh start. Things may be even better this time around.

Rethinking the Future

If you lose a part-time job, you'll probably find another one. When you're an adult, however, finding a new job won't always be easy. In the end, you may even decide to pursue a new career.

There was a time when most people worked at one job their entire lives. That's no longer true. Many people today change jobs or careers to suit their changing skills and interests. In addition, you can no longer count on having the same job or career for your whole life.

Jobs and careers are changing rapidly as technology, people's needs, and the world's resources change. Just think about this. Not so long ago, no one had even heard of many of the technology-related jobs we know today. These jobs include Webmaster and multimedia developer.

The Global Workplace

Research and Respect: Don't Leave Home Without Them

Don't whistle, keep your hands out of your pocket, know when to keep your distance, and accept business cards with two hands. How will you ever make it in another culture? It's easy: all it takes is a little research and respect.

Before you travel, take time to research the customs, practices, and history of the country you'll visit. You'll not only be prepared, you'll also impress your hosts by knowing a little bit about them. What if you do make a mistake anyway? Be respectful and have a good attitude. Ask your hosts to explain the correct etiquette, and respect the custom next time. Finally, be open to new experiences and enjoy them.

Internet Activity

Use the Internet and library resources to research a country in which you would be interested in working. Find out about the customs, history, and major businesses in this country. Go to the *Exploring Careers* Web site at exploring.glencoe.com for a list of Web sites to help you complete this activity.

Losing a job or being forced to change careers can be a shock. It's a blow to your self-esteem. You may worry about the future or be afraid to try again. Give yourself some time to adjust. Then get ready to rethink your future and revise your career plan. A positive attitude will help you succeed.

Looking for a New Job or Career

Being prepared and keeping an open mind can make all the difference when you're faced with job or career changes you did not choose. The sooner you start considering your options and making decisions, the sooner you'll be working again. To get started, ask yourself these questions:

- What do I want to do next?
- What new interests might lead me toward a new job or career?
- What skills and abilities do I already have?
- What skills and abilities would I like to develop?
- How can I get the education or training I need for a new job or career?
- What new short-, medium-, and long-term goals will I set for myself?

These kinds of questions will help you to assess yourself. They'll help you determine what you want to accomplish with your next step. If you get discouraged by your job search, remember that you have many resources. If your résumé is up to date and you've kept in contact with the people in your network, you may find yourself back in the workforce sooner than you think!

Loss or Opportunity? Losing a job is hard. *Why might the loss of a job be an opportunity?*

Are You Ready for Change?

How can you prepare for change? Continuing to learn throughout your life is one sure way to stay ahead of the curve. During your career, additional training and education will help you learn new skills and sharpen the skills you already have.

Figure 16.2 **ADJUSTING TO CHANGE**

No matter what changes occur in your life, you will have to adjust to them. Here are some positive tips for adjusting to change. *How can you use each tip in your life right now?*

A

Plan Ahead

If you know about a change in advance, prepare for it even if you do not want it to happen. It will be easier to adjust to the change. Perhaps you know you'll be transferring to a new school. Find out about the school before your first day. Visit if you can. Talk with people there. You'll feel more comfortable when the first day of school arrives.

B

Share Your Feelings

Use your support group. Talk to friends, family members, or other trusted people. If needed, find someone who's trained to help people with their problems. Teachers, school counselors, coaches, and religious advisers can help you handle change.

Continuing to learn can also help you to advance to a different level in your job and stay current with changes in your field. You will learn more about the importance of lifelong learning in Lesson 16.2. There are other strategies for being prepared for change. **Figure 16.2** offers some helpful tips for adjusting to change.

C

Find Something Positive About the Change

Looking for something positive can be challenging at times but also very rewarding, and often surprising. Remember that changes are part of life. They help you grow. Even the most painful changes can be the source of something positive. It does not help to keep thinking about what is wrong or different. It's better to learn from the experience.

D

Learn to Be Supportive

Pay attention to family members, friends, and coworkers. Notice when they are having a hard time. Figure out how you can help. You want people to be there for you. Learn to do the same for them. Reaching out to others will remind you that you're not alone.

Life Changes Make You Grow

Q: Big changes scare me—nothing good ever comes from them. Why can't things just stay the way they are?

A: Change happens whether we like it or not. Changes aren't always bad, though. Think about the good things that have entered your life. Some changes are harder than others. It helps to share your feelings about difficult changes. It also helps to look for the good in these changes. Perhaps you have to change to a new school. The silver lining might be that you will make more good friends at the new school. Facing changes—both good and bad—helps you grow as a person.

Build a Support Network

Another way to prepare for change is to build a support network. Friends, family members, teachers, and counselors can be a great source of support in times of change. You can go to them for advice. They will listen and offer encouragement. They will remind you that you are worthwhile. They will also often tell you the truth as they see it. Other people can be a good resource when you need reassurance or ideas. While you're at it, think about how you can support other people in your life.

Life is an adventure, filled with surprises. Along the way, you will experience all kinds of changes. Some will make you happy. Others will make you sad. No matter what changes are in store for you, you will have to deal with them. There's no getting around it. Change is part of life. Make the best of it.

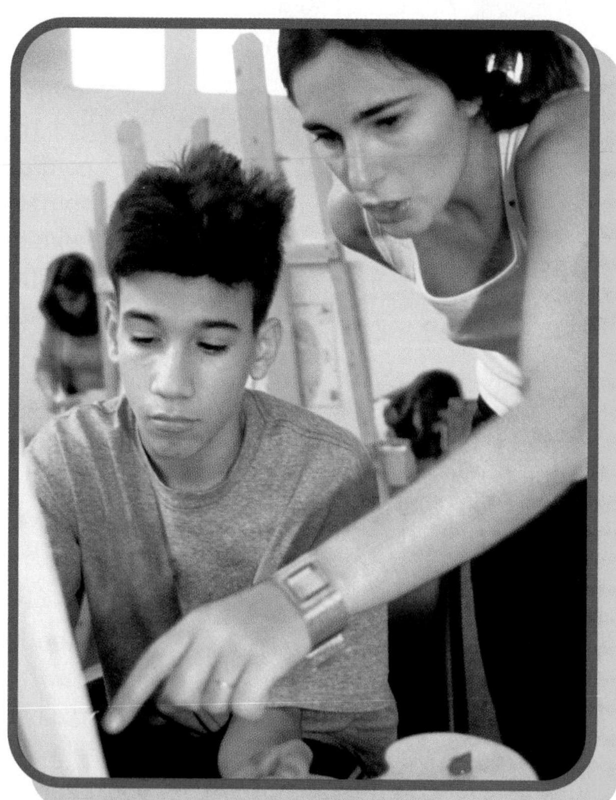

Learning Opportunities
It's always worthwhile to keep your skills up-to-date. *What learning opportunities do you take advantage of outside of school?*

Lesson 16.1 Review and Activities

Key Terms Review

1. Imagine you're a counselor who has to discuss life changes with a group of teens. Write down what you plan to say. Include the following terms.
   - **stepparent**
   - **blended family**

Check Your Understanding

Choose the correct answer for each item. Write your answers on a separate sheet of paper.

2. Personal changes beyond a person's control include ______.
   a. the death of a loved one
   b. graduation
   c. school
3. Many changes are ______. You can plan for them.
   a. unexpected
   b. predictable
   c. random

Critical Thinking

Use complete sentences to answer the following questions. Write your answers on a separate sheet of paper.

4. How might you prepare for future personal changes?
5. Think of an unwanted change in your life that led to something positive. How did it help you grow?
6. How can being prepared for change help you meet your goals?

Connecting to the Workplace

7. **Handling Stress** Kavi's mother is seriously ill. He is very worried about her. He finds it hard to sleep. Kavi works part-time. He is an excellent worker, but is falling behind at work because he can't concentrate. No one at work knows about Kavi's situation at home. His boss has been getting complaints and is concerned that Kavi is not doing his work. His coworkers are concerned about his health. Should Kavi share with others what he is going through? Explain.

Teamwork

8. **Create a Guide** Team up with a group of classmates. Create a guide for students who are going through difficult personal changes. Your guide should begin with a list of some changes young people experience. It should provide suggestions for how you can help yourself in each situation. It should also give tips for how friends and family members can help. Include a list of school and community resources in your guide. If possible, ask a school counselor to review your guide. Donate copies of your guide to the school library and to school counselors' offices.

Lesson 16.2

Lifelong Learning

Discover

- The importance of lifelong learning
- Why you should plan for the future
- The power of positive thinking
- How you can start to move toward the future

Why It's Important

If you continue to learn and think about the future, you can create the kind of life you want.

KEY TERMS

- **lifelong learning**
- **accomplishments**
- **fulfillment**

You started learning the day you were born. You will continue to learn your entire life—if you are willing. How can you be open to learning? Always be on the lookout for opportunities to learn new things. Know how and where to find the latest information and resources.

Be a Lifelong Learner

Be prepared for change by becoming a lifelong learner. **Lifelong learning** is all the learning activity you do throughout life. It can be formal, like the learning done in school. It can also be informal learning that you do on your own; for example, teaching yourself a new software program.

As a student, you can take advantage of learning opportunities outside of school. Look for workshops, special training courses, volunteer opportunities, and other apprenticeships. The Internet is another rich source of information for learning opportunities. You'll be amazed at the new things you discover about yourself, work, and other life experiences.

A Bright Future Thinking about the future? It helps to have a plan and a positive attitude. *What else do you need to move toward the future you imagine for yourself?*

Try This Activity

Learn for a Lifetime

Every day for a week, record every place or situation in which you learn something. Do you take classes outside of school? What do you learn from people in your family? Do you read books or the newspaper? What do you watch on television? Write down what you've learned in each of these learning environments.

Compare Learning Lists Share your learning list with a few classmates. What learning environments do you have in common? Find one learning environment on a classmate's list that you never thought of. Think about how you might add it to your list.

Make Plans Now

To be in charge of your life, you need to plan for the future. Your plan can start in your head. It works better, though, if you write down your plan. Keep your plan in a safe place. That way, you can refresh your memory by referring to it. You can see how well you're doing. You can also make changes in your plan when you want to.

Some people don't like to make plans. Maybe it's because they're afraid that things won't turn out the way they thought. In fact, the opposite is true. People who plan and set goals for themselves see things happen!

Do you have a plan? What are you waiting for? Chapter 5 gives you some hints about how to begin. Your plan now may include getting good grades or working part-time during the summer. It may also include graduating from high school or saving money for college. Lifelong learning should be in your plan. Also include a career goal in your plan.

A reasonable career goal right now might be to explore several careers that interest you. Talk to people who work in those careers. Do career research at the library and on the Internet. Research all of the careers that interest you so that you can be confident when you make your career decision.

Your ideas about your future may change as you explore careers and other things that interest you. Don't be afraid to change your goals and your plan as you need or want to.

Attitude COUNTS

Winning Gracefully

It's tough enough to be a good loser, but what about a good winner? In school and work, there will be many times when you win something through your good effort. Although you may feel like celebrating, remember to be considerate toward the people around you. Avoid bragging.

Cooperative Learning Activity

With a small group, take turns role-playing the following situations. Each group member should have the chance to role-play a "winner" and a "non-winner."

- Your friend did not make the volleyball team. You did.
- You got a bigger raise than your coworker.
- You got an "A" on your math test. Your study partner got a "C."

Be Positive!

Planning isn't the only way to think about the future. A positive attitude makes the future bright. It increases your chances of reaching any goal you set.

Let's face it. There is always something to complain about. It's raining. You wish you could drive. Your friend is mad at you for no reason. You left your lunch at home. You didn't do well on your last math test. You're tired of your hair. The list goes on and on.

Trade In Your Negative Thoughts

Have you ever thought about trading in your negative thoughts? When you find yourself saying or thinking negative things about yourself or anything else, stop! Replace those negative thoughts with positive ones.

If you have a negative thought, think about where the thought comes from. Do you think you're lazy because you don't always finish your homework? That could be a time management problem. Consider a solution to each problem.

Can you think of someone who has a great attitude? He or she is probably fun to be around. Such people have bad days like anyone else. In general, though, they're upbeat. They try to stay positive.

Enjoy Your Work You can tell this employee really enjoys her work. *Why do employers value a positive attitude?*

Think Positive
Have you heard of the expression "the power of positive thinking"? *What does this expression mean to you? Why is it important to be positive?*

Most people like to be around positive people. Employers are no exception. Parents look for baby-sitters who like children. Restaurants want to hire people who are friendly to customers. Businesses prefer employees who can stay positive—even under pressure.

Make Things Happen

A positive attitude is not only more fun—it also makes things happen. Forming positive images helps you take action toward your goals.

Begin by developing a positive attitude toward yourself. Take time to notice all your **accomplishments** —everything you do well. Take the time to document your accomplishments. Add to your accomplishment list regularly. They will contribute to your positive attitude. Accomplishments will also help you move forward into what you see for yourself in the future.

Move Toward Your Vision

In this book, you've taken a look at your interests, your values, your skills, your aptitudes, and your personality. You've started to explore careers. You've taken a peek inside the world of work. You've learned about making decisions and making plans. You've practiced setting both short- and long-term goals.

You can use the information in this book now. You can also turn to it later when you look for a full-time job and plan your career.

Career Opportunities

Transportation, Distribution, and Logistics

Workers in transportation, distribution, and logistics move goods from manufacturers to warehouses to stores. They transport goods by truck, rail, ship, and plane, and keep track of where items are all over the world.

Critical Thinking

What skills would be beneficial for a warehouse worker? Why?

WAREHOUSE WORKER

Local company seeks worker to load and unload shipments to warehouse, move materials using forklift, and track shipments. Must be dependable, hard-working, and able to lift at least 75 pounds. Warehouse experience a plus, but not required.

Think About the Future

The present is the perfect place to start thinking about the future. It's where you begin to take steps toward your goals. It's where you can really make a difference.

Many people worry so much about the future that they can't act in the present. You learned about the importance of goal-setting in Chapters 5 and 12. Goals help you act. Goals provide you with the motivation or drive to move forward every day. This drive comes from having a clear idea of the direction in which you want to go. It is much easier to get excited about what you are doing if you have a planned end result. Goals also help you stay in the present because each step begins there.

As you set your personal and career goals, remember the importance of small steps. If you move too fast toward a goal, it's easy to skip important steps. It's like trying to run a marathon when you've never run a mile.

Each small step toward a personal goal or a career goal is a small victory. That feeling of success encourages you to take another small step. Before you know it, you've arrived!

Try This Activity

Examine the Past to Learn About the Future

Change has a huge effect on society and on career opportunities. To understand how change can affect a career, select a career and study how it has changed over the past decade. Use print and online resources to find out how demand, job responsibilities, education and training requirements, and salaries have changed in a selected career choice.

Develop a Time Line Develop a time line covering the last ten years depicting change in your selected career choice. Compose a report explaining the changes that have occurred and how those changes have affected people employed in that career. In your report, predict how you think the career might change in the future decade.

Explore Possibilities

The world isn't discovered only by famous explorers. You're an important explorer too. You explore your own personal world as well as the world you share with other people.

Step by step, you're exploring the world around you. You may discover a career that no one else has ever imagined. You may invent something or do something that changes people's lives.

Right now you're exploring a world of possibilities, including many possible careers. Expect the best as you go forward. Expect your life to be happy. Expect to have loving relationships. Expect to succeed in school. Expect to find **fulfillment,** or satisfaction, in a job you love. Last but not least, expect that you have something special to offer the world, because you do.

Keep Exploring
You've just begun to explore the world of possibilities before you. *What tools or techniques can you use to explore careers?*

Lesson 16.2 Review and Activities

Key Terms Review

1. In a two-page essay, describe what makes your life fulfilling. Also imagine yourself in 20 years. Explain what you want your accomplishments to include. Use these terms in your essay.

- **lifelong learning**
- **accomplishments**
- **fulfillment**

Check Your Understanding

Choose the correct answer for each item. Write your answers on a separate sheet of paper.

2. A ______ can make things happen.

a. good plan
b. positive attitude
c. responsible person

3. As you set your goals, it's important to remember to ______.

a. take large steps
b. skip important steps
c. take small steps

Critical Thinking

Use complete sentences to answer the following questions. Write your answers on a separate sheet of paper.

4. Why is lifelong learning important?

5. Describe your career goal and describe how problem solving, decision making, and positive thinking will help you reach your goal.

6. Describe one thing you are doing now to explore career possibilities.

Character Building

7. Developing a Positive Attitude Jade had always planned to be a chef. When she graduated from culinary school, she got a job as an assistant chef. She now assists a famous chef at a top restaurant. Although she is learning a lot, she is grumpy because she spends most of her time washing vegetables. Help her replace her negative thoughts with positive ones. Write Jade a letter pointing out the positive aspects of her job that she should focus on and feel good about.

Community Involvement

8. Promote Positive Thinking Contact a local organization that is planning to hold a charity or volunteer event in your community, such as a graffiti removal day, a trash clean-up day, or a neighborhood tree planting event. Volunteer to help promote the event. Advertise the positives of participating in the event and making your community a better place. Use catchy slogans in your advertisements.

TRANSPORTATION, DISTRIBUTION, AND LOGISTICS

Transportation • Moving people, goods, and services

Distribution • The shipment of goods and services

Logistics • Coordinating the movement of people, goods, services, information, and money

Job Title	Work Description
Air Traffic Controller	Coordinates the movement of planes in the air
Airline Pilot	Flies airplanes and helicopters
Flight Attendant	Ensures that airplane passengers have a safe and comfortable flight
Locomotive Engineer	Operates locomotives in and between yards and stations
Logistics Manager	Oversees distribution operations
Material Moving Equipment Operator	Uses machinery to move heavy boxes, crates, and drum containers
Railroad Conductor	Supervises a train crew and is responsible for the safety of the train's passengers, cargo, and crew
School Bus Driver	Drives a school bus to take students to and from school
Truck Driver	Transports goods from producers to resellers or consumers
Vehicle Mechanic	Performs maintenance, makes repairs, and completes inspections

Exploration Activity

Transportation, Distribution, and Logistics Use library and Internet resources to research a career in the Transportation, Distribution, and Logistics career cluster. Write a report on the kinds of work, skills required, working conditions, training and education required, and career outlook.

Cooperative Learning Interview a classmate about the career he or she researched. Find out as much information about that career as you can during the interview. Then have your classmate interview you about the career you researched. Afterward, share what you learned with the class.

Chapter 16 Review and Activities

Chapter Highlights

Lesson 16.1 Personal changes beyond your control, such as divorce or death, can be difficult to deal with. It is important to seek help for difficult personal changes when needed.

Lesson 16.2 Lifelong learning, planning, and maintaining a positive attitude are good ways to create a bright future for yourself. Your plan may include both personal and career goals.

Key Concept Review

Use complete sentences to answer the following questions. Write your answers on a separate sheet of paper.

1. What are some personal changes you might choose?
2. What are some reasons why a person might lose a job?
3. Who besides friends and family members can help you adjust to change?
4. What do you need to do to be in charge of your life?
5. When can you make things happen—in the present or the future? Explain.

Critical Thinking

Use complete sentences to answer the following questions. Write your answers on a separate sheet of paper.

6. Why do you think change makes people nervous and uneasy?
7. When could you have helped yourself adjust to change by planning ahead?
8. How can you create a fulfilling life for yourself?
9. Would you call yourself a positive person? Why or why not?
10. What do you imagine you will be doing in five years and in 20 years?

Skill Building

11. **Thinking Skills—Seeing Things in the Mind's Eye**
    Think about how you could make your community a better place. Come up with a plan detailing how you can take action to make your community a better place. Break down your plan into small, manageable parts. List the small tasks needed to accomplish your ultimate goal.

12. Interpersonal—Teaches Others

Create or locate a picture book for younger students about life changes they may experience. Such changes may include divorce, remarriage, moving, illness, and death. Share your book with elementary school students.

Academic Applications

13. Language Arts

Write a rap or poem that talks positively about your future. Include details about the kind of work you'll be doing. You might also include your accomplishments. Record it to keep and play back some years from now.

14. The Arts

Choose a medium, such as painting or sculpture, and create an art piece that celebrates your accomplishments. When you complete your art project, share it with a friend or family member. Then display it in your bedroom so you can be reminded of your accomplishments.

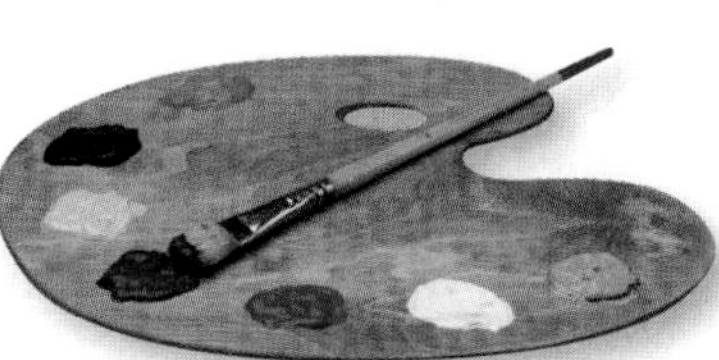

Personal Career Portfolio

Portfolio Cover Letter

- **Write** a cover letter to include with your portfolio.
- **Define** the audience of your letter before you start writing.
- **Introduce** yourself in the letter.
- **State** the purpose of your Personal Career Portfolio in the letter.
- **Describe** the documents in your Personal Career Portfolio.
- **Explain** why each document was included.
- **Highlight** the aspects of the portfolio that you feel best demonstrate your strengths.
- **Focus** on the skills the documents demonstrate and how those skills might be useful in the job or career you are seeking.
- **Customize** your portfolio cover letter for each job opportunity you pursue.
- **File** your portfolio cover letter as the first document in your Personal Career Portfolio.

Glossary

A

ability A skill that has been developed. (p. 9)

accomplishments Everything a person does well. (p. 353)

active listening Listening and responding with full attention to what's being said. (p. 201)

adaptability The ability or willingness to change in order to suit different conditions. (p. 68)

adaptability skills A person's ability to change in order to fit new circumstances that may arise. (p. 163)

addiction A physical or psychological need for a substance. (p. 229)

administration Setting the goals and rules of an organization, and then helping the organization reach the goals and keep to the rules. (p. 77)

agriculture Growing crops and raising animals for human use. (p. 19)

annual report A summary of a company's business for the year. (p. 118)

aptitude The potential a person has for learning a skill. (p. 9)

architecture Designing and constructing structures that enclose space to meet human needs. (p. 37)

arts The performing and visual arts, including dance, theater, music, painting, sculpture, and graphic design. (p. 57)

assess To judge. (p. 189)

attitude A person's basic outlook on life. (p. 68)

audience Anyone who receives information. (p. 199)

audio/video technology (a/v technology) The technology used to present information in sound or pictures on radio, television, CD, DVD, or the Internet. (p. 57)

B

backup plan An alternative course of action. (p. 73)

balance The situation when opposite sides or parts of something have the same weight, amount, or force. (p. 318)

benefits The "extras" an employer provides employees in addition to pay, such as insurance, paid time off, or child care. (p. 155)

blended family A family consisting of a parent, a stepparent, and one or more children. (p. 339)

body language The gestures, posture, and eye contact people use to express themselves. (p. 140)

brainstorming A method of shared problem solving in which all members of a group contribute ideas. (p. 186)

budget A plan for saving and spending money. (p. 297)

business Buying and selling goods and services. (p. 77)

business etiquette The rules of good workplace manners. (p. 161)

business plan A written proposal describing a new business to a potential lender or investor. (p. 283)

C

capitalism The free enterprise system; the economic system of the United States. (p. 273)

career A work history of one or more jobs in the same or related fields of interest. (p. 26)

career clusters Groups of similar occupations and industries. (p. 43)

career fair An event where employers offer career and employment information. (p. 107)

career interest areas General kinds of activities people do in many different careers. (p. 45)

chronological order Time order, or the order in which events happen. (p. 96)

citizen A person who is recognized by the government as having the rights and protections of a country. (p. 326)

civic minded Being concerned about and active in community affairs. (p. 329)

classifieds Newspaper advertisements organized in classes, or groups. (p. 110)

collaboration Working with others for a common purpose. (p. 184)

command economy A type of economic system in which there is no private enterprise and in which the government makes all of the key economic decisions. (p. 274)

commission Earnings based on how much a worker sells. (p. 155)

communication The exchange of information between senders and receivers. (p. 198)

communications The transmission of messages from one place or person to another through technology such as radio, television, satellites, and telephones. (p. 57)

community service Volunteer work that benefits the community. (p. 330)

compromise To give up something to settle a disagreement. (p. 179)

conflict A strong disagreement. (p. 177)

conflict resolution A step-by-step process used to settle disagreements. (p. 179)

construction Building structures. (p. 37)

consumers People who buy and use goods and services. (p. 274)

contact list A list of people one knows and will contact in order to build a network. (p. 107)

context clues Hints about the meaning of unfamiliar words or phrases provided by the words surrounding them. (p. 204)

cooperate To work with others to reach a common goal. (p. 161)

cooperative program (co-op) A program that combines school studies with paid work experience. (p. 55)

corporate culture The characteristics and customs that make a company unique. (p. 153)

cover letter A one-page letter a job seeker sends along with a résumé telling who he or she is and why he or she is sending a résumé. (p. 131)

coworkers People who work together in the workplace. (p. 151)

D

database A software program that stores data, or information, in different ways for easy searching, sorting, and organizing. (p. 114)

decision A choice one makes about what action to take. (p. 62)

decision-making process A series of steps used to identify and evaluate choices in order to arrive at a decision. (p. 70)

demand The amount of goods and services that consumers want to buy. (p. 278)

discretion The good judgment used when acting or speaking so as not to offend others. (p. 161)

distribution The shipment of goods and services. (p. 357)

E

e-commerce The buying and selling of goods and services via the Internet. (p. 33)

eating disorder A pattern of extreme eating behavior over time. (p. 229)

economic system A country's way of making choices about how to use its resources to produce and distribute goods and services. (p. 273)

Glossary

economic values Values that reflect the importance of money to a person's happiness. (p. 6)

economics The study of how people produce, distribute, and use goods and services. (p. 272)

economy The ways people make, buy, and sell goods and services. (p. 32)

education The process of teaching and learning. (p. 99)

emergency A serious event that happens without warning and calls for quick action. (p. 238)

empathize To try to see things from the other person's point of view and understand his or her situation. (p. 175)

employee Someone who works for a person or business for pay. (p. 150)

employer A person or business that pays a person or group of people to work. (p. 115)

empowerment The feeling of power and satisfaction that comes from being directly responsible for one's work decisions. (p. 185)

engineering Solving practical problems by combining the theories and principles of science and mathematics with technology. (p. 333)

entrepreneur A person who organizes and runs a business. (p. 281)

entry-level Lower-level. (p. 154)

ethics The rules of behavior that govern a group or society. (p. 163)

exchange A trade of one item for another. (p. 309)

exploratory interview A short, informal talk with someone who works in a career that one finds interesting. (p. 52)

F

F.I.C.A. The Federal Insurance Contribution Act, a law having to do with the taxes that are withheld from paychecks and contributed to the Social Security program. (p. 296)

finance Acquiring, investing, and managing money. (p. 121)

first aid The emergency care given to an injured or sick person before help arrives. (p. 239)

fixed expenses Expenses that people have already agreed to pay and that must be paid by a particular date. (p. 299)

flexible expenses Expenses that come irregularly or that people can adjust more easily than fixed expenses. (p. 299)

flextime A work schedule arrangement that allows workers to choose work hours that fit their particular needs. (p. 35)

food Substances consumed by living things for energy and growth. (p. 19)

Food Guide Pyramid A guideline created by the U.S. Department of Agriculture that shows the nutrients a person needs each day. (p. 225)

format The arrangement of something such as a document. (p. 127)

Form I-9 A form that verifies that a person is legally qualified to work in the United States. (p. 152)

free enterprise A type of economic system in which individuals or businesses may buy and sell goods and services and set prices with little government control. (p. 273)

fulfillment Satisfaction. (p. 355)

full-time Working at least 40 hours a week. (p. 27)

G

gender equity Equal employment opportunity for all, regardless of gender. (p. 34)

global economy All the world's economies and how they are linked. (p. 32)

goods Items that people buy. (p. 32)

government The institution through which the state keeps order in society, provides services to the public, and enforces the law. (p. 145)

grant Money for education provided by the government, schools, or private donors. (p. 302)

gross pay Total pay. (p. 296)

H

health The condition of both one's body and mind. (p. 224)

health science The science of maintaining and improving human health. (p. 169)

hospitality Lodging and food and beverage management and service. (p. 193)

human resources (H.R.) The department of a company or business that recruits employees, administers company policies, develops employee training programs, and manages employee records. (p. 166)

human services Services that improve people's quality of life and promote safe, healthy communities. (p. 219)

hygiene All the things people do to be clean and healthy. (p. 229)

I

images Pictures. (p. 208)

impulse buying Making a sudden, unplanned decision to buy. (p. 305)

income The amount of money a person receives or earns regularly. (p. 294)

income tax Tax paid to the government on income earned. (p. 296)

information technology The technology used to design, develop, set up, operate, and support computer systems. (p. 243)

initiative The willingness to do what needs to be done without being told to do it. (p. 162)

interest Money that banks pay depositors for use of their money. (p. 301)

interest inventory A checklist that points to one's strongest interests. (p. 3)

interests Favorite activities. (p. 2)

internship A temporary paid or unpaid position that involves direct work experience in a career field. (p. 54)

interview A formal meeting between a job seeker and an employer about a possible job. (p. 135)

J

job Work that a person does for pay. (p. 26)

job application A form that asks questions about a job seeker's skills, work experience, education, and interests. (p. 132)

job lead Information about a job opening. (p. 105)

job market The need for workers and the kinds of work available to them. (p. 32)

job shadowing Following a person on the job for a few days in order to learn about a particular career. (p. 54)

job sharing A flexible work arrangement that allows two part-time employees to divide one full-time job. (p. 35)

job-specific skills The skills necessary to do a particular job, like balancing a budget or programming a computer. (p. 11)

L

labor force All people over the age of 16 who work or are seeking work. (p. 32)

Glossary

law The set of rules and standards by which a society governs itself. (p. 267)

learning styles The different ways people naturally think and learn. (p. 15)

leisure Time to do what one likes. (p. 318)

letter of recommendation A letter written in support of a job seeker from a reference. (p. 133)

letter of resignation A formal letter that explains why and when an employee is leaving his or her job. (p. 265)

lifelong learning All the learning activity (both formal and informal) that one does throughout life. (p. 350)

lifestyle The way a person uses his or her time, energy, and other resources. (p. 27)

loan Borrowed money that must be repaid. (p. 302)

logistics Coordinating the movement of people, goods, services, information, and money. (p. 357)

long-term goal A challenging goal that takes a long time to achieve and may first involve the achievement of short- and medium-term goals. (p. 93)

M

management The direction or control of a business or enterprise. (p. 77)

manufacturing The process of making products by hand or by machine. (p. 289)

marketing The process of developing, promoting, and distributing goods and services to consumers. (p. 283 and p. 313)

mathematics The study of numbers and their relationships. (p. 211 and p. 333)

mediator Someone who helps opposing people or groups compromise or reach an agreement. (p. 179)

Medicare A health care program provided by the federal government primarily for retired persons. (p. 296)

medium-term goal A goal that is usually more challenging and takes longer to achieve than a short-term goal. (p. 93)

mentor An experienced coworker who answers the questions of a new employee and offers guidance to him or her. (p. 151)

minimum wage The lowest hourly wage an employer can legally pay for a worker's services. (p. 158)

N

natural resources Raw materials that occur naturally in the earth, such as minerals, metals, soil, and water. (p. 19)

net pay Take-home pay. (p. 296)

netiquette The accepted rules of conduct used on the Internet. (p. 216)

networking Communicating with people you know or can get to know to share information and advice. (p. 105)

notice An official written statement that one is leaving one's job. (p. 265)

nutrients The substances in food that the body needs to produce energy and stay healthy. (p. 225)

O

obstacle Something that stands in the way of a decision or action. (p. 63)

occupation A set of related job skills and experiences. (p. 26)

Occupational Safety and Health Administration (OSHA) A special branch of the U.S. Department of Labor in charge of setting safety standards and inspecting places of work to see that the standards are being followed. (p. 237)

orientation A program that introduces new employees to their new company and its policies and procedures, or ways of doing things. (p. 151)

outcome The result or effect of a decision or action. (p. 68)

outsourcing Using outside resources to perform activities traditionally handled by internal company staff. (p. 35)

overtime Extra pay for each hour worked beyond 40 hours a week. (p. 154)

P

part-time job A job in which a person works up to 30 hours a week. (p. 88)

performance reviews Meetings between an employee and his or her supervisor to evaluate how well the employee is doing his or her job. (p. 166)

personal career portfolio A collection of information about a person, including projects and work samples, that shows the person's skills and qualifications to employers. (p. 131)

personal fact sheet A list of basic information about a person's education, experience, qualifications, and skills. (p. 130)

personality The sum total of an individual's feelings, actions, habits, and thoughts. (p. 14)

pre-employment tests Tests given to an applicant by an employer to find out if the applicant fits the job. (p. 136)

prejudice A negative attitude toward a person or group that is not based on facts or reason. (p. 178)

previewing Reading only the parts of a written work that outline or summarize its content. (p. 204)

prioritize To put in order from first to last or from most important to least important. (p. 84)

procrastinate To put off deciding or acting. (p. 84)

producers Individuals or companies that make or provide goods and services. (p. 275)

profit The amount of money left after a business pays its expenses. (p. 275)

promotion A job advancement to a position of greater responsibility and authority. (p. 252)

public administration The administrative management of government and nonprofit organizations. (p. 145)

public safety Efforts to keep the public safe from crime, fire, and emergencies. (p. 267)

purpose Overall goal or reason. (p. 199)

R

raise An increase in pay. (p. 252)

references People who will recommend a job seeker to an employer. (p. 133)

referral Someone to whom one is referred, or directed. This person may have information about a job or job opening. (p. 108)

refund The return of money in exchange for a purchased item. (p. 309)

register To officially sign up as a qualified voter. (p. 328)

regulate Set rules for. (p. 274)

relationships A person's connections or dealings with other people. (p. 174)

research Investigating a subject and gathering information about it. (p. 50)

respect Consideration, especially for others. (p. 174)

résumé A summary of a job seeker's personal information describing education, skills, work experience, activities, and interests. (p. 127)

S

salary A fixed amount of money paid for a certain period of time. (p. 154)

sales The process of providing goods and services to consumers for a price. (p. 313)

scholarship Money for education awarded to students because of their need, or for academic or athletic achievement. (p. 301)

school-to-work program A program that brings schools and businesses together so that students can gain work experience and training. (p. 111)

science The systematic use of observations and experiments to gain knowledge about the world. (p. 211 and p. 333)

security Privately funded efforts to protect safety and private property at homes and businesses. (p. 267)

sedentary Spending much time sitting. (p. 226)

self awareness Knowing one's own thoughts, feelings, and actions. (p. 15)

self-esteem Recognition and regard for oneself and one's abilities. (p. 177)

self-motivation The drive to do something simply for the reward of feeling good and satisfied once it is accomplished. (p. 162)

service The process of performing tasks for consumers. (p. 313)

service learning A learning method in which students learn and develop through thoughtfully organized service to the community. (p. 55)

services Activities people do for others for a fee. (p. 32)

short-term goal A goal to start working on right away. (p. 93)

skill The ability to perform a task due to training and experience. (p. 9)

skimming Reading through a book or document quickly, picking out main ideas and key points. (p. 204)

Social Security A federal government program that provides benefits for people of all ages. (p. 296)

social skills The skills a person uses to interact with others. (p. 161)

socialist economy A type of economic system in which there is private enterprise, but the government controls key industries and makes many economic decisions. (p. 274)

spreadsheet A software program that arranges information, usually numbers, in rows and columns or displays information in graphs and other formats. (p. 215)

stepparent The spouse of one's mother or father following her or his remarriage. (p. 339)

stress The mental or physical tension that is the body's natural response to conflict. (p. 229)

subject Main topic or key idea. (p. 200)

supervisor The person who assigns, checks, and evaluates the work of an employee. (p. 151)

supply The amount of goods and services available for sale. (p. 278)

T

team A group of people who work together to set goals and make decisions to solve problems and put ideas into action. (p. 35)

team planning Working with others to set goals, assign tasks, and assess results. (p. 187)

technology The practical use of scientific knowledge (ideas, methods, tools, and materials) to get things done. (p. 3 and p. 333)

telecommute Working at home for a company. (p. 35)

temporary job A part-time or full-time job that lasts only a short while, such as for a couple of weeks or months. (p. 89)

time management Choosing how to spend one's time and creating a schedule for one's choices. (p. 321)

tourism Services involving travel planning, tourist information, guided tours, entertainment, recreation, and meeting and convention planning. (p. 193)

training Education in a specific skill or professional area. (p. 99)

transferable skills The general skills used in school and in various types of jobs. (p. 11)

transportation Moving people, goods, and services. (p. 357)

trend A change over a period of time. (p. 35)

V

values The ideas a person lives by and the beliefs that are important to that person. (p. 5)

volunteering Working without pay. (p. 54)

W

W-4 Form A form that instructs an employer about the amount of money to deduct from an employee's paycheck for taxes. (p. 152)

wages A fixed amount of money paid for each hour worked. (p. 154)

warranty A guarantee that a product meets certain standards of quality. (p. 308)

withhold To take out (as in money from a paycheck). (p. 296)

work permit A legal document that allows a minor to hold a job. It shows the number of hours the minor can work and the kinds of jobs he or she can hold. (p. 104)

work-study program A program that allows students to earn their education by working full- or part-time jobs in a related field while they are in school. (p. 302)

work values The things about work that are important to a person. (p. 6)

workers' compensation A government-run program that gives injured workers financial help to cover lost wages and medical expenses. (p. 238)

workforce diversity A wide variety of workers with different backgrounds, experiences, ideas, and skills in the workplace. (p. 35)

What Is the Career Clusters Appendix?

The Career Clusters Appendix provides you with additional information about career clusters. On this page and the next you'll find a basic introduction to the career clusters concepts of pathways, knowledge, and skills. Pages 370–377 provide a more detailed look at each of the 16 career clusters and at each individual cluster's pathways.

For more information about the 16 career clusters visit the career clusters series Web site at **careerclusters.glencoe.com**.

What Are Career Clusters?

Career clusters are groups of similar occupations and industries. By studying career clusters, you can learn about the exciting range of careers available in today's world of work. Career clusters were developed by the U.S. Department of Education as a way to help you identify your career interests and plan your career.

What interests you—art, veterinary science, counseling, space exploration, finance, teaching? Pick two or three career clusters that appeal to you and explore the various careers available within each. Once you start learning about a career cluster, you're sure to discover all kinds of exciting jobs that you didn't know existed. Studying career clusters will also help you to discover your interests and decide where you want your future to take you.

What Are Career Pathways?

Every career cluster is divided into a number of career pathways. A career pathway is an area of occupational interest within a career cluster. Each pathway contains a group of careers requiring similar academic and technical skills, as well as similar education, training, or certification.

Let's say you are interested in the Arts, Audio/Video Technology, and Communications career cluster. This cluster gives you six career pathways to choose from. You might choose the performing arts career pathway, perhaps becoming a dancer, musician, or actor; or you might be more drawn to a career in the journalism and broadcasting career pathway, perhaps becoming a television correspondent, newspaper reporter, or broadcast technician. There are many interesting jobs to explore within each career pathway. So go ahead and start exploring! There's a big world of work out there, and it's waiting for you!

Knowledge and Skills for Success

What skills do you need in order to succeed in the career you choose? The exact skills and knowledge you'll need will vary depending on the career cluster and the career pathway you choose.

There are three separate but interdependent types of skills essential to your career success: academic skills, employability skills, and occupational skills. Academic skills describe the knowledge of core subjects, such as English, math, and science, that provides the foundation for further learning. Employability skills describe the skills, such as teamwork and problem solving, necessary to be a successful employee in any industry. Occupational skills describe the skills and knowledge necessary to succeed in a particular industry and a particular occupation.

Jobs in each career pathway require a similar foundation of knowledge and skills. If you want to go into health science, for example, you'll need different knowledge and skills for a career in the diagnostic services pathway than you would for a career in the support services pathway.

No matter what career interests you, however, you'll need to develop a foundation knowledge and skills. These skills will help you prosper in any job, any career, and any industry. Make sure to develop your knowledge and skills in the areas listed on the next page.

Foundation Knowledge and Skills

Academic Foundations
- math
- science
- social studies (history, social science)
- language arts (English, foreign languages)
- learning skills
- research skills
- knowledge of career paths

Communication
- speaking skills
- active listening skills
- writing skills
- adapting communication to medium, context, and recipient
- knowledge of relevant terminology

Problem Solving and Critical Thinking
- thinking skills
- analytical skills
- decision-making skills
- logical reasoning skills
- distinguishing between fact and opinion
- creativity

Information Technology Applications
- computer hardware
- computer software
- Internet research methods
- electronic communication

Understanding Systems
- systems theory
- understanding organizational structures
- understanding team structures

Safety, Health, and Environmental Knowledge
- identifying safety and health hazards
- safety laws and regulations
- health laws and regulations
- environmental laws and regulations
- environmental awareness

Leadership and Teamwork
- understanding leadership styles
- developing attributes of leadership
- being an effective team member
- enthusiasm and self-motivation

Ethics and Legal Responsibilities
- professional conduct
- workplace ethics
- workers' rights
- workers' responsibilities

Employability and Career Development
- positive work habits
- self-knowledge
- career awareness
- career objectives
- personal qualities
- self-improvement

Technical Skills
- job-specific skills such as computer programming, budget analysis, journalistic writing, etc.

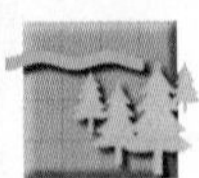

The Agriculture, Food, and Natural Resources Career Cluster

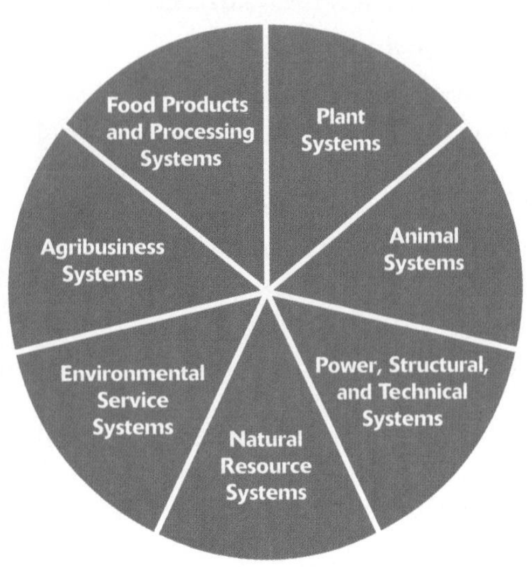

What Is the Agriculture, Food, and Natural Resources Career Cluster?

This career cluster prepares learners for careers in the planning, implementation, production, management, processing, and/or marketing of agricultural commodities and services, including food, fiber, wood products, natural resources, and other plant and animal products. It also includes professional, technical, and educational services.

Career Pathways in the Agriculture, Food, and Natural Resources Career Cluster

There are seven pathways in the Agriculture, Food, and Natural Resources career cluster, as shown in the diagram at left.

The Architecture and Construction Career Cluster

What Is the Architecture and Construction Career Cluster?

This career cluster prepares learners for careers in designing, planning, managing, building, and maintaining the built environment. People employed in this cluster work on new structures, restorations, additions, alterations, and repairs.

Career Pathways in the Architecture and Construction Career Cluster

There are three pathways in the Architecture and Construction career cluster, as shown in the diagram at right.

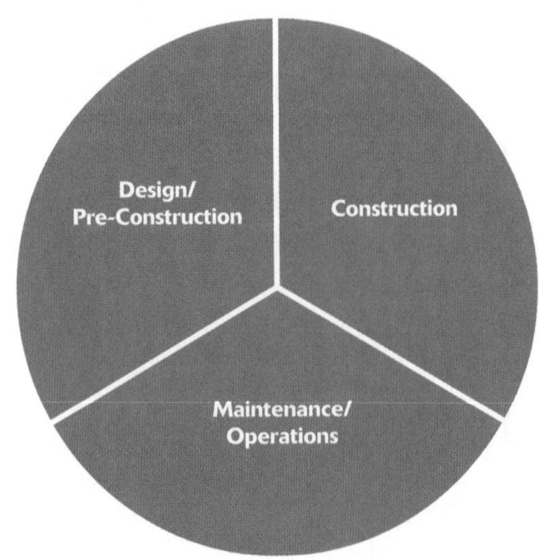

The Arts, Audio/Video Technology, and Communications Career Cluster

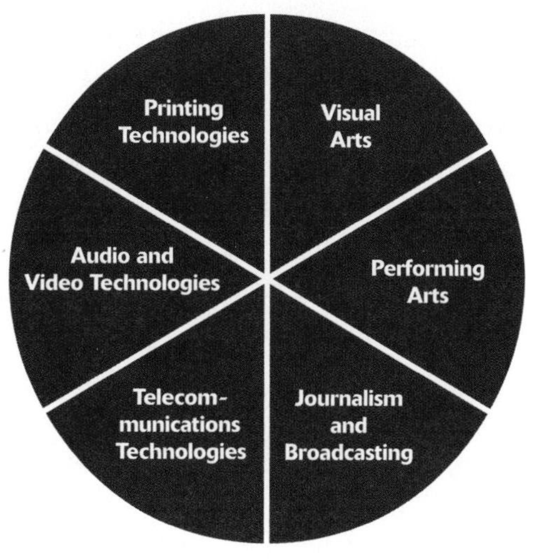

What Is the Arts, A/V Technology, and Communications Career Cluster?

This career cluster prepares learners for careers in designing, producing, exhibiting, performing, writing, and publishing multimedia content including visual and performing arts and design, journalism, and entertainment services. Careers in this cluster extend across nearly every discipline.

Career Pathways in the Arts, A/V Technology, and Communications Career Cluster

There are six pathways in the Arts, A/V Technology, and Communications career cluster, as shown in the diagram at left.

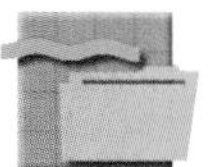

The Business, Management, and Administration Career Cluster

What Is the Business, Management, and Administration Career Cluster?

This career cluster prepares learners for careers in planning, organizing, directing and evaluating business functions essential to efficient and productive business operations. Business, management, and administration career opportunities are available in every sector of the economy.

Career Pathways in the Business, Management, and Administration Career Cluster

There are six pathways in the Business, Management, and Administration career cluster, as shown in the diagram at right.

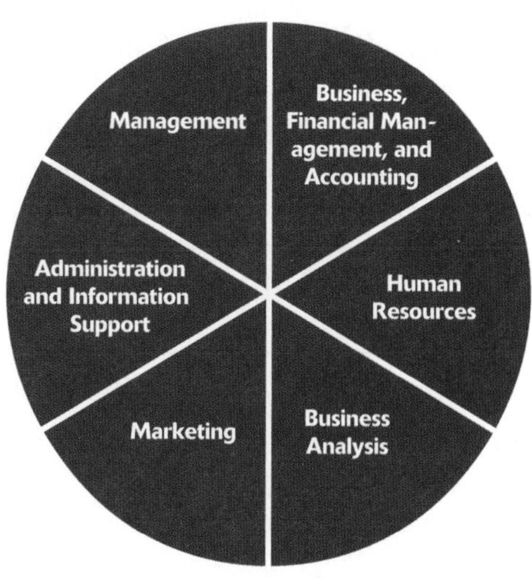

The Education and Training Career Cluster

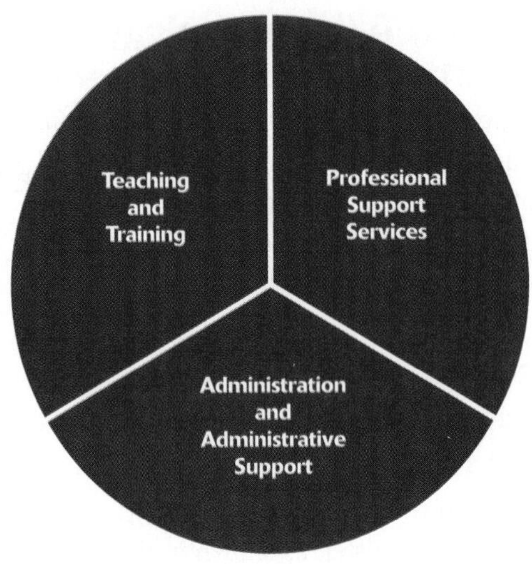

What Is the Education and Training Career Cluster?

This career cluster prepares learners for careers in planning, managing and providing education and training services, as well as related learning support services. Millions of learners each year train for careers in education and training in a variety of settings that offer academic instruction, vocational and technical instruction, and other education and training services.

Career Pathways in the Education and Training Career Cluster

There are three pathways in the Education and Training career cluster, as shown in the diagram at left.

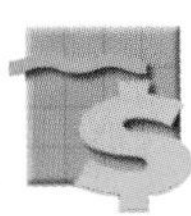

The Finance Career Cluster

What Is the Finance Career Cluster?

This career cluster prepares learners for careers in financial and investment planning, banking, insurance, and business financial management. Career opportunities are available in every sector of the economy and require specific skills in organization, time management, customer service, and communication.

Career Pathways in the Finance Career Cluster

There are four pathways in the Finance career cluster, as shown in the diagram at right.

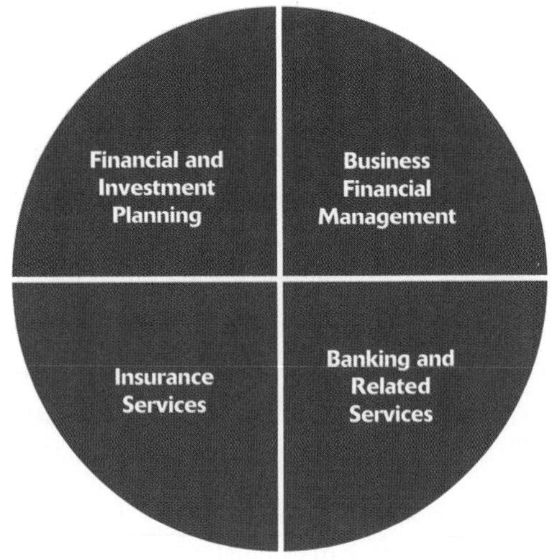

The Government and Public Administration Career Cluster

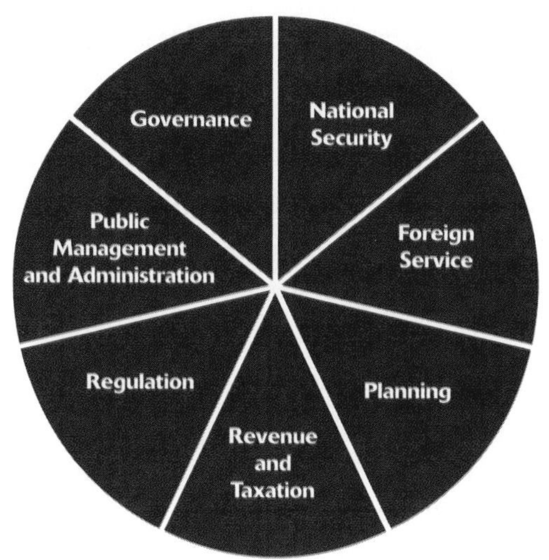

What Is the Government and Public Administration Career Cluster?

There are many opportunities in government in every career area. The Government and Public Administration career cluster focuses on those careers that are unique to government and not contained in another career cluster. There are some activities which are unique to the federal government. It defends us from foreign aggression; represents American interests abroad; deliberates, passes, and enforces laws; and administers many different programs. State and local governments pass laws or ordinances and provide vital services to constituents.

Career Pathways in the Government and Public Administration Career Cluster

There are seven pathways in the Government and Public Administration career cluster, as shown in the diagram at left.

The Health Science Career Cluster

What Is the Health Science Career Cluster?

This career cluster prepares learners for careers in planning, managing, and providing therapeutic services, diagnostic services, health informatics, support services, and biotechnology research and development. Jobs in this career cluster can require specific academic, technical, and communication skills.

Career Pathways in the Health Science Career Cluster

There are five pathways in the Health Science career cluster, as shown in the diagram at right.

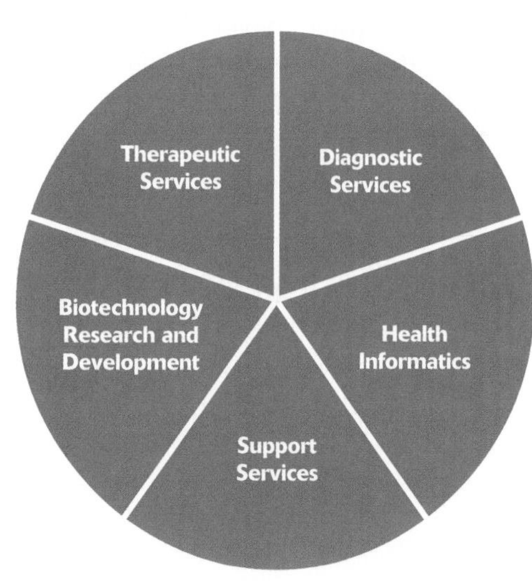

The Hospitality and Tourism Career Cluster

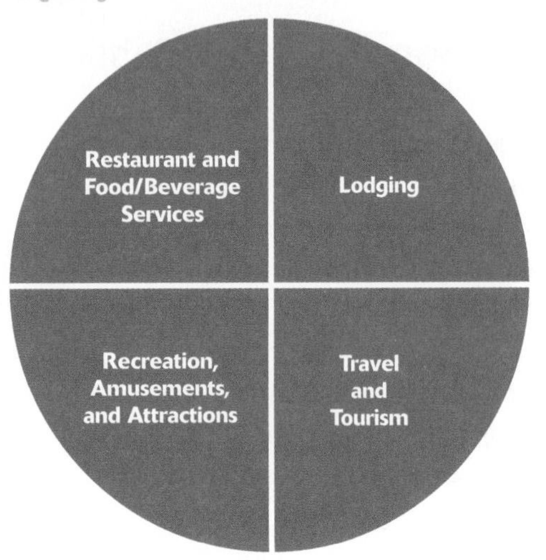

What Is the Hospitality and Tourism Career Cluster?

This career cluster prepares learners for careers in the marketing, management, and operations of restaurants and other food services, lodging, attractions, recreation events, and travel-related services. Hospitality operations are located in communities throughout the world.

Career Pathways in the Hospitality and Tourism Career Cluster

There are four pathways in the Hospitality and Tourism career cluster, as shown in the diagram at left.

The Human Services Career Cluster

What Is the Human Services Career Cluster?

This career cluster prepares learners for employment in career pathways related to families and human needs. Workers in this cluster are skilled in dealing with human behavior and relationships. Their knowledge helps individuals function in their communities.

Career Pathways in the Human Services Career Cluster

There are five pathways in the Human Services career cluster, as shown in the diagram at right.

The Information Technology Career Cluster

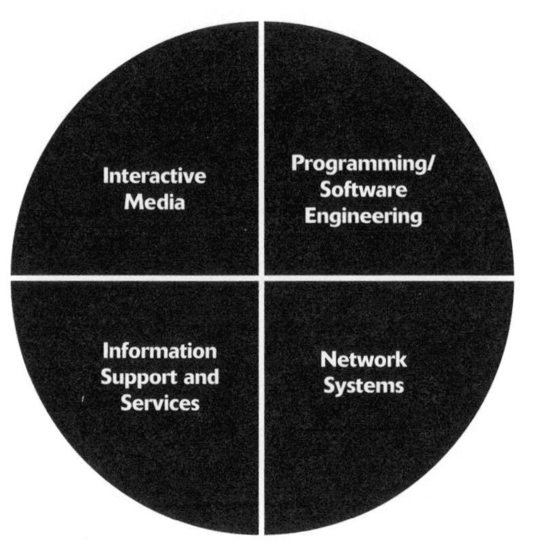

What Is the Information Technology Career Cluster?

This career cluster prepares learners for employment involving the design, development, support, and management of hardware, software, multimedia and systems integration services. Information technology, or *IT*, careers are available in every sector of the economy—from financial services to environmental services.

Career Pathways in the Information Technology Career Cluster

There are four pathways in the Information Technology career cluster, as shown in the diagram at left.

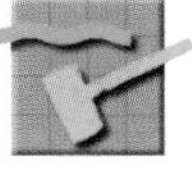

The Law, Public Safety, and Security Career Cluster

What Is the Law, Public Safety, and Security Career Cluster?

This career cluster helps prepare students for careers in planning, managing, and providing legal, public safety, and protective services, as well as homeland security. This includes professional and technical support services for these specialized occupations.

Career Pathways in the Law, Public Safety, and Security Career Cluster

There are five pathways in the Law, Public Safety, and Security career cluster, as shown in the diagram at right.

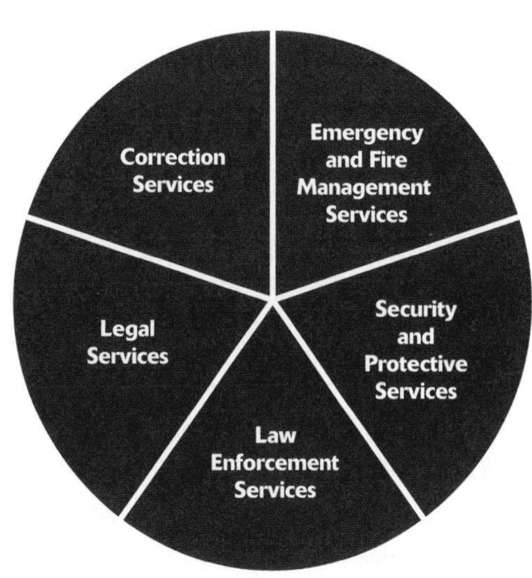

The Manufacturing Career Cluster

What Is the Manufacturing Career Cluster?

This career cluster helps prepare students for careers in planning, managing, and performing the processing of materials into intermediate or final products and related professional and technical support activities such as production planning and control, maintenance, and manufacturing/process engineering.

Career Pathways in the Manufacturing Career Cluster

There are six pathways in the Manufacturing career cluster, as shown in the diagram at left.

The Marketing, Sales, and Service Career Cluster

What Is the Marketing, Sales, and Service Career Cluster?

This career cluster prepares learners for careers in planning, managing, and performing marketing activities to reach organizational objectives. Workers in this cluster are usually excellent communicators who enjoy working with a wide variety of people.

Career Pathways in the Marketing, Sales, and Service Career Cluster

There are seven pathways in the Marketing, Sales, and Service career cluster, as shown in the diagram at right.

The Science, Technology, Engineering, and Mathematics Career Cluster

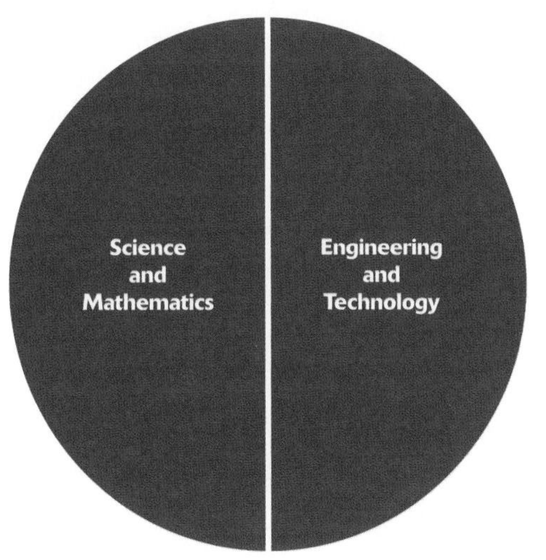

What Is the Science, Technology, Engineering, and Mathematics Career Cluster?

A career in science, technology, engineering, or mathematics is exciting, challenging, and ever-changing. Learners who pursue one of these career fields will be involved in planning, managing, and providing scientific research. Professional and technical services for this cluster include laboratory and testing services, and research and development services.

Career Pathways in the Science, Technology, Engineering, and Mathematics Career Cluster

There are two pathways in the Science, Technology, Engineering, and Mathematics career cluster, as shown in the diagram at left.

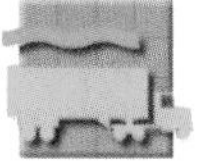

The Transportation, Distribution, and Logistics Career Cluster

What Is the Transportation, Distribution, and Logistics Career Cluster?

This career cluster exposes students to careers and businesses involved in the planning, management, and movement of people, materials, and products by road, air, rail, and water. It also includes related professional and technical support services such as infrastructure planning and management, logistic services, and the maintenance of mobile equipment and facilities.

Career Pathways in the Transportation, Distribution, and Logistics Career Cluster

There are seven pathways in the Transportation, Distribution, and Logistics career cluster, as shown in the diagram at right.

School-to-Work Applications and Connections

Academics Activities

Career Opportunities

Investigating Career Clusters

Character Building

Community Involvement

Connecting to the Workplace

Get Ready!

The Global Workplace

Skill Building Activities

Teamwork

Try This Activity

Index

Page numbers given in italics refer to charts or illustrations.

Index

Page numbers given in italics refer to charts or illustrations.

D

E

Index

Page numbers given in italics refer to charts or illustrations.

Index

Page numbers given in italics refer to charts or illustrations.

Index

Page numbers given in italics refer to charts or illustrations.

P

Index

Q

R

Index

Page numbers given in italics refer to charts or illustrations.

Index

Index

Page numbers given in italics refer to charts or illustrations.

Photo Credits

Cover Photography: Arthur Tulley/Getty Images(t); Gail Mooney/Masterfile(rt); Royalty Free/CORBIS(rb); Charles Thatcher/Getty Images (c); Stuart Hughes/Getty Images(lb); Jim Cummins/Getty Images(lc).

Randi Anglin/Syracuse Newspapers/The Image Works **92**; Bill Aron/PhotoEdit **162**, **310**(l); Paul Barton/Corbis **xiii**, **336–337**; Benelux Press/Getty Images **289**; Walter Bibikow/Getty Images **145**; Ed Bock/Corbis **viii**(r), **102–103**, **275**, **324**; Cleve Bryant/PhotoEdit **188**; Mark Burnett/Stock Boston **46**(b); Peter Cade/Getty Images **304**; Myrleen F. Cate/PhotoEdit **326**; Myrleen Ferguson Cate/PhotoEdit **89**; Ron Chapple/Getty Images **357**; Paul Conklin/PhotoEdit **54**; Corbis **311**(r); Elizabeth Crews/The Image Works **135**; David Kelly Crow/PhotoEdit **278**; Francisco Cruz/SuperStock **xvi**, **187**; Jim Cummins/Getty Images **xv**(t), **xii**(b), **316–317**; Bob Daemmrich Photography, Inc. **vi**(b), **40–41**, **108**, **272**; Bob Daemmrich/Stock Boston **xii**(t), **292–293**; Bob Daemmrich/The Image Works **104**, **183**, **219**, **227**, **255**, **345**; Mary Kate Denny/PhotoEdit **71**, **342**; ErikDreyer/Getty Images **277**; Steve Dunwell/Index Stock/PictureQuest **252**; Laura Dwight/PhotoEdit/PictureQuest **283**; John Eastcott and Yva Momatiuk/Stock Boston **9**; Paul Edmondson/Corbis **155**; Kenneth Ehlers/ImageState **313**; James Frank/Stock Connection/PictureQuest **70**; Hunter Freeman/Getty Images **5**(r); Tony Freeman/PhotoEdit **xv**, **190**, **228**, **239**, **257**, **329**; Stephen Frisch/Stock Boston **46**(cl); Tim Fuller **26**(l), **26**(r), **27**(l), **27**(r); Michelle Gabel/Syracuse Newspapers/The Image Works **355**; Mark Gamba/Corbis **236**; Getty Images **47**(cl); Spencer Grant/PhotoEdit **30**, **208**(t); Spencer Grant/Stock Boston **307**; Jeff Greenberg/Photo Researchers **72**; Jeff Greenberg/PhotoEdit **348**; Mike Greenlar/The Image Works **50**; Tom Grill/Corbis **267**; David Grossman/The Image Works **24**; David M.Grossman/Photo Researchers **205**; Charles Gupton/Corbis **x**(t), **196–197**; Ted Horowitz/Corbis **46**(cl); Richard Hutchings/PhotoEdit **229**; IFA/eStock/PictureQuest **260**; IT Stock Int'l/eStock/PictureQuest **14**; Alan Jakubek/Corbis **177**; Riley/Getty Images **185**;Reed Kaestner/Corbis **126**; Bonnie Kamen/PhotoEdit **311**(l); Howard Kingsnorth/Getty Images **2**; Lisette Le Bon/SuperStock **xi**(t), **42**, **52**, **246–247**; Lester Lefkowitz/Corbis **243**; James Levin/Getty Images **157**(cl); Mark Lisk/Pictor/PictureQuest **ix**(cl), **172–173**; David Lok/SuperStock **299**; Richard Lord/PhotoEdit **48**; Dennis MacDonald/PhotoEdit **138**, **150**; David Madison/Getty Images **234**; Felicia Martinez/PhotoEdit/PictureQuest **203**; Joseph McNally/Getty Images **57**; Michael Melford/Getty Images **47**(cr); Roy Morsch/Corbis **176**; Mug Shots/Corbis **47**(b), **338**; Michael Newman/PhotoEdit **84**, **111**, **158**, **198**, **305**, **320**; Jonathan Nourok/PhotoEdit **230**; Dominic Oldeshaw **116**, **117**; Dominic Oldeshaw **94**(l), **94**(r), **95**(l), **95**(r); Dominic Oldshaw **240**, **241**(l), **241**(r); Lori Adamski Peek/Getty Images **11**; Jose Luis Pelaez/Corbis **156**(cl); PhotoDisc/Getty Images **127**, **174**, **308**; Pictor/PictureQuest **226**; David Pollack/Corbis **208**(b); Paul Redman/Getty Images **77**; Nancy Richmond/The Image Works **4**; Marc Romanelli/Getty Images **5**(l); Francesco Ruggeri/Getty Images **121**; Chris Ryan/Getty Images **37**; Andy Sacks/Getty Images **19**; Chuck Savage/Corbis **ix**(cr), **148–149**; Ian Shaw/Getty Images **99**; James Shaffer/PhotoEdit **55**; Rhoda Sidney/Stock Boston **viii**(l), **124–125**; Juan Silva Productions/Getty Images **352**; Ariel Skelley/Corbis **156**(cr), **251**; Jeff Smith/ImageState **333**; Jeff Smith/PhotoSmith **140**(l), **140**(r), **141**(l), **141**(r), **180**(l), **180**(r), **181**(l), **181**(r); **284**(l), **284**(r), **285**(l), **285**(r), **322**(l), **322**(r), **323**(tl), **323**(tr), **323**(b); Lee Snider/The Image Works **294**; Joseph Sohm;ChromoSohm Inc./Corbis **331**, **353**; Tom Stewart/Corbis **xi**(b), **82**, **258**, **270–271**; Stockbyte/PictureQuest **vii**(t), **60–61**; SuperStock **169**; SW Productions/brandXpictures **214**, **248**; Syracuse Newspapers/The Image Works **237**; Charles Thatcher/Getty Images **xv**(b); Bob Thomas/Getty Images **193**; Steve Torregrossa **64**(bl), **64**(c), **64**(cl), **64**(cr), **65**(c), **65**(cl), **65**(cr), **262**(t), **262**(b), **263**(tl), **263**(tr), **263**(b), **346**(l), **346**(r), **347**(t), **347**(b); Bill Tucker/ImageState **vii**(b), **80–81**; Steve Vidler/SuperStock **32**; Franco Vogt/Corbis **160**; Dana White/PhotoEdit **118**; Dana White/PhotoEdit **63**; Dusty Willison/ImageState **106**; David Young-Wolff/Getty Images **v**, **x**(b), **xx**, **1**, **222–223**, **339**; David Young-Wolff/PhotoEdit **vi**(t), **22–23**, **85**, **113**, **133**, **136**, **152**, **156**(b), **157**(cr), **167**, **175**, **178**, **211**, **224**, **306**, **310**(r), **318**, **327**, **340**, **350**; David Young–Wolff/ PhotoEdit/PictureQuest **189**; Yellow Dog Productions/Getty Images **259**, **281**.